Subhash Chandra Bose

Subhash Chandra Bose

Dr. C.P. Raj
Dr. Ved Prakash

AMIGA PRESS. INC
Delhi -110051

AMIGA
PRESS INC.
AMIGA PRESS INC.
Registered Office:
19 DBS Building, Ansari Road, Darya Ganj, Delhi. 110002, India
Phone: +91-11-23283333 Email: amigapress@gmail.com

This edition is published by Amiga Press.Inc

ISBN : 978-93-84533-27-4

First Published 2018

Reprint 2026

Printed at : Replika Press Pvt. Ltd.

Preface

Bose was elected president of the Indian National Congress for two consecutive terms but resigned from the post following ideological conflicts with Mahatma Gandhi. Bose believed that Mahatma Gandhi's tactics of nonviolence would never be sufficient to secure India's independence, and advocated violent resistance. He established a separate political party, the All India Forward Bloc and continued to call for the full and immediate independence of India from British rule. He was imprisoned by the British authorities eleven times. His stance did not change with the outbreak of the Second World War, which he saw as an opportunity to take advantage of British weakness.

At the outset of the war, he fled India and travelled to the Soviet Union, Germany and Japan seeking an alliance with the aim of attacking the British in India. With Japanese assistance he reorganised and later led the Indian National Army, formed from Indian prisoners-of-war and plantation workers from Malaya, Singapore and other parts of South-East Asia, against British forces. With Japanese monetary, political, diplomatic and military assistance, he formed the Azad Hind Government in exile, regrouped and led the Indian National Army to battle against the allies in Imphal & Burma during the World War II.

The Indian National Army, from the time it came into public perception in India around the time of the Red Fort Trials, and from the time it found its way into the works of Military Historians around the world, has been the subject of a number of projects, both of academic, historical and of popular nature. Some of these are critical of the army, some-especially of the ex-INA men are biographical or autobiographical, while still others are works of history and politics that tell the story of the INA. A large number of these give a large analysis of Subhash Chandra Bose and his work with the INA.

The origins of the idea of raising an armed force that would fight its way into India to bring down the Raj goes back to the First World War, when the Ghadar Party and the nascent embryo of the Indian Independence League formulated plans to initiate rebellion in the British Indian Army from Punjab to Hong Kong with German Support. This plan failed after the information was leaked to British Intelligence, but only after the Hong Kong Garrison had rebelled. However, during World War II, all the three major Axis Powers, at some stage of their campaign against Britain, sought to support/exploit the armed revolutionary activities within India and aided the recruitment of a military force from disaffected Indian prisoners of war captured while serving with the British Commonwealth forces and Indian expatriates, of which the most famous, and successful, was probably the Indian National Army that came into being with Japanese Support in the Far East. Italy had in 1942 created the Battaglione Azad Hindoustan, with ex-Indian Army personnel and Italians previously resident in India and Persia, that ultimately served under Ragruppamento Centri Militari. However, these efforts proved unsuccessful, given the overtly propagandist nature of their efforts that ultimately found little acceptance among the constituent soldiers, and the lack of a leadership that would deemed legitimate by the troops. By November 1942, following the defeats in El Alamein, the Italian efforts had failed.

The book will prove an informative and most useful asset for students, scholars and teachers in this field.

—Editor

Contents

Preface (*v*)

1. **Introduction** 1
Actions during the II World War; The Escape; Attempts of Assassination; Disappearance and Alleged Death; Authoritarian Rule; Bose Mystery ; The Disappearance Theories; Did Netaji Really Die?

2. **Bose, Indian National Army and Freedom of India** 25
Commemorations; Works on the INA; The First INA; The Second INA; Troop Strength; Order of Battle; Command Structure; Literary Works; Indische Legion; Uniform and Standard; Legacy of the Free India Legion; A Liberation Army; Government Administration and the War

3. **Vision of Bose and National Integration** 54
The Fundamental Problems of India; Glimpses of Netaji; Bose and National Integration

4. **Mission and Leadership of Bose** 77
Netaji-Symbol of National Integration; How Transparent!; Proclamation of the Provisional Government of Azad Hind; Modern Views of Bose

5. **Political Work, Ideology and Views of Bose** 115
Political Works and Views; Mass Mobilization; Women's Equality; Commitment to Youth; Netaji's Earlier Activities

6. **Mutiny in the British Indian Army** 139
Indian National Army of Liberation in the East; British Military

7. **Bose, Forward Bloc and Imphal Campaign** 171
Formation of the Forward Bloc; Forward Bloc Today; The Imphal Campaign

8. **Famous Speeches of Bose** 203
Battle of Imphal and Adherence to Fundamentals by Netaji ; Netaji Subhash Chandra Bose the Greatest Revolutionary and Socialist Leader; India will be Free

Bibliography 225

Index 227

1

Introduction

Subhash Chandra Bose, generally known as Netaji (lit. "Respected Leader"), was one of the most prominent and highly respected leaders of the Indian Independence Movement against the British Raj.

Bose was elected president of the Indian National Congress for two consecutive terms but resigned from the post following ideological conflicts with Mahatma Gandhi. Bose believed that Mahatma Gandhi's tactics of nonviolence would never be sufficient to secure India's independence, and advocated violent resistance. He established a separate political party, the All India Forward Bloc and continued to call for the full and immediate independence of India from British rule. He was imprisoned by the British authorities eleven times.

His stance did not change with the outbreak of the Second World War, which he saw as an opportunity to take advantage of British weakness. At the outset of the war, he fled India and travelled to the Soviet Union, Germany and Japan seeking an alliance with the aim of attacking the British in India. With Japanese assistance he reorganised and later led the Indian National Army, formed from Indian prisoners-of-war and plantation workers from Malaya, Singapore and other parts of South East Asia, against British forces. With Japanese monetary, political, diplomatic and military assistance, he formed the Azad Hind Government in exile, regrouped and led the Indian National Army to battle against the allies in Imphal and Burma during the World War II.

His political views and the alliances he made with Nazi and other militarist regimes opposed to the British Empire have been the cause of arguments among historians and politicians, with some accusing him of Fascist sympathies and of Quislingist actions, while most others in India largely sympathetic towards his inculcation of realpolitik as a manifesto that guided his social and political choices. He is believed to have died on 18 August 1945 in a plane crash over Taiwan. However, contradictory evidence exists regarding his death in the accident.

Early Life

Subhash Chandra Bose was born in 1897 to an affluent Bengali family in Cuttack, Orissa in India. His father, Janakinath Bose, was a public prosecutor who believed in orthodox nationalism, and later became a member of the Bengal Legislative Council. Bose was educated at Ravenshaw Collegiate School, Cuttack, Scottish Church College, Calcutta and Fitzwilliam College at Cambridge University. In 1920, Bose took the Indian Civil Services Entrance Examination and was placed fourth with highest marks in English. However, he resigned from the prestigious Indian Civil Service in April 1921 despite his high ranking in the merit list, and went on to become an active member of India's independence movement. He joined the Indian National Congress, and was particularly active in its youth wing.

Still, Bose's ideals did not match those of Mahatma Gandhi's single belief in nonviolence. He, therefore returned to Calcutta to work under Chittaranjan Das, the Bengali freedom fighter and co-founder (with Motilal Nehru) of the Swaraj Party.

In 1921, Bose organised a boycott of the celebrations to mark the visit of the Prince of Wales to India, which led to his imprisonment. In April 1924, Bose was elected to the post of Chief Executive Officer of the newly constituted Calcutta Corporation, In October that year, Bose was arrested on suspicion of terrorism. At first, he was kept in Alipore Jail and later he was exiled to Mandalay in Burma (where earlier Bal Gangadhar Tilak had spent 6 years in prison). On January 23, 1930, Bose was once again arrested for leading an "independence procession", protesting against British rule in India. After his release from jail on September 25, he was elected as the Mayor of the City of Calcutta.

Over a span of 20 years, Bose was incarcerated eleven times by the British, either in India or in Rangoon. During the mid 1930s he was exiled by the British from India to Europe, where he championed India's cause and aspiration for self-rule before gatherings and conferences.

After his father's death, the British authorities allowed him to land at Calcutta's airport only for the religious rites, which would be followed by his swift departure. He travelled extensively in India and in Europe before stating his political opposition to Gandhi. During his stay in Europe from 1933 to 1936, he met several European leaders and thinkers. He came to believe that India could achieve political freedom only if it had political, military and diplomatic support from outside, and that an independent nation necessitated the creation of a national army to secure its sovereignty. Subhash Chandra Bose married Emilie Schenkl, an Austrian born national, who was his secretary, in 1937. According to Schenkl, she and Bose were secretly married in Bad Gastein on 26 December 1937. They had one daughter, Anita, born in 1942. Bose wrote many letters to Schenkl during the period 1934–42, of which many have been published in the book *Letters to Emilie Schenkl*, edited by Sisir Kumar Bose and Sugata Bose.

Bose became the president of the Haripura Indian National Congress in 1938, against Gandhi's wishes. Gandhi commented "Pattavi's defeat is my own defeat. Anyway, Subhash Bose is not an enemy of the country". Gandhi's continued opposition led to the latter's resignation from the Working Committee, and the possibility that the rest of the CWC would resign. In the face of this gesture of no-confidence, Bose himself resigned, and was left with no alternative but to form an independent party, the All India Forward Bloc. Bose also initiated the concept of the *National Planning Committee* in 1938.

Indian National Army

The Indian National Army (INA) was originally founded by Capt. Mohan Singh in Singapore in September 1942 with Japan's Indian POWs in the Far East. This was along the concept of—and with support of—what was then known as the Indian Independence League, headed by expatriate nationalist leader Rash Behari Bose? The first INA was, however disbanded in December 1942 after disagreements between the Hikari Kikan and Mohan singh, who came to believe that the Japanese High Command was using the INA as a mere pawn and Propaganda tool. Mohan Singh was taken into custody and the troops returned to the Prisoner-of-War camp. However, the idea of a liberation army was revived with the arrival of Subhash Chandra Bose in the Far East in 1943. In July, at a meeting in Singapore, Rash Behari Bose handed over control of the organisation to Subhash Chandra Bose. Bose was able to reorganise the fledging army and organise massive support among the expatriate Indian population in South East Asia, who lent their support by both enlisting in the Indian National Army, as well as financially in response Bose's calls for sacrifice for the national cause. At its height it consisted of some 85,000 regular troops, including a separate women's unit, the Rani of Jhansi Regiment (named after Rani Lakshmi Bai), which is seen as a first of its kind in Asia.

Even when faced with military reverses, Bose was able to maintain support for the Azad Hind movement. Spoken as a part of a motivational speech for the Indian National Army at a rally of Indians in Burma on July 4, 1944, Bose's most famous quote was "Give me blood, and I shall give you freedom!". In this, he urged the people of India to join him in his fight against the British Raj. Spoken in Hindi, Bose's words are highly evocative. The troops of the INA were under the aegis of a provisional government, the Azad Hind Government, which came to produce its own currency, court and civil code, and was recognised by nine Axis states—Germany, Japan, Italy, the Independent State of Croatia, Wang Jingwei's Government in Nanjing, Thailand, a provisional Government of Burma, Manchukuo and Japanese-controlled Philippines. Recent researches have shown that the USSR too had recognised the "Provisional Government of Free India". Of those countries, five were authorities established under Axis occupation. This government participated as a delegate or observer in the so called Greater East Asia Co-Prosperity Sphere.

The INA's first commitment was in the Japanese thrust towards Eastern Indian frontiers of Manipur. INA's special forces, the Bahadur Group, were extensively involved in operations behind enemy lines both during the diversionary attacks in Arakan, as well as the Japanese thrust towards Imphal and Kohima, along with the Burmese National Army led by Ba Maw and Aung San. A year after the islands were taken by the Japanese, the Provisional Government and the INA were established in the Andaman and Nicobar Islands with Lt. Col. A.D Loganathan appointed its Governor General. The islands were renamed *Shaheed* (Martyr) and *Swaraj* (Self-rule). However, the Japanese Navy remained in essential control of the island's administration. During Bose's only visit to the islands in late in 1943, when he was carefully screened from the local population by the Japanese authorities, who at that time were torturing the leader of the Indian Independence League on the Islands, Dr. Diwan Singh (who later died of his injuries, in the Cellular Jail). The islanders made several attempts to alert Bose to their plight, but apparently without success. Enraged with the lack of administrative control, Lt. Col Loganathan later relinquished his authority to return to the Government's head quarters in Rangoon.

On the Indian mainland, an Indian Tricolour, modelled after that of the Indian National Congress, was raised for the first time in the town in Moirang, in Manipur, in Northeastern India. The towns of Kohima and Imphal were placed under siege by divisions of the Japanese, Burmese and the *Gandhi* and *Nehru* Brigades of I.N.A. during the attempted invasion of India, also known as Operation U-GO. However, Commonwealth forces held both positions and then counter-attacked, in the process inflicting serious losses on the besieging forces, which were then forced to retreat back into Burma.

Bose had hoped that large numbers of soldiers would desert from the Indian Army when they would discover that INA soldiers were attacking British India from the outside. However, this did not materialise on a sufficient scale. Instead, as the war situation worsened for the Japanese, troops began to desert from the INA. At the same time Japanese funding for the army diminished, and Bose was forced to raise taxes on the Indian populations of Malaysia and Singapore, sometimes extracting money by force. When the Japanese were defeated at the battles of Kohima and Imphal, the Provisional Government's aim of establishing a base in mainland India was lost forever. The INA was forced to pull back, along with the retreating Japanese army, and fought in key battles against the British Indian Army in its Burma campaign, notable in Meiktilla, Mandalay, Pegu, Nyangyu and Mount Popa. However, with the fall of Rangoon, Bose's government ceased be an effective political entity. A large proportion of the INA troops surrendered under Lt. Col Loganathan when Rangoon fell. The remaining troops retreated with Bose towards Malaya or made for Thailand. Japan's surrender at the end of the war also led to the eventual surrender of the Indian National Army, when the troops of the British Indian Army were repatriated to India and some tried for treason...

His other famous quote was, "Delhi chalo", meaning "On to Delhi!". This was the call he used to give the INA armies to motivate them. "Jai Hind", or, "Glory to India!" was another slogan used by him and later adopted by the Government of India and the Indian Armed Forces.

ACTIONS DURING THE II WORLD WAR

Bose advocated the approach that the political instability of wartime Britain should be taken advantage of—rather than simply wait for the British to grant independence after the end of the war (which was the view of Gandhi, Nehru and a section of the Congress leadership at the time). In this, he was influenced by the examples of Italian statesmen Giuseppe Garibaldi and Giuseppe Mazzini. His correspondence reveals that despite his clear dislike ...for British subjugation, he was deeply impressed by their methodical and systematic approach and their steadfastly disciplinarian outlook towards life. In England, he exchanged ideas on the future of India with British Labour Party leaders and political thinkers like Lord Halifax, George Lansbury, Clement Attlee, Arthur Greenwood, Harold Laski, J.B.S. Haldane, Ivor Jennings, G.D.H. Cole, Gilbert Murray and Sir Stafford Cripps.

He came to believe that a free India needed Socialist authoritarianism, on the lines of Turkey's Kemal Atatürk, for at least two decades. Bose was refused permission by the British authorities to meet Mr. Ataturk at Ankara for political reasons. It should be noted that during his sojourn in England, only the Labour Party and Liberal politicians agreed to meet with Bose when he tried to schedule appointments. Conservative Party officials refused to meet Bose or show him the slightest courtesy due to the fact that he was a politician coming from a colony, but it may also be recalled that in the 1930s leading figures in the Conservative Party had opposed even Dominion status for India. It may also be observed here that it was during the regime of the Labour Party (1945-1951), with Attlee as the Prime Minister, that India gained independence.

THE ESCAPE

On the outbreak of war, Bose advocated a campaign of mass civil disobedience to protest against Viceroy Lord Linlithgow's decision to declare war on India's behalf without consulting the Congress leadership. Having failed to persuade Gandhi of the necessity of this, Bose organised mass protests in Calcutta calling for the 'Holwell Monument' commemorating the Black Hole of Calcutta, which then stood at the corner of Dalhousie Square, to be removed. A reasonable measure of the contrast between Gandhi and Bose is captured in a saying attributable to him: "If people slap you once, slap them twice". He was thrown in jail by the British, but was released following a seven-day hunger strike. Bose's house in Calcutta was kept under surveillance by the CBI, but their vigilance left a good deal to be desired. With two court cases pending, he felt the British would not let him leave the country before the end of the war. This set the scene for Bose's escape to Germany, via Afghanistan and the Soviet Union. Bose had never been to Afghanistan, and could not speak the local tribal language (Pashto).

Bose escaped from under British surveillance at his house in Calcutta. On January 19, 1941, accompanied by his nephew Sisir K. Bose, Bose gave his watchers the slip and journeyed to Peshawar. With the assistance of the Abwehr, he made his way to Peshawar where he was met at Peshawar Cantonment station by Akbar Shah, Mohammed Shah and Bhagat Ram Talwar. Bose was taken to the home of Abad Khan, a trusted friend of Akbar Shah's. On 26 January 1941, Bose began his journey to reach Russia through India's North West frontier with Afghanistan. For this reason, he enlisted the help of Mian Akbar Shah, then a Forward Bloc leader in the North West Frontier Province. Shah had been out of India *en route* to the Soviet Union, and suggested a novel disguise for Bose to assume. Since Bose could not speak one word of Pashto, it would make him an easy target of Pashto speakers working for the British. For this reason, Shah suggested that Bose act deaf and dumb, and let his beard grow to mimic those of the tribesmen.

Supporters of the Aga Khan helped him across the border into Afghanistan where he was met by an Abwehr unit posing as a party of road construction engineers from the Organization Todt who then aided his passage across Afghanistan via Kabul to the border with Soviet Russia. Once in Russia the NKVD transported Bose to Moscow where he hoped that Russia's traditional enmity to British rule in India would result in support for his plans for a popular rising in India. However, Bose found the Soviets' response disappointing and was rapidly passed over to the German Ambassador in Moscow, Count vonder Schulenburg. He had Bose flown on to Berlin in a special courier aircraft at the beginning of April where he was to receive a more favourable hearing from Joachim von Ribbentrop and the Foreign Ministry officials at the Wilhelmstrasse.

ATTEMPTS OF ASSASSINATION

In 1941, when the British learned that Bose had sought the support of the Axis Powers, they ordered their agents to intercept and assassinate Bose before he reached Germany. A recently declassified intelligence document refers to a top-secret instruction to the Special Operations Executive (SOE) of British intelligence to murder Bose. In fact, the plan to liquidate Bose has few parallels, and appears to be a last desperate measure against a man who had thrown the British Empire into a panic.

In Germany

Having escaped incarceration at home by assuming the guise of a Pashtun insurance agent ("Ziaudddin") to reach Afghanistan, Bose travelled to Moscow on the passport of an Italian nobleman "Count Orlando Mazzotta". From Moscow, he reached Rome, and from there he travelled to Germany, where he instituted the Special Bureau for India under Adam von Trott zu Solz, broadcasting on the German-sponsored Azad Hind Radio. He founded the *Free India Centre* in Berlin, and created the Indian Legion (consisting of some 4500 soldiers) out of Indian prisoners of war who had previously fought for the British in North Africa prior to their capture by Axis forces. The Indian Legion was attached to the Wehrmacht, and later transferred to the Waffen SS; its members swore their allegiance to both Hitler and Bose to secure India's independence. He was also, however, prepared to envisage an invasion of India via the U.S.S.R. by Nazi troops, spearheaded by the Azad Hind Legion; many have questioned his judgment here, as it seems unlikely that the Germans could have been easily persuaded to leave after such an invasion, which might also have resulted in an Axis victory in the War.

The lack of interest shown by Hitler in the cause of Indian independence eventually caused Bose to become disillusioned with Hitler and he decided to leave Nazi Germany in 1943. Bose had been living together with his wife Schenkl in Berlin from 1941 until 1943, when he left for southeast Asia. He travelled by the German submarine *U-180* around the Cape of Good Hope to Imperial Japan (via Japanese submarine *I-29*). Thereafter the Japanese helped him raise his army in Singapore. This was the only civilian transfer across two submarines of two different navies in World War II.

DISAPPEARANCE AND ALLEGED DEATH

Officially, Bose died in a plane crash over Taiwan, while flying to Tokyo on 18 August 1945. However, his body was never recovered, and many theories have been put forward concerning his possible survival. One such claim is that Bose actually died in Siberia, while in Soviet captivity. Several committees have been set up by the Government of India to probe into this matter.

In May 1956, a four-man Indian team (known as the Shah Nawaz Committee) visited Japan to probe the circumstances of Bose's alleged death. The Indian government did not then request assistance from the Government of Taiwan in the matter, citing their lack of diplomatic relations with Taiwan.

However, the Inquiry Commission under Justice Mukherjee, which investigated the Bose disappearance mystery in the period 1999-2005, did approach the Taiwanese government and obtained information from the Taiwan Government that no plane carrying Bose had ever crashed in Taipei. The Mukherjee Commission also received a report originating from the US State Department, supporting the claim of the Taiwan Government that no such air crash took place during that time frame.

The Mukherjee Commission submitted its report to the Indian Government on November 8, 2005. The report was tabled in Parliament on May 17, 2006. The probe said in its report that Bose did not die in the plane crash and the ashes at Renkoji temple are not his. However, the Indian Government rejected the findings of the commission.

Political Views

Bose's earlier correspondence (prior to 1939) also reflects his deep disapproval of the racist practices of, and annulment of democratic institutions in Nazi Germany. He also, however, expressed admiration for the authoritarian methods (though not the racial ideologies) which he saw in Italy and Germany during the 1930s, and thought they could be used in building an independent India.

Bose had clearly expressed his belief that democracy was the best option for India. The pro-Bose thinkers believe that his authoritarian control of the Azad Hind was based on political pragmatism and a post-colonial recovery doctrine rather than any anti-democratic belief.. However, during the war (and possibly as early as the 1930s) Bose seems to have decided that no democratic system could be adequate to overcome India's poverty and social inequalities, and he wrote that an authoritarian state, similar to that of Soviet Russia (which he had also seen and admired) would be needed for the process of national rebuilding. Accordingly some suggest that Bose's alliance with the Axis during the war was based on more than just pragmatism, and that Bose may have been a Fascist, though not a Nazi; alternatively, others consider he might have been using populist methods of mobilization common to many postcolonial leaders. After the Independence of India, Subhash Chandra Bose did not get much importance, as the Gandhi-influenced Congress Party came to rule.

A high point in Bose's "military career" came in July 1943 in Singapore. At a mass meeting there on July 4, Rash Behari Bose (no relation) handed over to him the leadership of the Indian Independence League. The next day, Subhash Bose reviewed for the first time the soldiers of the Indian National Army (INA), which then comprised 13,000 men. In his address to the troops, which is a good example of his speaking style, he cited George Washington and Giuseppi Garibaldi as examples of men who led armies that won independence for their respective countries. Bose went on:

"Soldiers of India's army of liberation!...

"Every Indian must feel proud that this Army—his own Army—has been organized entirely under Indian leadership and that, when the historic moment arrives, under Indian leadership it will go to battle...

"Comrades! You have voluntarily accepted a mission that is the noblest that the human mind can conceive of. For the fulfilment of such a mission, no sacrifice is too great, not even the sacrifice of one's life...

"...Today is the proudest day of my life. For an enslaved people, there can be no greater pride, no higher honour, than to be the first soldier in the army of liberation. But this honour carries with it a corresponding responsibility, and I am deeply conscious of it. I assure you that I shall be with you in darkness and in sunshine, in sorrow and in joy, in suffering and in victory. For the present, I can offer you nothing except hunger, thirst, privation, forced marches and death. But if you follow me in life and in death, as I am confident you will, I shall lead you to victory and freedom. It does not matter who among us will live to see India free. It is enough that India shall be free, and that we shall give our all to make her free.

"May God now bless our Army and grant us victory in the coming fight!"

This "Free India Army" ("*Azad Hind Fauj*") would not only "emancipate India from the British yoke," he told the soldiers, but would, under his command, become the standing national army of the liberated nation.

Choreography for Impact

As his staging at the 1930 Calcutta session of the Congress party suggest, Bose understood early on the importance of political choreography and the aesthetics of mass meetings. After his visits to Fascist Italy and National Socialist Germany, he was even more mindful of the importance for any successful broad-based political movement of mass meetings, marches, visual symbols, and ceremonial or liturgical rituals. For example, at the 51st session of the Congress party at Haripura in 1938, Bose made sure that his entrance as the new Congress president would be spectacular. Escorted by 51 girls in saffron saris (the number corresponding with the number of the Congress session), he was seated in an ancient chariot drawn by 51 white bullocks, and taken on a two hour procession through 51 specially-constructed gates, accompanied by 51 brass bands. Political choreography of this type—although not to this extreme degree—was very evident at all mass rallies (which sometimes attracted crowds numbering as many as 200,000) of the Forward Bloc party that Bose formed in 1939. Carefully chosen symbols, slogans and songs, coupled with a flood of written propaganda, were used in an unsuccessful attempt to make the Forward Bloc into a mass party.

Even during the last years of the war, when he was in South East Asia heading the Provisional Government of Free India and the INA, he continued to choreograph carefully all of his rallies, meetings and ceremonies, in order to maximize their impact. He also realized that his own role in this choreography was central. Even in the hottest tropical weather, for instance, he wore an imposing military uniform, including forage cap, khaki tunic and jodhpurs, and shiny, knee-length black boots. Moreover, whenever, he travelled "he demanded all the rights and privileges of a head of state. On his road travels in Malaya, for example, he insisted on a full ceremonial escort; Japanese military jeeps mounted with sub-machineguns, a fleet of cars, and motorcycle outriders." Historian Mihir Bose argues persuasively that such carefully planned actions were manifestations not of megalomania, but rather of Subhash Bose's effort to create a sense of unity transcending class, caste and origin among the large and diverse populations of Indians in South-East Asia, to increase their political awareness, to arouse and inspire both them and his INA troops, and to show the world that he regarded himself as a political leader of substance and importance.

This naturally raises the question of Bose's leadership style. In the passage from *The Indian Struggle* quoted above at length, he expressed his belief in what he called "the dictatorship of the party" (the party being the governing body of a free India), but he did not specify the precise nature of the party's leadership, or whether it, too, would be dictatorial. Most importantly, he did not state whether he saw himself as the party leader, or comment directly on what role he intended for himself in a free India. Nonetheless, clues about these details can be gleaned from other sections of *The Indian Struggle* and from the speeches and statements Bose made at various times throughout his career.

Determined Leadership

Bose clearly admired strong, vigorous, military-type leaders, and in *The Indian Struggle* he listed several whom he particularly respected. These included Hitler, Mussolini, Stalin and even a former British Governor of Bengal, Sir Stanley Jackson. Nowhere in this book is there any criticism of these individuals (three of them dictators) for having too much power, yet another man is chastised for this: Mahatma Gandhi. Bose admired Gandhi for many things, not least his ability to "exploit the mass psychology of the people, just as Lenin did the same thing in Russia, Mussolini in Italy and Hitler in Germany." But he accused Gandhi of accepting too much power and responsibility, of becoming a "Dictator for the whole country" who issued "decrees" to the Congress. According to Bose, Gandhi was a brilliant and gifted man, but, unlike Mussolini, Hitler and the others mentioned, a very ineffectual leader. Gandhi had failed to liberate India because of his frequent indecision and constant willingness to compromise with the Raj (something Bose said he would never do).

It is clear that Bose—who believed from his youth that he was destined for greatness —saw himself as a "strong" leader in the mold of those named above. "I ask those who have any doubts or suspicions in their minds to rely on me," he told the Indian Independence League Conference in Singapore on July 4, 1943. He continued:

"I shall always be loyal to India alone. I will never deceive my motherland. I will live and die for India. .. The British could not bring me to submission by inflicting hardships on me. British statesmen could neither induce me nor deceive me. There is no one who can divert me from the right path."

Bose was decisive, aggressive and ambitious, and even as a university student, these features of his personality attracted many devoted followers. Dilip Kumar Roy, his companion during his days as a student at Cambridge, referred to him as "strength-inspiring," and the absolute leader of the Indian student population.

Bose's militarism, ambition and leadership traits do nót necessarily indicate (contrary to popular opinion) that he was a leader in the fascist mold. If they did, one would have to consider all personalities with similar traits—Winston Churchill, for example—as "fascist." In this regard, it is worth noting that during his many years as head of various councils, committees and offices, and during 15-month tenure as president of the Indian National Congress (February 1938 to May 1939), Bose never acted in an undemocratic manner, nor did he claim powers or responsibilities to which he was not constitutionally or customarily entitled. Neither did he attempt in any way to foster a cult of his own personality (as, it could be argued, Gandhi did).

However, after he assumed control of the INA in July-August 1943, Bose's leadership style underwent a transformation. First, he allowed a cult of his personality to flourish among the two million or so Indians living in South East Asia. Prayers were regularly said on his behalf, and his birthday celebrations were—like Gandhi's in India—major festivals. He was invincible, according to one Indian myth from this period, and could not be harmed by bombs or bullets. An image of Bose that stressed his strength of character, military prowess, and willingness to sacrifice for a free India was intentionally promoted in propaganda broadcasts and printed material. With his approval, the title *Netaji* ("Revered Leader") was added to his name in all articles about him appearing in the newspapers of the Indian Independence League; even his staff officers were permitted to address him with this title. By the end of the war, few Indians in South Asia still referred to him by name; he was always respectfully called *Netaji.*

AUTHORITARIAN RULE

Second, in contrast to his statement at the 1938 Haripura session of the Congress party (quoted above)—that leaders would be elected from below—Bose proclaimed, on October 21, 1943, the formation of the Provisional Government of Azad Hind ("Free India"). While retaining his post as Supreme Commander of the Indian National Army, he announced that he was naming himself Head of State, Prime Minister, and Minister for War and Foreign Affairs. (The most important of these positions—Head of State—he anticipated retaining in a free India.) These appointments involved no democratic process or voting of any kind. Further, the authority he exercised in these posts was dictatorial and often very harsh. He demanded total obedience and loyalty from the Indians in south Asia, and any who opposed him, his army or government faced imprisonment, torture, or even execution.

Additionally, if wealthy Indians did not contribute sufficient funds to Bose's efforts, they risked confiscation of their property. Bose's threats were taken very seriously, and had the desired effect: funds did pour in. His INA troops were obliged to swear an oath of loyalty to both the Provisional Government and to him personally. He ordered the summary execution of all-INA deserters, and also prepared (but was never able to implement) law codes for the entire population of India. These laws, which stipulated the death penalty for a range of offences, were to come into force when the INA, together with the Japanese Army, entered India to fight against the British. With regard to his leadership style during this 1943-45 period, in fairness to Bose is should be pointed out that the entire world was then engulfed in a horrendous war, and political and military leaders everywhere, on all sides, adapted extraordinarily authoritarian and repressive measures. Some of the measures and policies adapted by the wartime government of the United States, for instance, were as oppressive and as severe as any planned or implemented by Bose.

A New India

Bose clearly anticipated that the British would be driven out of India in an armed struggle (under his leadership), and that a social and political revolution would begin the moment the Indian people saw British rule under attack in India itself. This revolution, he believed, would bring an end to the old caste system and traditional social hierarchy, which would be replaced by an egalitarian, casteless and classless society based on socialist models. This process would require very careful guidance, with a firm hand, to prevent anarchy and chaos.

Bose had, in fact, held these beliefs since the early 1930s, as Mrs. Kitty Kurti, a close German friend of Bose, revealed in her anecdotal memoir. At a June 1933 meeting attended by Kurti, Bose explained that:

> *Besides a plan of action which will lead up to the conquest of power, we shall require a programme for the new state when it comes into existence in India. Nothing can be left to chance. The group of men and women who will assume the leadership of the fight with Great Britain will also have to take up the task of controlling, guiding and developing the new state and, through the state, the entire Indian people. If our leaders are not trained for post-war*

> *leadership also there is every possibility that after the conquest of power a period of chaos will set in and incidents similar to those for the French Revolution of the 18th century may be repeated in India. ... The generals of the wartime period in India will have to carry through the whole programme of post-war reforms in order to justify to their countrymen the hopes and aspirations that they will have to rouse during the fight. The task of these leaders will not be over till a new generation of men and women are educated and trained after the establishment of the new state and this new generation are able to take complete charge of their country's affairs.*

This explains what Bose meant in *The Indian Struggle* when he wrote (as quoted above) of the need for a strong, single-party government, "bound together by military discipline" with "dictatorial powers for some years to come, in order to put India on her feet."

Only an very strong government, strict discipline, and dictatorial rule would, according to Bose, prevent the anticipated revolution from falling into chaos and anarchy. That is why the government would not—"in the first years after liberation"—"stand for a democracy in the Mid-Victorian sense of the term."

It would use, whatever military force was necessary to maintain law and order, and would not relinquish authority or re-establish more regular forms of government until it felt confident that "the work of postwar social reconstruction" had been completed and "a new generation of men and women in India, fully trained and equipped for the battle of life" had emerged.

Bose clearly anticipated that authoritarian rule would not last beyond the period when social reconstruction was completed, and law and order were established—when India was "on its feet," as he often wrote. As he frequently stated, Bose aimed for nothing less than the formation of "a new India and a happy India on the basis of the eternal principles of liberty, democracy and socialism."

He rejected Communism (at least as it was practiced in the Soviet Union) principally because of its internationalism, and because he believed that the theoretical ideal found in the writings of Marx could not be applied, without modification, to India. Still, he maintained socialist views throughout his adult life, and, on very many occasions, expressed his hope for an egalitarian (especially classless and casteless) industrialized society in which the state would control the basic means of production.

He was opposed to liberalism, believing that greater emphasis should be placed on social goals than on the needs or desires of individuals. Individual wishes, he reasoned, must be subordinated to the needs of the state, especially during the struggle for independence and the period of reconstruction immediately following liberation.

Nonetheless, having himself been imprisoned eleven times and sent into exile three times, he was fully committed to upholding the rights of minority intellectual, religious, cultural and racial groups. He hoped for an "all-round freedom for the Indian people—that is, for social, economic and political freedom," and would, he said "wage a relentless war against bondage of every kind till the people can become really free."

It could be argued that he was not as committed to the principle of democracy as he was to socialism and freedom (as he defined it). While he extolled democracy on numerous occasions, at other times his words suggest a belief that other parties would have a place, in a free India, only as long as they were "working towards the same end, in whole or in part," as his governing party.

Political pluralism did not appeal to him at all. He seems to have envisioned a free India that was more authoritarian than democratic. His own actions as head of the Provisional Government of Azad Hind illustrate a lack of regard for the democratic process.

BOSE MYSTERY

It's amazing how Netaji Subhash Chandra Bose continues to be in news after his disputed death. In a way, this has been in defiance of successive Indian governments who would rather want the people to sideline him as they have. A recent BBC online poll named Bose the third most popular leader in South Asia after Jinnah and Gandhi. Strikingly, as per the same poll, the stalwarts like Jawaharlal Nehru, Indira Gandhi and the inimitable Atal Bihari Vajpayee don't even blip on the radar anymore.

The coming months will see Subhash making a comeback of a sort. India's longest running political controversy is heading towards its grand finale. For five years the media and the lawmakers in India have adopted a touch and go sort of approach towards the inquiry of Justice MK Mukherjee into the "death" of Subhash Bose. Not any longer. The commission, formed in 1999 following a court order, is gearing up to present its report by November. The government will have to present it in parliament along with an action taken report. All those of you who have interest in either politics, or history, or intrigue, or mystery better watch out: It doesn't get any bigger than this.

Psst ...Top Secret!

Let this impression be trashed at the outset that the Netaji mystery belongs to a different era. No doubt it started in 1945; but it has been simmering till date. The controversy is a bombshell and that's what the official records hint at. Netaji is supposed to have died at the end of Second World War, and yet the Indian Government continues to sit on files about him. And they are wary of approaching the British and Russian governments to release the papers they are keeping to themselves.

But why so much of precaution over some details about man who ceased to be a problem to his adversaries in and outside India decades back? This is for you Gen-X dudes: Some of the classified Netaji files maintained by the Government of India are of mid-1990s vintage! That is, post-Rajiv Gandhi period. Perish the idea ... "Oh, such an old story, what is the fuss now!" The Government of India wouldn't agree. They think there is something about Netaji that can spell big time trouble even now. That's why they refused to hand over several Top Secret files to the Mukherjee Commission. Why would they be doing so? Well, in the case of two Narasimha Rao period files, they reasoned that the "disclosure of the nature and contents of these documents would ... hurt the sentiments of the people at large and may evoke wide-spread reactions .... Diplomatic relations with friendly countries may also be adversely affected if the said documents are disclosed."

Should not we demand to know what these documents have to say? How on earth some bits about a dead man affect India's relations with other countries? Should not we ask our government to state facts? Don't we have a right to know what happened to the man who liberated us?

Pre-conceived Notions

It's cynicism exemplified when people say, "How long we can go on inquiring?" If Americans, for instance, were to be besotted with same defeatist thinking, they would not have become the great power they are. Indeed they don't give up. How can one leave out in cold those who fight for one's country? Last year only the US Government asked the Indian Government to help them trace out their missing World War II airmen. Netaji went missing while waging war for freedom for us and we don't want to know what happened to him. What is it if not brazen ungratefulness?

Those who dismissively say that "there have been commissions after commissions" have no idea whatsoever what sort of frauds were played on the nation by the previous "commissions". In 1956, Shah Nawaz Khan, a Congress MP and a secretary to then Railway Minister, headed a committee—a puppet on a string, actually. There are reasons to believe that he did what he was told by Nehru government. After his "command performance" Shah Nawaz was made a minister. GD Khosla, who headed a commission in early 1970s, was a friend of Nehru's to start with. He wrote the biography of Prime Minister Indira Gandhi even as he inquired into Netaji's disappearance. Can you imagine such things happening now? Both these panels declared that Netaji had died in a plane crash in Taiwan. Never mind that they did not bother to know what the Taiwan Government thought much as people wanted them to.

"But the issue is dead!" Ok, for argument's sake, if that be the case, it is going to COME ALIVE. A Commission of Inquiry headed by a former judge of the Supreme Court of India is going to handover a report to Home Minister Shivraj Patil, who, at the moment, doesn't seem to be at ease with the direction the Commission is heading to. The report will have to be discussed by the Cabinet before being presented in Parliament for a free for all debate. It is inevitable that Netaji mystery will become a hot topic.

Perplexing Past

Funny how people jump to conclusions. "My grandfather was in the INA and he said Netaji died and, therefore I believe so." This is how some give their verdict on the issue the nation is debating for 6 decades. If only it were that easy. There were over 50,000 people aligned with the Provisional Government of Free India and only a handful knew what happened to Netaji in his last known days. The rest were in as much dark as the Indians back home. They all heard stories ... Netaji died or Netaji escaped. The truth, or inkling of it, came out after interrogations and inquiries, whose reports are not in public domain.

On August 25, 1945 the Indian newspapers broke the news that Netaji had died in a freak plane crash in Taipei (then Taihoku) on August 18th. He had been flying to Tokyo to work out the INA's surrender when this happened. The British would believe none of it. Viceroy Wavell noted in his diary on 23 August that "I wonder if the Japanese announcement of Subhash Chandra Bose's death in a air-crash is true. I suspect it very much, it is just what should be given out if he meant to go underground..." They dispatched their crack intelligence teams to South-East Asia. The findings were bewildering. Netaji was not heading to Tokyo. Months before the world war staggered to a halt, he'd begun planning a new chapter of his war on colonialism. He saw the Cold War coming and reached out to the USSR. The British intelligence got clear information that Subhash was going to Russia at the time of his death. The Japanese had given out a false story about his destination. The survivors of the crash were rounded up and records were captured. The pictured that emerged was of deceit. Eyewitnesses were found to be lying and records appeared as if they had been planted.

Americans chipped in with help. In fact it were they who had the best knowledge. They reached Taiwan in September 1945 and guess what they found. " ... there is no direct evidence that Subhash Chandra Bose was killed in a airplane crash ... despite the public statements of the Japanese to that effect." This, stated the State Department, ten months after Netaji's "death". What really happened? "The D.I.B. during his recent visit to London mentioned the receipt ... of information to the effect that Subhash Bose was alive in Russia." This is from a May 1946 report and D.I.B. means, the Director of Intelligence Bureau Sir Norman Smith.

The Government of free India knew about the Soviet connection to the Netaji mystery. But all they did was to dilly-dally and state that no inquiry was required. It took ten years of pressure before Prime Minister Nehru agreed to inquire into the matter. This must be hammered: the government never wanted to probe Netaji's fate. From Shah Nawaz to Monoj Mukherjee, each time they were forced to. Isn't it revolting?

Present Perfect

Thank God for Mukherjee Commission! Or shall we thank Mikhail Gorbahev? The fall of the USSR brought the Netaji issue out. In mid-1990s the Russians themselves began saying that Subhash was with them after his death. The matter reached India and the press did rake it up. But Narasimha Rao, with Pranab Mukherjee in tow, would not say a thing. A patriotic fellow moved to Calcutta High Court and the court found the matter to be wide open for inquiry. The government was chided and told to form a commission of inquiry to find out where and how Netaji had died. Mercifully, at the time the verdict came, the NDA was in power.

The inquiry of the Mukherjee Commission in past five years has been pathbreaking. They have found out, among others, that the Government of India, at the PMO level, indulged in systematic, unlawful destruction of evidence concerning the Netaji death case. The government did not want any inquiry in Taiwan, which is precisely what Justice Mukherjee did. The result: the ROC Government ruled out the very occurrence of the crash that we had been told over decades had killed Netaji.

Indian Government also did not want any inquiry in Russia; but that is happening now. After much pulls and pressures, the Mukherjee Commission will visit Russia from September 20 onwards. However, that's not a good enough development. The Government's communication to the commission suggests that they won't do anything to help the commission access security and intelligence related classified papers in Russia, said to be containing definite information about Netaji's "post-death" life. Time has come for us, the people of India, to demand from our Government something that they should have done decades back: For God's sake, request the Head of the Russian Government to state facts. The people of India must know what happened to their liberator.

THE DISAPPEARANCE THEORIES

Netaji was killed in a plane crash in Taipei

"This is the most commonly heard version and has much to go by it. There were witnesses to the crash and Bose's death. His ashes are enshrined in Tokyo's Renkoji temple. The most wellknown INA veterans, researchers and Bose family members vouch for it. The government of independent India said repeatedly it so happened. Two probes by the government proved just this."

Netaji Actually Escaped to the USSR

"No, this version did not come up later on. The 'escape' theory was born in 1945 itself and got a new lease of life in early 1990s. A section of INA veterans, researchers, bulk of the Bose family and members of various offshoots of Forward Bloc have all believed it. An 'international blackmail' is read along with this line of thinking. Netaji, some say, was dispatched to a Siberian gulag. They believe Soviets kept him alive for some time to do business with independent India. Slowly India wriggled out of the western influence and sided with the Soviet bloc during the cold war."

Netaji Returned to India

"Bose is believed to have surreptitiously slipped into India as hermit named Bhagwanji and never surfaced. This tale has been vehemently refuted by almost all the researchers, INA veterans and Bose kin. On gut feeling, one would go with them. Some detractors of the Bhagwanji theory level a most serious charge on the Government of India. It is alleged that to divert people's attention from Bose's incarceration, and possible elimination, in the USSR, the Intelligence Bureau under Prime Minister Jawaharlal Nehru, the protege of Bose's rival Mohandas Gandhi, planted several holy men across the country, beginning with the infamous Shoulmari Baba. People either went gaga about these fake 'Netajis' or scoffed at the very controversy. This also helped hush up the Soviet connection altogether."

A Brief History of Governmental Flip-flop on Netaji Mystery

The year 1997 was a watershed for Netaji mystery. The Calcutta High Court was approached by lawyer Rudra Jyoti Bhattacharjee, who wanted the Government to take some actions over the Subhash Bose death case. While the court heard arguments and counterarguments, it came to know what exactly the Central Government thought of the matter.

"The Government of India has ... maintained and is maintaining even now that a further probe is required and the information that Netaji died in the plane crash on August 18, 1945 is full of loopholes, contradictions and, therefore inconclusive."

With that background in mind, Chief Justice Prabha Shankar Mishra ordered the Central Government on 30 April 1998 that it should "launch a vigorous enquiry in accordance with law by appointing, if necessary, a Commission of Inquiry as a special case for the purpose of giving an end to the controversy".

After an year of deliberations, in which the then Home Minister LK Advani, Home Secretary Kamal Pande, Principal Secretary to the Prime Minister Brajesh Mishra, Attorney General Soli Sorabjee took a leading part, the government agreed and notified that "Central Government is of the opinion that it is necessary to appoint a commission of Inquiry for the purpose of making an in-depth inquiry into a definitive matter of public importance". It also underlined that "there is widespread feeling among the public that the issue of finding the truth about Netaji still remains".

That same notification dated 14 April 1999 assigned the following points of inquiry to the commission headed by Justice MK Mukherjee, a retired judge of the Supreme Court of India:

(a) whether Netaji Subhash Chandra Bose is dead or alive;

(b) if he is dead, whether he died in the plane crash, as alleged;

(c) whether the ashes in the Japanese temple are ashes of Netaji;

(d) whether he has died in any other manner at any other place and, if so, when and how;

(e) if he is alive, in respect of his whereabouts.

Even a casual look at the above would convince any reasonable person that the government in 1999 had no clue about Netaji's fate. And nor were they in a position to confirm whether or not the ashes in Tokyo were of Netaji's. Or else, there was no need to put all these queries to the commission.

Quite naturally, the government did not make a case of its own before

Mukherjee Commission as the inquiry proceeded. Soon, evidence contrary to the air crash theory emerged and, as a result, in February 2005 the government's counsel had to argue against the Taipei crash theory during the argument session. So much so, the counsel gave the Government of India the credit for helping confirm the information, originally obtained by yours truly, from Taiwan Government that no plane carrying Bose had ever crashed in Taipei.

Then twist in the tale came. Justice Mukherjee submitted his report to Home Minister in November 2005, concluding that there was no air crash, Netaji flew towards the USSR and the ashes kept in the Renkoji Temple were of a Japanese solider.

Logically speaking, this vindicated the stand taken by three successive governments, viz, United Front, NDA and the Congress, which was firmly in the saddle when the government counsel made the above submissions.

So, don't you think that there was some sort of partisan politics during the Vajpayee era. The BJP seems to be in unison with the Congress over the Subhash Bose death case. That's why you haven't heard anything on this matter from their senior leaders, with the notable exception of Dr. Murli Manohar Joshi.

Coming back to the moot point, the government took more than 7 months to study the report and did a somersault. They rejected the main finding in a single line and, in a way, asserted that Netaji had died following an air crash in Taipei, and the ashes in Renkoji temple were indeed his. The nation was not told what new information had come their way in those months warranting them to change their-long standing stance supported by the finding of a commission of inquiry appointed by them following a court order. Lawyers can tell better, but should think that the government's action is legally untenable and it would be a travesty of justice to let it prevail.

DID NETAJI REALLY DIE?

Did Netaji Really Die at Formosa?

This is a question which has been asked umpteen number of times with no satisfactory answer available. This has also been debated time and again by both Netaji loyalists as well as the media and the people of India at large.

Here we will try to explore this mystery, but by no means it is the definitive article on his death.

After dropping of the atom bomb in Hiroshima on August 8, 1945 and Nagasaki on August 9, the Japanese surrendered. But Netaji was not willing to do that since he was fighting to free India from the British.

According to Gordon, Bose flew to Bangkok on August 16, 1945 and to Saigon on August 17. He was accompanied by Col. Habibur Rehman, Col. Pritam Singh, Major Abid Hasan, S.A. Ayer and Debnath Dass. Bose had hoped to take all of them, but in vain. In Saigon, the plans had to be changed. Bose was told that only one place was available in the aircraft which was to leave for Taipei and then Dairen (Manchuria). One more seat was secured for him.

Among his Japanese co-passengers accompanying Bose in the aircraft was the Lieutenant-General Shidei, a Japanese expert on the Soviet Union who was to fly to Dairen to take command of the Kumantang army to work out the surrender. In a bomber of the 97-2 (sally type), Netaji and Col. Habibur Rehman boarded the aircraft with two heavy suit cases filled with gold and jewellery. There were ten other Japanese in the plane which took off from Tourane on August 18, 1945 between 5 and 5.15 a.m. and flew to Taipei (Japanese Taihoku).

The aircraft again took off from Taipei and just after rising to the height of 30 feet, it burst into flames and crashed. This was on August 18, at about 5 p.m. Bose received extensive burns over his whole body, the more serious ones on the head, chest and thighs. He was in a state of semi-consciousness. In a truck, he was driven up to the hospital. Dr. Yoshimi Tameyoshi who attended on Netaji state, "When he (Netaji) was laid on the bed, his injuries was cleaned with oil and dressed. During the first-four hours, he was unconscious". Later, when he gained consciousness the doctor asked him, 'Whether there was any statement, will or such matter he wanted to make' Bose answered, 'Nothing'.

—Dr. Tameyoshi added,' After the fourth hour he appeared to be sinking into unconsciousness.' At about 23.20 hours, Subhash Chandra Bose died. Apart from the injuries received about there were abrasions on his elbows and knees."

Dr. Yoshimi Tameyoshi's statement is a first-class eye-witness account to establish Subhash Chandra Bose's death on August 18, at Takhoku. This statement was brought to light by the noted archivist and historian Dr. T.R. Sareen from the achieves of Public Records Office records. Dr. Gordon, by using this source, has established Bose's death. We have to note that this statement forms a part of British records submitted to Captain A.R. Turner in-charges of War Crimes Liaison Branch (Formosa).

The major question arises is whether the statement given by Taneyoshi's is factual or not. Remember that the Britishers were the victor's, and history is written by the winners. Also he could have been pressurised by the Britishers to give such a statement so that a major headache, at least for the time being, could be avoided.

But things are not as simple as said above. There are many big questions which have been left unanswered.

These include—Whether Netaji was really there in the plane at the time of the crash? Was he mortally injured after the crash? Did he somehow escape before or after the crash? Are the ashes at Renkoji temple really his? Was Goomnami Baba really Netaji? Was the crash done by the British intelligence? Was he really captured by the Russians and kept in captivity? If Netaji survived than where did he really went after that and why didn't he made himself public? Where did he disappear?

The first enquiry was setup almost immediately by Lord Wavell, the Viceroy, to look into the disappearance of Netaji. It is believed that after an extensive inquiry they came to the conclusion that Netaji had died. Though no official report have ever been made in this regard. The first Indian enquiry relating to Netaji's death was commissioned by the Government of India (GOI) under Shah Nawaz Khan, a Railway Minister in the Union Government. He quickly declared that Netaji Subhash Chandra Bose had died at Formosa on the 18th of August, 1945. This decision seemed to be given with a lot of haste and without the necessary investigation. While it is undoubted that he was a great soldier, one of the three most important INA figures after Netaji, but did he really had the skills to carry out an investigation of this nature?

Then came the Khosla enquiry. It was commissioned by the GOI under Prime Minister Mrs. Indira Gandhi. It was a one member commission chaired by G.D. Khosla, a retired Chief Justice of the Punjab High Court. It visited many important places like Singapore, Bangkok and Rangoon and interviewed many people.

It is said that the relationship between Netaji Subhash Chandra Bose and Khosla were not great. Both of them met in England, when Netaji was giving the ICS examination. It is said that Netaji and Mr. Khosla had a small fight when Netaji returned to India, but Khosla was still keen on giving the exam.

There was a further loss of credibility, because Khosla was said to be very close to the Nehru family and it is historic that in the later years, Netaji and Pandit Nehru were not on the best of terms.

Also Khosla didn't visit many key places like Formosa, which caused a further dent in his credibility.

After four years he gave the verdict that Netaji Subhash Chandra Bose had died at Formosa. For this he relied on the medical report of Dr. Yoshimi

Taneyoshi, Captain of the Imperial Japanese army, the surgeon incharge when Netaji was reported to have succumbed.

But this report was rejected by many eminent persons outside the Congress, including Morarji Desai.

The BJP (Bhartiya Janta Party) led NDA (National Democratic Alliance) has instituted the latest such inquiry by setting up Justice J.C. Mukherjee commission.

But a significant amount of time has passed since the incident and most of the documents relating to the period, include those of crashes in Formosa, are not available. Also many key witnesses or those believed to have information in that regard are no longer alive, which will hamper the commission.

But at the same time technology has improved dramatically over the years. DNA testing can be (and have been) done. After the Mukherjee commission's report is made public it may be possible to authoritatively say whether the Renkoji ashes or Goomnami Baba have anything to do with Netaji Subhash Chandra Bose.

2

Bose, Indian National Army and Freedom of India

A further controversy exists, especially within India, with regards to the attitude and treatment towards the Indian National Army (INA) by the Post 1947 Governments of India as well as the omission of the events of September 1945-46 from the historical records of the Freedom Movement.

Nehru, in 1948, refused to readmit the men of the INA to the Indian Army after independence. He cited the break in the service of the ex-INA men, as well as the effects on the Indian Army of taking ex-INA troops into their ranks. However, it has been noted that as late as 1948, considerable pro-INA sentiments existed in the army as well as public psyche, attracting strong dissatisfactions from members of Nehru's cabinet, Defence Minister Sardar Baldev Singh is on record as having commented on the need to strengthen the morale of the Indian army "which in recent months has been somewhat tried for internal discipline and perverse lauding of the "Indian National Army" and its role in the war against the Allies in Asia."

Also, although Nehru promised pensions, the men of the INA were however not eligible for the Freedom Fighters Pension till 1972. A number of people, notably ex-members of the INA and sympathetic groups have accused the Nehru, Mountbatten, and subsequently successive Congress governments, of largely ignoring and not-recognising the role of the INA, as well as the events surrounding it between 1945-46, in the history of the Independence movement.

These have been compounded by a number of conspiracy—theories and news reports in the past on agreements between the Indian political leadership to hand over its leader Subhash Chandra Bose as a War Criminal if he was found to be alive. Other historians have suggested a systemic bias of the. Later historians have, however, argued that given the political aim and nature of the entire Azad Hind movement especially the Indian National Army, Nehru's decisions may have been to prevent politicisation of the army and assert civilian authority over the military.

Further criticisms have been made in recent years for the general hardships and apathy surrounding the conditions of ex-INA troops including, for example, the circumstances surrounding the death and funeral of Ram Singh Thakur, the composer of India's National Anthem. Also, criticisms have been made for not recognising as freedom-fighters for India the expatriate Indians, notably Burmese Indians, who joined the INA and were not repatriated to India at the end of the war. Most are not recognised as Indian citizens, and not recognised as citizens in their adopted countries, effectively being stateless people.

COMMEMORATIONS

Memorials

Subhash Chandra Bose laying foundation stone of INA War Memorial, Singapore, 8 July 1945.

- The INA War Memorial at Singapore to commemorate the *"Unknown Warrior"* of the INA. Started on 8 July 1945 the memorial was situated at the Esplanade Park. It was destroyed on Mountbatten's orders when allied troops reoccupied the city. The words inscribed upon the War Memorial were the motto of the INA: *Ittefaq* (Unity), *Etmad* (Faith) and *Kurbani* (Sacrifice).
- The Former Indian National Army Monument, was established in 1995 by the National Heritage Board of Singapore at the site where the old memorial stood with financial donations from the Indian community in Singapore. The site is now officially one of the Historical sites in Singapore.
- The Indian National Army Memorial at Moirang, Manipur commemorates the place where the flag of Azad Hind was raised by Col. Shaukat Hayat Malik. Moirang was the first Indian Territory captured by the INA. The memorial suffered damage in an insurgent attack in 2004 when the Statue of the Springing Tiger on the entrance was blown up.
- *Swatantrata Sainani Smarak* (Memorial to the soldiers of the Independence Army) is an Indian National Army (INA) memorial at the Salimgarh Fort, at Delhi, adjacent to the Red Fort, on the banks of the Yamuna. The site has been neglected for a number of years now

and fallen into disrepair. Its exhibits include the Indian National Army uniform worn by Colonel Prem Sahgal, riding boots and coat buttons of Colonel Gurbaksh Singh Dhillon, photographs of Subhash Chandra Bose. In addition, a separate gallery also holds material and photographs from excavations carried out by the Archaeological Survey of India inside the fort in 1995.

Postage and Philately

- Jai Hind, the INA's battle cry, became Independent India's first commemorative post mark on 15 August 1947.
- The first postage stamp issued by Independent India shows the Indian Flag with the letters Jai Hind in the top right hand corner.

These were a pat of the *Jai Hind* series of stamps issued on 15 August 1947.

- Commemorative postage stamps were issued by the Indian government in 1968 and 1993 respectively to commemorate the 25th and the 50th anniversaries of the establishment of Azad Hind at Singapore.

The Indian Postal Department also includes the six unused Azad Hind Stamps in its commemorative book *India's Freedom Struggle through India Postage Stamps*.

WORKS ON THE INA

The Indian National Army, from the time it came into public perception in India around the time of the Red Fort Trials, and from the time it found its way into the works of Military Historians around the world, has been the subject of a number of projects, both of academic, historical and of popular nature. Some of these are critical of the army, some—especially of the ex-INA men are biographical or autobiographical, while still others are works of History and politics that tell the story of the INA. A large number of these give a large analysis of Subhash Chandra Bose and his work with the INA.

THE FIRST INA

Japan, as well as South East Asia was a major refuge for Indian nationalists living in exile before the start of World War II who formed strong proponents of militant nationalism and also influenced Japanese policy significantly. Although Japanese intentions and policies with regards to India were far from concrete at the start of the war, Japan had sent intelligence missions, notably under Major I Fujiwara, into South Asia even before the start of the World

War II to garner support from the Malayan Sultans, overseas Chinese, the Burmese resistance and the Indian movement.

These missions were successful establishing contacts with Indian nationalists in exile in Thailand and Malaya, supporting the establishment and organisation of the Indian Independence League. At the outbreak of World War II in South East Asia, 70,000 Indian troops were stationed in Malaya. After the start of the war, Japan's spectacular Malayan Campaign had brought under her control considerable of Indian Prisoners of War, notably nearly 55,000 after the Fall of Singapore. The conditions of service within the British Indian Army as well as the conditions in Malaya had fed dissension among these troops. From these troops, the First Indian National Army was formed under Mohan Singh Deb and received considerable Japanese aid and support. It was formally proclaimed in September 1942 and declared the subordinate military wing of the Indian Independence League in June that year. The unit was dissolved in December 1942 and Mohan Singh was arrested and exiled to Pulau Ubin after apprehensions of Japanese motives with regards to the INA led to disagreements, distrust and subsequently open hostility between Mohan Singh and INA leadership on one hand, and the leagues leadership, most notable Rash Behari Bose and the Japanese military command on the other. A large number of the initial volunteers chose to revert to Prisoner of War Status and large number of these were subsequently sent to work in the Death Railway or in New Guinea. From the end of December 1942 to February Rash Behari Bose struggled to hold the INA together.

THE SECOND INA

In a series of meetings between the INA leaders and the Japanese in 1943, it was decided to cede the leadership of the IIL and the INA to Subhash Chandra Bose, since a number of the officers and troops who had returned to PoW camps, or had not volunteered in the first place, made it known that they would be willing to join the INA only on the condition that it was led by Bose. Bose had, at the start of the war in Europe, escaped from house arrest to make his way to Germany, reaching Berlin on 2 April 1941. In Germany he convinced Hitler, in a series of conferences, to support the cause of Indian Independence, forming the Free India Legion and the Azad Hind Radio By early 1943, Bose had turned his attention to Southeast Asia.

With its large overseas Indian population, it was recognised that the region was fertile ground for establishing an anti-colonial force to fight the Raj. In January 1943, the Japanese invited Bose to lead the Indian nationalist movement in East Asia. He accepted and left Germany on 8 February. After a three-month journey by submarine, and a short stop in Singapore, he reached Tokyo on 11 May 1943, where he made a number of radio broadcasts to the Indian communities, exhorting them to join in the fight for India's Independence.

On 15 February 1943, the Army itself was put under the command of Lt. Col. M.Z. Kiani. The former ranks and badges were revived. A policy forming body was formed with the Director of the Military Bureau, Lt. Col Bhonsle, in charge and clearly placed under the authority of the IIL. Under Bhonsle served Lt. Col. Shah Nawaz Khan as Chief of General Staff, Major P.K. Sahgal as Military Secretary, Major Habib Ur Rahman as commandant of the Officers' Training School and Lt. Col. A.C. Chatterji (later Major A.D. Jahangir) as head of enlightenment and culture.

On 4 July 1943, two days after reaching Singapore, Subhash Chandra Bose assumed the leadership of the IIL and the INA in a ceremony at Cathay Building. Bose's influence was notable. His appeal not only re-invigorated the fledgling INA, which previously consisted mainly of POWs, his appeals also touched a chord with the Indian expatriates in South Asia as local civilians-ranging from barristers to plantation workers – had no military experience joined the INA, doubled its troop strength. An Officers' Training School for INA officers, led by Habib Ur Rahman, and the Azad School for the civilian volunteers were set up to provide training to the recruits. A youth wing of the INA, composed of 45 Young Indians personally chosen by Bose and affectionately known as the Tokyo Boys, were also sent to Japan's Imperial Military Academy to train as fighter pilots. Also, possibly the first time in Asia, and even the only time outside the USSR, a women's regiment, the Rani of Jhansi regiment was raised as a combat force.

TROOP STRENGTH

Although there are slight variations in estimates, the INA is considered to have comprised about 40,000 troops when it was disbanded. The following is an estimate attributed to Lt. Colonel G.D. Anderson of British intelligence:

> *There were 45,000 Indian troops from Malaya captured and assembled in Singapore when the Japanese captured it. Of these, about 5,000 refused to join the First INA. The INA at this time had 40,000 recruits. The Japanese were prepared to arm 16,000. When the "first INA" collapsed, about 4,000 withdrew. The Second INA, commanded by Subhash Chandra Bose, started with 12,000 troops. Further recruitment of ex-Indian army personnel added about 8,000-10,000. About 18,000 Indian civilians enlisted during this time. In 1945, at the end of the INA, it consisted of about 40,000 soldiers.*

ORDER OF BATTLE

The exact organisation of the INA and its troop strength is not known, as Fay notes, since its records were destroyed by the withdrawing Azad Hind Government before Rangoon fell. .Fay's account of the INA gives the following account.

- The 1st Division was under Mohammed Zaman Kiyani. It drew a large number of ex-Indian army PoWs who had joined Mohan Singh's first INA. In addition, it also drew PoWs who had not joined in 1942. The 1st division consisted of:
  - The 2nd Guerrilla regiment, or the Gandhi Brigade under Col. Inayat Kiani, consisting of two infantry battalions.
  - The 3rd Guerrilla regiment, or the Azad Brigade under Col. Gulzara Singh, consisting of three battalions.
  - The 4th Guerrilla regiment, or the Nehru Brigade. This unit was later under the command of Lt. Col G S Dhillon.
  - The 1st Guerrilla regiment, or the Subhash Brigade under Col. Shah Nawaz Khan, consisting of three infantry battalions. This unit was the first and the major commitment of the INA to the U Go Offensive.

The 1st Division was lightly armed. Each battalion was composed of five Companies of infantry. The individual companies were armed with six antitank rifles, six Bren guns and six Vickers machine guns. Some NCOs carried hand grenades, while men going forward on duty were issued British stocks of hand grenades by senior officer of the Bahadur groups attached to each unit. Mortars were available, but Fay points out these were not available at battalion level.

- The 2nd Division under Aziz Ahmed. The 2nd division was formed to a large extent after the Imphal offensive had started, and drew a large remnant of the Hindustan Field Force of the First INA. The 2nd Division consisted of.
  - The 1st Infantry Regiment, later to be merged with the 5th Guerrilla regiment to form the 2nd Infantry Regiment. The 1st Infantry drew a large number of civilian volunteers from Burma and Malaya, and came to ve equipped with the lions share of the heavy armament that the INA possessed.
  - The 5th Guerilla regiment, later to be renamed the 2nd Infantry Regiment under Col Prem Sahgal. This unit drew a large number of the remnants of the Hindustan Field Force.

- An additional 3rd Division of the INA was composed chiefly of local volunteers in Malaya and Singapore. This unit disbanded before Japan Surrendered. There was also a motor transport division, but this known to not have had a significant capability or resources.
- The Rani of Jhansi Regiment, under Lakshmi Sahgal, composed of female volunteers from Malaya and Burma.

COMMAND STRUCTURE

The INA in Operation

As the Japanese offensive opened, the INA sent its first forces into battle. The INA's own strategy was to avoid set-piece battles for which it lacked arms, armament as well as manpower. Initially, it sought to obtain arms as well as increase its ranks from British Indian soldiers expected to defect to patriotic cause.

Once the Japanese forces were able to break the British defences at Imphal, the INA would cross the hills of North-East India into the Gangetic plain, where it was to work as a guerrilla army and expected to live off the land, garner support, supplies, and ranks from amongst the local populace to ultimately touch off a revolution.

Prem Kumar Sahgal, an officer of the INA once Military secretary to Subhash Bose and later tried in the first Red Fort trials, explained that although the war itself hung in balance and nobody was sure if the Japanese would win, initiating a popular revolution with grass-root support within India would ensure that even if Japan lost the war ultimately, Britain would not be in a position to re-assert its colonial authority, which was ultimately the aim of the INA and Azad Hind.

1944

The plans decided between Bose and Kawabe envisaged the INA was to be assigned an independent sector of its own in the U Go offensive and no INA unit was to operate less than a battalion strength. For operational purposes, the Subhash Brigade was assigned under the command of the Japanese general Head Quarters in Burma.

Advance parties of the Bahadur Group also went forward with the advanced Japanese units early during the offensive. As Japan opened its offensive towards India, the INA's first division, consisting of four Guerrilla regiments, was divided between the diversionary Ha Go offensive in Arakan 1944, with one battalion reaching as far as Mowdok in Chittagong.

A Bahadur group unit, led by Shaukat Malik, took the border enclave of Moirang in early April. The main body of the first division was however committed to the U Go Offensive directed towards Manipur, initially successfully protecting the Japanese flanks against Chin and Kashin guerrilas as the Mutaguchi's three divisions crossed the Chindwin river and the Naga Hills, and later directed towards the main offensive through Tamu in the direction of Imphal and Kohima.

However, by the time Khan's forces left Tamu, the offensive had been held, and the troops were redirected to Kohima. By the time Khan's forces reached Ukhrul in the vicinity of Kohima, Japanese forces had began their slow withdrawal Kohima.

The first division suffered the same fate as did Mutaguchi's Army when the siege of Imphal was broken. With little or no supplies and supply lines deluged by the Monsoon, harassed by Allied air-dominance and local Burmese irregulars, the INA began withdrawing when the 15th Army and Burma Area Army began withdrawing, and suffer the same terrible fate as wounded, starved and diseased men succumbed during the hasty withdrawal into Burma.

The INA lost a substantial amount of men and materiel in the retreat, and a number of units were disbanded or used to feed the newly formed units of the second division.

1945

As the allied Burma campaign began the following year, however, the INA remained committed to the defence of Burma, and was a part of the Japanese defensive deployments.

The second division, tasked with the defence of Irrawaddy and the adjoining areas around Nangyu, was instrumental in opposing Messervy's 7th Indian Division when it attempted to cross the river at Pagan and Nyangyu during Irrwaddy operations. Later, during the Battles of Meiktila and Mandalay, the 2nd division was instrumental in denying the British 17th Division the area around Mount Popa that would have exposed the Flank of Kimura's forces attempting to retake Meiktila and Nyangyu.

Ultimately however, the division was obliterated. As the Japanese situation became precarious, Azad Hind withdrew from Rangoon with Ba Maw's government and the Japanese forces for Singapore along with the remnants of the first division and the Rani of Jhansi Regiment. Nearly 6000 troops amongst the surviving units of the Army remained in Rangoon under A.D Loganathan surrendered as Rangoon fell, and helped keep order till the allied forces entered the city.

The only Indian territory that the Azad Hind govt controlled were the Indian territories that fell during the Imphal offensive, and the islands of Andaman and Nicobar. However, the latter two were bases for the Japanese Navy, and the navy never really fully relinquished control. Enraged with the lack of administrative control, the Azad Hind Governor, Lt. Col Loganathan later relinquished his authority to return to the Government's head quarters in Rangoon. The Japanese forces is said to have carried out torture on thousands of local inhabitants during the occupation, and some historians inexplicably apportion the blame to Subhash Bose's provisional government.

End of the INA

As the Japanese withdrawal from Burma progressed, the other remnants began a long march over land and on foot towards Singapore, along with Subhash Chandra Bose. The withdrawing forces suffered casualties regularly in clashes with Aung San's Burmese resistance, as well as Chinese guerrillas who harassed the Japanese troops. At the time of Japan's surrender in September 1945, Bose left for Manchuria to attempt to contact the advancing Soviet troops, and was reported to have died in an air crash near Taiwan.

LITERARY WORKS

The first literary works on the INA were published as early as 1946. Some were works of fiction with the INA as the central theme and subject, others the records of the INA that the authors were able to obtain from the ex-servicemen, or from what information was available from the trials and from what the British Intelligence possessed and that the authors had access to. Some of the literature focused on the first INA trial itself. The notable work on INA include

- *Two Historic Trials at Red Fort* by Moti Ram. (New Delhi: Roxy Printing Press, 1946). This was one of the first published account of any sort of the INA and describes the Trial of Major General Shah Nawaz Khan, Col Prem Sahgal, and Col G.S Dhillon that took place between November and December, 1946. Moti Ram was the staff correspondent of the Hindustan Times at the first Red Fort Trial and wrote his book on what information was available at the trial, and from interviews with the defendants, Sahgal, Khan and Dhillon. The book also provides an account of the 1858 trial of Bahadur Shah Zafar.
- *Jai Hind, the Diary of a Rebel Daughter of India. Bombay, 1945* (fiction) by Amritlal Seth. The book is a work of fiction narrating the story of a recruit of the Rani of Jhansi Regiment. It is believed to be loosely based on the story of Lakshmi Sahgal.

- *The Day of the Scorpion* and *The Towers of Silence,* second and third respectively of Paul Scott's *Raj Quartet* that mentions *Jiffs* in the political and social context in which the term found use in the Eastern Army during the war.
- *The Glass Palace* by Amitav Ghosh chronicles the fictional life of a Rangoon Teak trader and describes the occupation of Rangoon and the Indian perspectives and efforts In the book, Uma Dey is a widow and Indian Independence League activist. Her appearance in the later half of the book is used as a device to characterize the postcolonial divisions for the remainder of the novel. The novel describes the Burma front in some detail, examining the motivations of those Indian officers who joined the INA and those who did not)

Historical literary works on the INA includes

- *My memories of I.N.A. & its Netaji'* by Shah Nawaz Khan.
- *The Indian National Army-Second Front of the Indian Independence Movement* by Kalyan Ghosh.
- *Jungle Alliance: Japan and the Indian National Army.* by Joyce C Lebra.
- *The Forgotten Army: India's Armed Struggle for Independence, 1942-45.* by Peter Fay.

Visual Media

Notable works on the INA in the visual and electronic media include

- *The War of The Springing Tiger* (1984)-made by Granada Television for Channel 4. It examines the role of the Indian National Army during the Second World War. The documentary focuses on a number of aspects, including why the PoWs chose to join the INA, its role in the Burma and Imphal Campaign, as well as exploring its role in the independence movement. The documentary took contributions from Lakhsmi and Prem Sahgal.
- *The Forgotten Army*-(1999)-Film India. This was a documentary directed by Kabir Khan and produced by Akhil Bakshi following their famous *Azad Hind Expedition* in 1994-95. The expedition retraced the route taken by the troops of the INA from Singapore to Imphal and ends at Red Fort, where the famous trial of the officers were held. The expedition team had among its members Col G.S Dhillon who himself was one of the famous accused in the first trial, Captain Lakshmi Sahgal, who commanded the Rani of Jhansi Regiment and was also the minister in Charge of Women's affairs in the Azad Hind Govt and Captain S.S. Yadava, an INA veteran and once the general secretary of All India INA Committee, as well as prominent members of the

Indian Parliament. The expedition met, and honoured, a number of INA veterans residing in South East Asia. The then Indian Prime Minister PV Narasimha Rao sent through the expedition team goodwill messages to the heads of state of the countries it went through. The documentary went on to win the Grand Jury Prize at the Film South Asia festival in 1999.

- *Hitler's secret Indian army* (2004)-BBC-By Mike Thomson. This traces briefly the story of Bose's Azad Hind Legion in Europe, but does not attempt to distinguish or explain the differences between the Legion and the INA.
- *Historical Journey of the Indian National Army*-From the National Archives of Singapore.
- *Indian National Army in East Asia*-Hindustan Times.

Cinema

INA has also been the source of or a significant context of a number of movies in a number of Indian languages. Notable amongst these include

- *Pahla Admi*, a 1950 film by Bimal Roy and INA veteran Nazir Ahmed.
- *Samadhi*, a 1950 Hindi film by Ramesh Saigal. The movie was a fictional drama set in Singapore around the time the second INA was rising. The lead character of Shekhar, played by Ashok Kumar, is a young recruit to the INA.
- *Indian*, a 1996 Tamil film directed by S. Shankar. The plot describes one of the main character, Senapathy, as an ex-soldier in the INA.
- *Netaji: The Forgotten Hero*, a 2004 movie by Shyam Benegal, traces the last five years of Subhash Chandra Bose, who was the Supreme Commander of the second INA and was instrumental in reorganising it. The film describes the story of the INA but focuses on its leader. The film was also widely noted for A R Rahman's music.

In music, *Kadam Kadam Badaye Ja...*, the INA's marching song, has since become a famous patriotic song in India. Today, it is in use as the Regimental quickmarch of the Indian Army as well as its Para Regiments. The music was composed by Ram Singh Thakur, from whose composition was later derived the tune for India's national anthem *Jana Gana Mana.*

Other mentions of the INA in popular culture abound through India, including

- The Azad Hind Fauj Marg, in New Delhi, is named after the INA, and houses the Netaji Subhash Institute of Technology named after Netaji Subhash Chandra Bose.

INDISCHE LEGION

The Legion Freies Indien, or the Indische Legion, variously known as the Tiger Legion, the Free India Legion (in English), the Azad Hind Legion, and the Indische Freiwilligen-Legion Regiment 950 or the I.R 950 (*Indisches Infanterie Regiment 950*) was an Indian armed unit raised in 1941 attached to the Wehrmacht, ostensibly according to the concept of an Indian Liberation force during World War II by Subhash Chandra Bose in Nazi Germany.

The initial recruits were Indian student volunteers resident in Germany at the time, and a handful from the Indian PoWs captured by Rommel during his North Africa Campaign. It would later draw a larger number of Indian PoWs as volunteers.

Raised initially as an assault group that would form a pathfinder to a German/Indian invasion of the western frontiers of British India, only a small contingent was ever put to its original intended purpose when a hundred of the Legionnaires were parachuted into eastern Iran to infiltrate into India through Baluchistan and commence sabotage operations against the British in preparation for the anticipated national revolt.

A majority of the troops of the Free India Legion were only ever stationed in Europe—mostly in non-combat duties—from Netherlands, to Atlantic Wall duties in France till the Allied invasion of France. A small contingent, including the leadership and the officer corps, was also transferred to Azad Hind after its formation and saw action in the INA's Burma Campaign.

Although it has been alleged to have been a collaborationist Heer Unit, the unit was not deployed as a part of the German War effort or defences in Europe but did see actions against British and Polish troops and also undertook anti-partisan operations in Italy in 1944.

At the time of the surrender of the Third Reich in 1945, remaining troops of the Free India Legion made efforts to march to Neutral Switzerland over the Alps, but these efforts proved futile as they were captured by American and French troops and eventually shipped back to India to face charges of treason.

Background

The origins of the idea of raising an armed force that would fight its way into India to bring down the Raj goes back to the First World War, when the Ghadar Party and the nascent embryo of the Indian Independence League formulated plans to initiate rebellion in the British Indian Army from Punjab to Hong Kong with German Support. This plan failed after the information was leaked to British Intelligence, but only after the Hong Kong Garrison had rebelled.

However, during World War II, all the three major Axis Powers, at some stage of their campaign against Britain, sought to support/exploit the armed revolutionary activities within India and aided the recruitment of a military force from disaffected Indian prisoners of war captured while serving with the British Commonwealth forces and Indian expatriates, of which the most famous, and successful, was probably the Indian National Army that came into being with Japanese Support in the Far East. Italy had in 1942 created the Battaglione Azad Hindustan, with ex-Indian Army personnel and Italians previously resident in India and Persia, that ultimately served under Ragruppamento Centri Militari. However, these efforts proved unsuccessful, given the overtly propagandist nature of their efforts that ultimately found little acceptance among the constituent soldiers, and the lack of a leadership that would deemed legitimate by the troops. By November 1942, following the defeats in El Alamein, the Italian efforts had failed.

However, at this time in India, although the Congress party had passed resolutions conditionally supporting the fight against fascism, Indian public opinion was more hostile at Britain's unilateral decision to declare India a belligerent on the side of the Allies. Among the more rebellious amongst Indian political leaders of the time was Subhash Chandra Bose, who was viewed as a potent threat enough that when the war started, the Rajput him under arrest, and later, house arrest.

Bose escaped from under British surveillance at his house in Calcutta on January 19, 1941, with the help of family members, members of his party—the Forward Bloc-and later the Abwehr, he made his way through Afghanistan to the Soviet Union. Once in Russia the NKVD transported Bose to Moscow where he hoped that Russia's traditional enmity to British rule in India would result in support for his plans for a popular rising in India.

However, Bose found the Soviets' response disappointing and was rapidly passed over to the German Ambassador in Moscow, Count von der Schulenberg, who arranged for Bose to be sent to Berlin at the beginning of April where he met Rippentrop and later, Hitler. In Berlin, Bose set up the Azad Hind Radio and the Free India Centre which commenced broadcasting to Indians in short wave frequencies. The Azad Hind Radio broadcasts were estimated to have regularly been received by 30,000 Indians who possessed the requisite receiver. However, soon, Bose's aim became to raise an army that he imagined would march to India's NWFP with German forces through the Caucasus and trigger the downfall of the Raj.

Origin

The first troops of the Free India Legion were derived from Rommel's Indian PoWs captured at El Mekili, Libya during the Battles for Tobruk.

Initially a core group of 27 officers were selected in May 1941 and flown to Berlin. A larger PoW camp of about 10,000 was also set up in Annaburg where Subhash Bose met Indian PoWs. From these, a group of approximately 6,000 men were transferred to the Frankenburg Camp, from which a further core of 300 soldiers were sent to Königsbrück for training and induction. It was at Königsbrück that uniforms were issued, in German feldgrau with the badge of the Leaping Tiger of Azad Hind. The formation of the Indian National Army was announced by the German Propaganda Ministry in January 1942. It did not, however, take oath until 26 August 1942, as the Legion Freies Indien of the German Army. By May of 1943, the numbers had been swelled, aided by the enlistment as volunteers of Indian expatriates in Germany.

Organization

The British Indian Army, possibly as an extension of the divide and rule policy, organized regiments and units on the basis of religion and regional identity. Bose, from very early on, sought to eradicate this practice to build on an unified Indian identity. Consequently, the Free India Legion was organized as mixed units so that Muslims, Hindus, Sikhs, Jats, Rajputs, Marathas and Garhwalis all served side-by-side. Approximately two-thirds of the Legion's members were Muslim and one-third Hindu and other religions, including a large number of Sikhs.. That Bose's idea of developing a unified nationalist identity was successful is evident from the fact that when Himmler proposed in late 1943—after Bose's Departure to the Far East—that the Muslim soldiers of the I.R. 950 be recruited into the 13th Waffen Mountain Division of the SS Handschar (1st Croatian) that was formed at the time, the head of the SS Head office Gottlob Berger was obliged to point out that while the Bosnians perceived themselves as people of an European identity, the Muslims perceived themselves as Indians.

UNIFORM AND STANDARD

The uniform issued to the Free India Legion were the standard German Army uniform of feldgrau in winter and Khaki in Summer. Additionally, the troops wore on their right upper arm a specially designed arm badge in the shape of the shield with three horizontal stripes of the saffron, white and green-the colours of the flag of Azad Hind—and featuring a leaping tiger on the white middle band. The legend Freies Indien inscribed in black featured on a white background above the tricolor. A saffron, white and green transfer was also worn on the left side of their helmets. Sikhs in the Legion were permitted to wear a turban, of a colour appropriate to their uniform as dictated by their religion instead of the usual peaked field cap.

The standard of the Free India Legion-presented as regimental colours in 1942-featured the same design as the arm badge of the IR 950 consisting of saffron, white and green horizontal bands in the stated order from top to bottom. The white middle band was approximately three times the width of the two colored bands. The words "AZAD" and "HIND" in white were inscribed over the saffron and green bands respectively. Also over the white middle band featured a leaping tiger. This is essentially the same design that the Azad Hind Government later adopted as their flag, although photographic evidence shows that the later Indian National Army, at least during the Burma Campaign, may not have carried it as their Battle Standard, opting for the Flag of the Congress instead.

Structure and Units

Free India Legion was organized as a standard German army infantry regiment of three battalions of four companies each, with, at least initially all the commissioned officers German. It has been later referred to as Panzergrenadier Regiment 950 (indische), indicating the unit was partially motorized. It was equipped with 81 motor vehicles and 700 horses. In this structure, the legion came to consist of

- I. Bataillon | Infanterie Kompanien 1 to 4
- II. Bataillon | Infanterie Kompanien 5 to 8
- III. Bataillon | Infanterie Kompanien 9 to 12
- 13th Infanteriegeschütz Kompanie (Infantry-Gun Company | consisting of six 7.5cm leichtes Infanteriegeschütz 18)
- 14th Panzerjäger Kompanie (Anti-tank Company | consisting of six Panzerabwehrkanone)
- 15th Pionier Kompanie (Engineer Company)
- Ehrenwachkompanie (Honour Guard Company)

It also consisted of Hospital staff and Training and Maintenance Staff (Ausbildungs und Betreutungsstab)

Freies Indien in Operation

It is doubtful that Subhash Chandra Bose envisaged the Free India Legion (or Azad Hind Legion as it came to be more popularly known by the time he left Germany for the far east) as an army sufficient or strong enough to conduct a campaign across Persia into India on its own. Instead, most historians accept that the IR 950 was to become the path finder would precede a much larger Indo-German force in a caucasian campaign into the western frontiers of British India that would encourage public resentment of the Raj and incite the British Indian army into revolt.

To this end, Operation Bajadere was launched in January 1942 when a detachment of the Freies Indien, numbering about one hundred and having trained with the German Special Forces, were paradropped into Eastern Persia tasked to infiltrate into India through Baluchistan. They were also tasked to commence sabotage operations in preparation for the anticipated national revolt. Information passed on to Abwehr headquarters in Berlin from their office in Kabul indicate that they were successful.

Following German defeat in Europe at Stalingrad and in North Africa at El Alamein it became clear that an Axis assault through Iran or even USSR was unlikely. Bose had in the mean time travelled to the Far East where the Japanese troops were threatening India. Bose's army in the South Asia, the Indian National Army successfully engaged the allies along with the Japanese 15th Army in Burma and ultimately entered India through Moirang to lay siege on Imphal. The German Naval High Command at this time made the decision to transfer the leadership and a segment of the Freies Indien to the Azad Hind Government in South Asia and on 21 January, it was formally made a part of the Indian National Army.

Holland and France

A majority of the troops of the Indian Legion, however, were to remain in Europe through the war and was never utilized in their original perceived role over Persia and Central Asia. The Legion was transferred to Zeeland in the Netherlands in April 1943 as part of the Atlantic Wall duties and later to France in September 1943, attached to 344 Infanterie-Division, and later the 159 Infanterie-Division of the Wehrmacht.

From Beverloo in Belgium, I Battalion was reassigned to Zandvoort in May 1943 were they stayed till relieved by Georgian troops in August. In September 1943, the battalion was deployed on the Atlantic coast of Bordeaux on the Bay of Biscay. The II Battalion moved from Beverloo to the island of Texel in May 1943 and stayed there till relived in September of that year. From here, it was deployed to Les Sables d'Olonne in France.. The III Battalion remained at Oldebroek as Corps Reserve till the end of September 1943. Where they gained a "wild and loathsome" reputation amongst the natives.

Indische Freiwilligen Legion der Waffen

The legion was stationed in the Lacanau region of Bordeaux at the time of the Normandy landings and remained there for up to two months after D-Day. On the 8th of August its control was transferred to the Waffen SS (as was that of every other volunteer unit of the Wehrmacht).

Command of the legion was very shortly transferred from Kurt Krapp to Heinz Bertling. The Indian personnel noticed a change of command was at hand and started to complain.

Noting he wasn't "wanted" Bertling kindly refused the assignment and headed back to Berlin. On 15 August, 1944, the unit pulled out of Lacanau to make its way back to Germany.

It was in the second leg of this journey, from Poitier to Chatrou that it suffered its first combat casualty (Lt. Ali Khan) while engaging French Regular forces in the town of Dun. The unit also engaged with allied armour at Nuis St. Georges while retreating across the Loire to Dijon. It was regularly harassed by the French Resistance, suffering two more casualties (Lt. Kalu Ram and Capt. Mela Ram). The unit moved from Remisemont, through Alsace, to Oberhofen near the town of Heuberg in Germany in the winter of 1944, where it stayed till March 1945.

Italy

II Battalion, 9th Company, of the Legion also saw action in Italy. Having been deployed in the spring of 1944, it faced the British 5th Corps and the Polish 2nd Corps before it was withdrawn from the front to be used in antipartisan operations. It surrendered to the Allied forces April 1945, still in Italy.

End of the Legion Freies Indien

With the defeat of the Third Reich imminent in May 1945, the Indian Legion sought sanctuary in neutral Switzerland. The remainder of the unit undertook a desperate march along the shores of Lake Constance, attempting to enter Switzerland via the alpine passes. This was, however, unsuccessful and the Legion was captured by US and French forces and delivered to British and Indian forces in Europe. There is some evidence that some of these Indian troops were shot by French Moroccan troops in the town of Immenstadt after their capture. The captured troops would later be shipped back to India where a number of the troops would stand trial for treason. It is alleged that a number of the Indian soldiers were shot by French troops before their delivery to British Forces.

LEGACY OF THE FREE INDIA LEGION

The integral associations of the Free India Legion with Nazi Germany and (later) Japan means its legacy is judged from two distinct view points- one of a collaborationist army of the Third Reich, and the other as the realization of a liberation army against the British Raj in India.

The Free India Legion was conceived with the same doctrine as the Indian National Army and the entire Azad Hind movement, it has found little exposure since the end of the war even in Independent India, possibly due to a perception that their fight was far removed from the Battlefields of Burma, a land much closer to India where the troops of the INA fought and died and caught the public imagination. To consider the legacy of Free India Legion, however, one has to consider both the Azad Hind Movement (of which the Legion was possibly a birth mother, and certainly an integral plan of Bose's initial plans) and the events that happened at the time, both in and away from the public eye.

Abandoned by its proclaimed leader, the politician Subhash Chandra Bose, and disillusioned by his naive assessment of the political situation the legion surrendered to the British and the Americans soon after.

Perceptions as Collaborators

In considering the history of the Free India Legion and the ramifications of its creation, the most controversial aspect comes to be its integral link to the Nazi Germany, with a prevailing perception among some historians that they were mere mercenaries and collaborators of the Third Reich by the virtue of their uniform, oath and field of operation. To properly assess this, one has to first assess what actions it is that may be termed collaborationist. Throughout Europe, during and after the war, collaboration came to be defined broadly as; being party to the Nazi philosophy of Aryan-and even more so, German- supremacy as a race; actively supporting and participating in the Nazi atrocities against *inferior* races and occupied people in support of furthering the Nazi ideology, and; actively supporting the Nazi war effort.

As a prologue to the main debate on these issues, it is necessary to consider the views of the founder and leader of the Free India Legion, Subhash Chandra Bose (for Bose was the life blood of the entire Free India Movement in Germany, and later in South Asia). Bose, in 1931, had organized and led protest marches against the Japanese invasion of Manchuria and of China itself in 1938 when he was Congress president. In 1937 he published an article attacking Japanese Imperialism in the Far East, although he betrayed some admiration for other aspects of the Japanese regime. Bose's earlier correspondence (prior to 1939) also reflects his deep disapproval of the racist practices of, and annulment of democratic institutions in Nazi Germany. He also, however, expressed admiration for the authoritarian methods (though not the racial ideologies) which he saw in Italy and Germany during the 1930s, and thought they could be used in building an independent India .

However, this does not address whether the men of the Freies Indien were party to or in collaboration with the Nazi machinery. In these contexts, it is doubtful that the Indian PoWs were party to or held any loyalty to the Nazi ideology of racial supremacy. Although, the Nazis regarded Indians as members of the Aryan race, the small number of Indians and their particular usefulness in Germany's situation resulted in Indians not receiving the best treatment. It is also fallacious to say that the soldiers of the Free India Legion were mere mercenaries who fought with the Reich, for money or power. Indeed, when the first PoWs were brought to Annaburg camp and met by Subhash Chandra Bose, there was marked open hostility towards him as a Nazi propaganda puppet.

Subsequent to this, at a time when Bose's efforts and views had gained more sympathy, a persistent query among the (then) PoWs had been "How would the Legionary stand in relation to the German soldier?". Neither were they prepared to fight Germany's war for Germany's people for Germany's interests. Italy had in 1942 created the Battaglione Azad Hindoustan, with Indian PoWs captured by Italy, and Italians previously resident in India and Persia and led by an Indian resident in Rome for a long-time, Iqbal Shedai, whose rallying cry was to raise an Indian Unit to fight for India.

In November 1942 the unit was three hundred and fifty strong, having been trained by Italian officers. Much has been said of the "dubious loyalty" of this unit. On 9 November, after the Allied landing in North Africa, the Italian high command made the decision to send the men to Libya to fight the allies instead of to India to fight for India's freedom, contrary to Shedai's promises. The men refused to go and mutinied, insisting that they were only willing to fight for the Indian cause Shedai refused to intervene. Consequently, the Centro Militare India was disbanded. The men of the Battaglione Azad Hindustan are later said to have been either integrated into the Free India Legion or sent back to PoW camps. In another instance, immediately prior to the first deployment of the Free India Legion in Holland in April 1943, after departure of I Battalion from Koenigsbrueck, two Companies within the II Battalion refused to move. The Free India Centre-incharge of the Legion after the departure of Bose in January 1943 for South Asia-came to face a number of grievances, prime of which stood out two in particular; some were influenced by a rumour that Netaji had abandoned them and had gone off leaving them entirely in German hands; a second grievance was a perception that the Wehrmacht was now going to use them in the Western Front, instead of sending them to the East to fight for India's liberation. Even in the east, where the Indian National Army took its colossal shape, the first efforts under Capt. Mohan Singh came to nought essentially because Rash Behari Bose, who led the Indian Independence League (of which the first INA in the east was integrally linked) lost credence among the troops, appearing as a Japanese pawn. These goes to show that the men never possessed loyalty either to the Fascist or the Nazi cause or ideology and that their motivation was to fight for India' liberation, their loyalty lay to India. They were unwilling to fight for an alien nation and for a cause that was distant to the sacrosanct one for which they had abandoned their oath to the King Emperor.

These, at the least, indicate that the Free India Legion was not a lovechild of desire to serve the Reich or its philosophy, wed to an opportunity to do so. If anything, Bose sought from early on to ensure that the troops were seen and treated as equal to their German counterparts.

As for having participated in the Nazi war effort, in Europe the unit's deployments in Holland and France appear to be solely for training purposes, according to Bose's plans for the unit to be trained in some aspects of coastal defence. Bose had also had the German High Command committed to not deploying the unit for purposes of German military interests and strategy.. Indeed after the invasion of France by the Allies, the unit was ordered back to Germany. It has been suggested that the unit participated in atrocities, especially in the French town of Ruffec. This may require more authentication. The allegations that the Free India Legion was nothing more than a collaborationist Heer unit is, therefore a very simplistic view of a formation of men who possibly imagined themselves as patriots and pioneers and not as Nazis or collaborators. However, the effects of the limited actions the unit undertook in anti-partisan role in Italy also ought to be considered while making a definitive conclusion.

A LIBERATION ARMY

The Free India Legion did not engage in its original conceived role in the western front of British India, so it is not possible to hold any arguments as to whether they did-or could have-fulfilled the destiny that the men of the Legion had dreamt of. Moreover, the Legion was, and still remains, far removed from public perception in India because it did not engage its enemy, the British

Raj as did the Indian National Army in Burma, which was much closer to the home of the common Indian. Even the 9th Company's engagements in Italy with British forces are hardly known outside those circles with an interest in World War II history.

Was, then, Bose's plans for Azad Hind Legion too grandiose for its own capability? In terms of military capability, that answer is a definitive yes, for the fate of Free India Legion was tied like a corpse to that of the Axis. But in political terms, to consider the Azad Hind Legion a paper tiger can be debated, for it ignores a number of events that occurred within India and more specifically the British Indian Armed Forces in the post-war demobilisation scenario. To consider the effects that the legion had, it is necessary however, to consider the effects that the *entire* Azad Hind movement (for they were a part of the same strategy and movement) had on the culmination of British Raj in India.

After the war ended, the stories of the INA and the Free India Legion were seen as so inflammatory that, fearing mass revolts and uprisings—not just in India, but across its empire—the British Government forbid the BBC from broadcasting their story.. The Raj also brought to trial soldiers and officers of the INA (as well as the Free India Legion, of which not much is known). However, the stories of the trials at the Red Fort filtered through. The Raj observed with alarm the turnaround in the perception of Azad Hind and its army as traitors and collaborators to the greatest among the patriots.

During the trial, inspired to a large extent by the stories of the INA soldiers that were going around the country at the time mutiny broke out in the Royal Indian Navy(the mutiny had other underlying social and political causes as well; see article), incorporating ships and shore establishments of the RIN throughout India, from Karachi to Bombay and from Vizag to Calcutta. The most significant, if disconcerting factor for the Raj, was the significant militant public support that it received..

A wave of nationalist sentiments swept through the Indian troops who had fought with the allies and were in the process of being de-mobilized. The navy mutiny was followed up by another among the ground crew in the Royal Indian Air Force.

Another Army mutiny took place at Jabalpur during the last week of February 1946, soon after the Navy mutiny at Bombay. This was suppressed by force, including the use of the bayonet by British troops. It lasted about two weeks. After the mutiny, about 45 persons were tried by court martial. 41 were sentenced to varying terms of imprisonment or dismissal. In addition, a large number were discharged on administrative grounds.

In the after-effect of the mutiny, Weekly intelligence summary issued on the 25th of March, 1946 admitted that the Indian army, navy and air force units were no longer trust worthy, and, for the army, "only day to day estimates of steadiness could be made". It was decided that; if wide-scale public unrest took shape, the armed forces (including the airforce-for Quit India had shown how it could turn violent) could not be relied upon to support counter-insurgency operations as they had been during the Quit India movement of 1942, and drawing from experiences of the Tiger Legion and the INA, their actions could not be predicted from their oath to the King emperor .

Reflecting on the factors that guided the British decision to relinquish the Raj in India, Clement Attlee, the then British Prime Minister, cited several reasons, the most important of which were: which were the INA activities of Netaji Subhash Chandra Bose, which weakened the Indian Army-the foundation of the British Empire in India-and the RIN Mutiny that made the British realize that the Indian armed forces could no longer be trusted to prop up the *Raj*.

Although Britain had made, at the time of the Cripps' Mission in 1942, a commitment to grant dominion status to India after the war; these events and views held in 1946 by the administrations of the Raj would suggest to the reader that, contrary to the usual narrative of India's independence struggle, (which generally focuses on Congress and Mahatma Gandhi), the INA and the revolts, mutinies, and public resentment it germinated were an important factor in the complete withdrawal of the Raj from India.

In the same breath, whether awarded any credit for India's independence or not, the events at the time show that the strategy of Azad Hind (derived from the embryo of the Free India Legion) of achieving independence from Britain by fermenting revolts and public unrests-although a militarily a failure-remains, politically a significant and historic success.

Azad Hind Radio

Azad Hind Radio was a radio service that was started in leadership of Netaji Subhash Chandra Bose in Germany in 1942 to unite Indians to fight for freedom. Though initially based in Germany, its headquarters were shifted to Singapore and later Rangoon following the course of the war in South-East Asia. Following Netaji's departure to South East Asia, the German operations were continued by A.C.N. Nambiar, the head of the Indian Legion (in Germany) and later Ambassador of the Arzi Hukumate Azad Hind in Germany.

The radio broadcast weekly news bulletins in English, Hindi, Tamil, Bengali, Marathi, Punjabi, Pashtu, and Urdu only as these were the languages of the people volunteering and serving the Indian Legion in Germany and the Indian National Army in South-East Asia. The majority of the volunteers spoke these Indian languages only.

Azad Hind Radio served to counter the misinformation and blackout of politically sensitive information as done by the BBC. As a retort and response to the periodic misinformation on the conditions prevalent in British India, as broadcast by the BBC, Netaji had on the Azad Hind Radio referred the British Broadcasting Corporation as the "Bluff and Bluster Corporation."

Arzi Hukumat-e-Azad Hind

Arzi Hukumat-e-Azad Hind the Provisional Government of Free India), or simply Azad Hind, was an Indian Government-in-Exile established in Singapore in 1943. It was a part of a political movement originating in the 1940s outside of India with a purpose of freeing India from British Rule. Established by Indian nationalists-in-exile during the latter part of the Second World War in Singapore with monetary, military and political assistance from Imperial Japan, ostensibly to posit and portray legitimacy for the campaign of the Indian National Army as a liberation force against British Rule in India. Founded on October 21, 1943,the government was inspired along the concepts of Netaji Subhash Chandra Bose who was also the leader of the government and the Head of State of this Provisional Indian Government in Exile. The government proclaimed authority over Indian civilian and military personnel in South-East Asian British colonial territory and prospective authority over Indian territory to fall to the Japanese forces and the Indian National Army during the offensive to India during the Second World War. The government of Azad Hind had its own currency, court and civil code, and in the eyes of many Indians its existence gave a greater legitimacy to the independence struggle against the British.

However, while it possessed all the nominal requisites of a legitimate government, it lacked large and definite areas of sovereign territory until the government assumed control of the Andaman and Nicobar Islands from Japan in 1943 and the occupation of parts of Manipur and Nagaland. Throughout its existence, it remained heavily dependent on Japanese support.

Immediately after the formation of the government-in-exile, Azad Hind declared war against the Anglo-American allied forces on the Indo-Burma Front. Its army, the "Azad Hind Fauj", (Indian National Army or the *INA*) went into action against the British Indian Army and the allied forces alongside the Imperial Japanese Army in the Imphal-Kohima sector. The INA was to make its mark in the battle of Imphal where along with the Japanese 15th

Army it breached the British defences in Kohima, reaching the salient of Moirang before Allied air dominance and compromised supply lines forced both the Japanese and the INA to lift the siege.

The existence of Azad Hind was essentially coterminous with the existence of the Indian National Army. While the government itself continued until the civil administration of the Andaman Islands was returned to the jurisdiction of the British towards the end of the war, the limited power of Azad Hind was effectively ended with the surrender of the last major contingent of INA troops in Rangoon.

The supposed death of Bose is seen as culmination of the entire Azad Hind Movement.

The allies at the time, as also some postwar historians claim the government as a puppet state on the grounds of the lack of universal political recognition (the government was not recognised by allied governments and Vichy France), almost ineffective control of the Andaman and Nicobar Islands, as well as the continued dependency on Japan for support and survival.

The legacy of Azad Hind is, however, open to judgment. After the war, the Raj observed with alarm the turnaround in the perception of Azad Hind and its army as traitors and collaborators to "the greatest among the patriots". Given the tide of militant nationalism that swept through India and the resentment and revolts it inspired, it is arguable that its overarching aim-to germinate public resentment and revolts within the Indian forces of the British Indian Army to overthrow the Raj was ultimately, if belatedly for Azad Hind, successful.

Establishment

The direct origins of Azad Hind can be linked to two conferences of Indian expatriates from across South-East Asia, the first of which was held in Tokyo in March of 1942. At this conference, convened by Rash Behari Bose, an Indian expatriate living in Japan, the Indian Independence League was established as the first move towards an independent Indian state politically aligned with the Empire of Japan. Rash also moved to create a sort of liberation army that would assist in driving the British from India—this force would later become the Indian National Army. The second conference, held later that year in Bangkok, invited Subhash Chandra Bose to participate in the leadership of the League. Bose was living in Germany at the time and made the trip to Japan via submarine.

Rash Behari Bose, who was already ageing by the time the league was founded, struggled to keep the league organized and failed to secure resources for the establishment of the Indian National Army. He was replaced as president of the Indian Independence League by Subhash Chandra Bose; there is some controversy as to whether he stepped down of his own volition or by pressure from the Japanese who needed a more energetic and focused presence leading the Indian nationalists.

Bose arrived in Tokyo on June 13, 1943, and declared his intent to make an assault against the eastern provinces of India in an attempt to oust the British from control of the subcontinent. Bose arrived in Singapore on July 2nd, and in October of 1943 formally announced the establishment of the Provisional Government of Free India.

In defining the tasks of this new political establishment, Subhash declared: "It will be the task of the Provisional Government to launch and conduct the struggle that will bring about the expulsion of the British and their allies from the soil of India."

Bose, taking formal command of the demoralized and undermanned Indian National Army from Rash Bose, turned it into a professional army with the help of the Japanese. He recruited Indian civilians living in Japanese-occupied territories of South-East Asia, and incorporated vast numbers of Indian POWs from British forces in Singapore, Malaya and Hong Kong to man the brigades of the INA.

Ministers

The Provisional Government of Free India consisted of a Cabinet headed by Netaji Subhash Chandra Bose as the *Head of the State, The Prime Minister and the Minister for War and Foreign Affairs*.

Captain Doctor Lakshmi Swaminathan (later married as Lakshmi Sehgal) was the *Minister in Charge of Women's Organization*. She held this position over and above her command of the *Rani Jhansi Regiment*, a brigade of women soldiers fighting for the Indian National Army. For a regular Asian army, this women's regiment was quite visionary; it was the first of its kind established on the continent. Dr. Lakshmi was one of the most popular and prosperous gynaecologists in Singapore before she gave up her fabulous practice to lead the troops of the Rani of Jhansi Regiment. Other public administration ministers of the Provisional Government of Free India included:

- Mr. S. A. Ayer—the Minister of Broadcasting and Publicity
- Lt. Col. A. C. Chatterji—the Minister of Finance

The Indian National Army was represented by Armed Forces ministers, including:

- Lt. Col. Aziz Ahmed
- Lt. Col. N. S. Bhagat
- Lt. Col. J. K. Bhonsle
- Lt. Colonel Guizara Singh
- Lt. Col. M.Z. Kiani
- Lt. Col. A. D. Loganathan
- Lt. Col. Ehsan Qadir
- Lt. Col. Shahnawaz Khan

The Provisional Government was also constituted and administered by a number of Secretaries and Advisors to Subhash Chandra Bose, including:

- A.N. Sahay-Secretary
- Karim Ghani
- Debnath Das
- D.M. Khan
- A. Yellapa
- J. Thivy
- Sirdar Isher Singh
- A. N. Sarkar—the government's official Legal Advisor.

All of these Secretaries and Advisory officials held Ministerial rank in the Provisional Government.

The extent of the Provisional Government's day-to-day management of affairs for Azad Hind is not entirely well-documented, so their specific functions as government officials for the state outside of their positions as support ministers for Subhash Chandra Bose is not entirely certain.

Recognition

Azad Hind had diplomatic relations with nine countries: Nazi Germany, the Empire of Japan, Fascist Italy, the Independent State of Croatia, Wang Jingwei's Government in Nanjing, Thailand, Burma, Manchukuo and the Philippines.

On the declaration of its formation in Singapore, President Eamon de Valera of the Irish Free State sent a note of congratulations to Bose. Vichy France, however, although being an Axis collaborator, never gave formal political recognition to Azad Hind.

Recent researches have shown that the USSR too had recognised the Provisional Government of Free India. This government participated as a delegate or observer in the Greater East Asia Co-Prosperity Sphere.

GOVERNMENT ADMINISTRATION AND THE WAR

The same night that Bose declared the existence of Azad Hind, the government took action to declare war against the United States and Britain. The government consisted of a Cabinet ministry acting as an advisory board to Subhash Bose, who was given the title "Netaji" (translating roughly to "leader") and was no doubt the dominant figure in the Provisional Government. He exercised virtual authoritarian control over the government and the army. With regards to the government's first issuances of war declarations, the "Cabinet had not been unanimous about the inclusion of the U.S.A. Bose had shown impatience and displeasure—there was never any question then or later of his absolute authority: the Cabinet had no responsibility and could only tender advice..."

At the end of October of 1943, Bose flew to Tokyo to participate in the Greater East Asia Conference as an observer to Japan's Greater East Asia Co-Prosperity Sphere; it could not function as a delegate because India had technically fallen outside the jurisdiction of Japan's definition of "Greater East Asia", but Bose gave speeches in opposition to Western colonialism and imperialism at the conference. By the end of the conference, Azad Hind had been given a limited form of governmental jurisdiction over the Andaman and Nicobar Islands, which had been captured by the Imperial Japanese Navy early on in the war.

Once under the jurisdiction of Azad Hind, the islands formed the government's first claims to territory. The islands themselves were renamed "Shaheed" and "Swaraj", meaning "martyr" and "self-rule" respectively. Bose placed the islands under the governorship of Lt. Col A. D Loganathan, and had limited involvement with the official governorship of the territory, instead involving himself in plans to expand the Indian National Army, ensure adequate men and materiel, and formulate its course of actions and the administrations and relations of the Indian population in South East Asia and determining Japanese designs in India and his provisional government. In theory the government itself had the power to levy taxes on the local populace, and to make and enforce laws: in practice they were enforced by the police force under Japanese control. Indians were willing to pay these taxes at first, but became less inclined to do so towards the end of the war when the Provisional Government enacted legislation for higher wartime taxes to fund the INA. During his interrogation after the war Loganathan admitted that he had only had full control over the islands' vestigial education department, as the Japanese had retained full control over the police force, and in protest he had refused to accept responsibility for any other areas of government. He was powerless to prevent the Homfreyganj massacre of the 30th January 1944, where forty-four Indian civilians were shot by the Japanese on suspicion of spying. Many of them were members of the Indian Independence League, whose leader in Port Blair, Dr. Diwan Singh, had already been tortured to death in the Cellular Jail after doing his best to protect the islanders from Japanese atrocities during the first two years of the occupation.

Azad Hind's military forces in the form of the INA saw some successes against the British, and moved with the Japanese army to lay siege to the town of Imphal in Eastern India. Plans to march towards Delhi, gaining support and fresh recruits along the way, stalled both with the onset of monsoon season and the failure to capture Imphal. British bombing seriously reduced morale, and the Japanese along with the INA forces began their withdrawal from India.

In addition to these setbacks, the INA was faced with a formidable challenge when the troops were left to defend Rangoon without the assistance of the Japanese in the winter of 1944-45. Loganathan was relocated from the Andaman Islands to act as field commander. With the INA garrison about 6,000 strong, he manned the Burmese capital in the absence of any other police force or troops during the period between the departure of the Japanese and the arrival of the British. He was successful in maintaining law and order to the extent that there was not a single case of dacoity or of loot during the period from April 24th to May 4th, 1945.

Indian Areas under the Administration of the Provisional Government

Almost all of the territory of the Provisional Government lay in the Andaman Islands, although the Provisional Government was allowed some authority over Indian enclaves in Japanese-occupied territories. Provisional Government civil authority was never enacted in areas occupied by the INA; instead, Japanese military authority prevailed and responsibility for administration of occupied areas of India was shared between the Japanese and the Indian forces.

The Defeat of the INA and the Collapse of the Provisional Government

Left to defend Rangoon from the British advance without support from the Japanese, the INA was soundly defeated. Bose had fled Burma and returned to Singapore before the fall of Rangoon; the government Azad Hind had established on the Andaman and Nicobar Islands collapsed when the island garrisons of Japanese and Indian troops were defeated by British troops and the islands themselves retaken. Bose himself was killed in a plane crash departing from Taiwan attempting to escape to Russia. The Provisional Government of Free India ceased to exist with the deaths of the Axis, the INA, and Netaji Bose in 1945.

The troops who manned the brigades of the Indian National Army were taken as prisoners of war by the British. A number of these prisoners were brought to India and tried by British courts for treason, including a number of high ranking officers such as Colonel Gurbaksh Singh Dhillon. The defense of these individuals from prosecution by the British became a central point of contention between the British Raj and the Indian Independence Movement in the postwar years.

3

Vision of Bose and National Integration

THE FUNDAMENTAL PROBLEMS OF INDIA

Netaji addresses students of the Tokyo University in November 1944. I do not propose to speak to such a distinguished gathering on the commonplace things that you hear and read about India. I think it would be far better if I speak to you on the more fundamental problems of India. Having being a student of philosophy myself, I am naturally more interested in fundamental problems. I hope you will also agree with me that I should rather speak to you today on some of the fundamental problems that face my country, both in the present as well as in the future.

In my travels abroad, I have often found that people generally have a wrong and sometimes a rather funny idea about my country. For instance, among the people in Europe, the general idea about India is that it is a land in which three things can be found: Snakes, Fakirs and Maharajas. Among those who have been influenced by British propaganda, the general idea about India is that it is a country where people are always fighting among themselves, and where the strong hand of Britain is required in order to maintain peace and order among the people.

If you approach the Orientalists in Europe, that is, the experts in Indology, you will find that they look upon India as a land of mystics and philosophers, a land which at one time produced a very rich philosophy, but which is today as dead as the ancient civilizations of Egypt and Babylon. Now the question is, "what is India in reality?" No doubt we have a very ancient civilization, but unlike other ancient civilizations, such as Egypt or Babylon, Phoenicia or even Greece, the ancient culture and civilization of India is not dead. It still lives in the present. And we Indians of today think the same thoughts fundamentally, the same thoughts and have the same feelings, the same ideals of life, as our forefathers who lived 2,000 or 3,000 years ago. In other words, there is a continuity, historical and cultural continuity, extending from ancient times till the present day-which is in some ways a very remarkable thing in history. Now, in order to understand India, this fundamental fact should first be understood, namely, that the India of the past is not dead. India of the past lives in the present, and will live in the future.

Against this background, this ancient background, we see changes in our national life from age to age. During the last 3,000 years, people have come into India from outside with new ideas, some times with new cultures. All these new influences, ideas and cultures have been gradually absorbed into the national life of India, so that in spite of the fact that, fundamentally we have the same culture and civilization as we had several thousand years ago, we have nevertheless changed and moved with the times. Today, in spite of our ancient background, we are able to live in a modern world and adapt ourselves to that world.

Those who have been influenced, whether consciously or unconsciously by British propaganda, have the impression that India was very easily conquered by the British and also that after the British conquest of India our country was for the first time politically unified. Both these notions are entirely wrong and without foundation.

In the first place, it is not true that India was easily conquered by the British. It took British 100 years, from 1757 to 1857, to finally subjugate India. Secondly, it is also an entirely wrong notion to think that India was politically unified by the British. The fact is that India was for the first time politically unified nearly 2,500 years ago under the Buddhist Emperor, Asoka the Great. In reality, India of the time of Asoka the Great was even larger than the India of today. Asoka's India included not only modern India, but also Afghanistan and a part of Persia. After the time of Asoka, India has gone through many ups and downs in her national life. There have been periods decay, followed by periods of progress and national upheaval. But through these ups and downs in our national life, we have been able, in the long run, to keep our progress. About 1000 years after Ashoka, India again reached the zenith of progress under the Gupta Emperors. This was followed by another glorious epoch in Indian history about nine hundred years later under the Mogul Emperors. Therefore, it is worth remembering that the British notion that we have been unified politically under British rule is entirely wrong. All that the British have tried to do is to divide the Indian people and to weaken, disarm and emasculate them.

I shall now present before you a problem which will interest scientists, and in particular students of sociology. The question is whether the Indian people have any right to live as a free nation. In other words, have they the strength and the vitality left in them to live and to develop themselves as a free nation? I personally hold the opinion that if a nation once loses its vitality, its inner vitality, then it has no right to exist. And even if it does continue to exist after loosing its vitality, that existence will have hardly any worth or value for mankind. The only reason why I stand for India's freedom and believe as a free nation we shall have a glorious future is that I believe that we have sufficient vitality left in us to live as free men and develop as a nation.

Now, if I have to answer this question as to whether sufficient vitality is left in us, I shall have to answer two questions: firstly, has our nation any creative faculty and secondly, is it prepared to fight and die in order to preserve its existence? These two tests have applied to India.

With regard to the first question, we have seen that in spite of the British rule in India, in spite of innumerable restrictions and disadvantages which follow from foreign rule, we have been able to give numerous proofs during the century that in different departments of our national life we still have creative power. The number of philosophers and thinkers produced in India under British rule, the number of writers and poets that enslaved India has produced, the artistic revival in India in spite of British rule, the scientific progress made by the Indian people in spite of so many difficulties in the way of their education, the standard already attained by our leading scientists as compared with scientists in different parts of the world, the industrial progress made by India as a result of her own effort and initiative and last but not the least, the distinction which we have attained in the field of sports, all these go to show that in spite of being politically subjugated the vitality of the nation has remained intact.

If under foreign rule and in spite of the obstacles and restrictions that follow from foreign rule, we could give so much proof of our creative faculty, then it stands to reason that when India is free and when the masses of the Indian people are afforded educational facilities, they will be able to give much better proof of their intellectual calibre and creative faculty in different walks of life.

I have just referred to the first test of a nation's vitality, namely, creative faculty. I shall now consider the second test, namely, as to whether the Indian people are able to fight and to die for the sake of freedom. On this point I should like to say, first of all, that, since the last great fight that they had with the British in 1857, the Indian people have not given up the struggle against the enemy, even for one day.

Unfortunately, owing to what I would call the folly of our forefathers, after our final defeat in 1857, the leaders in those days had allowed themselves to be disarmed. Whatever, difficulty we have subsequently experienced in winning back our freedom has been due to largely our having been disarmed. But though owing to the mistake of the leaders the people were disarmed, nevertheless they continued to fight for their freedom in other ways.

I shall not take up your time unnecessarily by giving a description of all the methods that have been used in India against the British. I will only say this, that all the methods that have been tried by revolutionists in different parts of the world for the achievement of their own independence have been tried in India. At the beginning of the century, particularly after the victory of Japan over Russia in 1904 and 1905, the freedom movement in India got a new impetus and since then, during the last 40 years, our revolutionaries have been studying very closely the methods of revolutionaries in other countries and they have tried to adopt as many of their methods as possible.

They have tried also to manufacture secretly arms and explosives for the achievement of independence. As a development of this struggle for freedom, India tried a new experiment-Civil Disobedience or Passive Resistance—of which the best exponent was Mahatma Gandhi. Though personally I believe that this method will not succeed in bringing us complete independence, there is no doubt that it has greatly helped to rouse and unify the Indian people and also to keep up a movement of resistance against the foreign government. I should, therefore, say that the fact that in spite of all the difficulties that result from foreign rule, a nation can produce a new method and practice that method with a large measure of success is also a proof of that nation's vitality. It shows that, that nation does not accept enslavement as a settled fact and is determined to struggle against it and to work out new methods for achieving independence.

I have, as a revolutionary, made a very close study of the revolutionary movements in other countries, and I can say without any exaggeration that since 1857 we have used every possible method of revolutionary struggle. In the course of this struggle, tremendous sacrifices have been made and many have given their lives. There was, however, one method that still remained for us to take up and that was the organization of a real modern national army.

That work we had not done up till recently because it was impossible to do that inside India under the eyes of the British army and the British police. But the moment this war gave the Indian people an opportunity of organizing a modern Indian national army outside India they at once seized it. As a result of that effort, and with the help of the Japanese Government and the armed forces of Japan, they have been able to build up this army. So my point is that throughout our revolutionary struggle against the British Government and their armed forces we have shown sufficient initiative, creative power and vitality and have made tremendous sacrifices. We now hope that under the conditions, and with the advantages the war has given us, we shall be able, after all, to fulfil our national aspirations and win freedom for India.

Having replied to the question regarding the vitality of the Indian people and their right to live as a free nation, I shall now attempt a sociological analysis of modern India, you have to take note of the three important factors. The first factor is the ancient background, that is, the ancient culture and civilisation of India, of which the Indian people of today are conscious, and of which they feel proud. The second factor is the struggle which has gone on without any break or interruption since we were finally overpowered by the British. And the third factor consists of certain influences which have come into India from outside.

Modern India is composed of its ancient background, the unbroken national struggle against Britain, and the impact of influences from abroad.

I shall now deal, in some detail with the influences which have reacted on India from outside and which have been responsible, to some extent, in making modern India what it is today? Among these outside influences, the first factor is the influence of western thought which was crystallized in Liberalism, Constitutionalism and Democracy.

In other words, since 1857, modern liberal and democratic thought has been influencing the intellectuals of India to a large extent.

From the beginning of the present century, a new factor came into operation. After the victory of Japan over Russia in 1904-05, the eyes of the Indian people were opened to a new movement in Asia—the movement for the revival of not merely of Japan—of other Asiatic countries. Since then, Indian thought has been greatly interested in Asiatic revival. During the last 40 years we have been thinking not merely of what was happening inside India, but also of what was happening in other parts of Asia?

Another important factor which had influenced our mind consisted of the struggles that have gone on in different parts of the world. Indian revolutionaries studied the Risorgimento Movement in Italy inder the leadership of Mazzini and Garibaldi and the struggle of the Irish people against their British oppressors. In Russia, before the last World War, there was, as you know, a movement against the Czar called Nihilist movement. That also was studied. And nearer India the new awakening of China under the leadership of Dr. Sun Yatsen was also studied very closely and with great interest by the Indian revolutionaries.

Thus, Indian revolutionaries have been exceedingly receptive to the influences exerted by revolutionary struggles abroad. Then during the last World War, when the revolution broke out in Russia and, as a result of it, a new government-the Soviet Government—came into existence, the work of that government was studied with great interest in our country.

People in India has not been interested so much in the Communist movement as in the work of reconstruction of Soviet Russia—in rapid industrialisation of that country and also in the way in which the Soviet Government solved the problems of the minorities. It is this constructive achievement of the Soviet Government which was studied with great interest by people in our country. As a matter of fact, intellectuals like our poet Tagore, who had no interest in Communism as such, were profoundly impressed when they visited Russia in the work of educational reconstruction in that country. Then there is another influence which came to India form outside in more recent times—I mean, the new movement in Europe headed by Italy and Germany called Fascism or National Socialism. This movement was also studied by our revolutionaries.

I have just dealt with some of the influences that have reached India form different parts of the world, form England, France, Japan, China, Russia, Germany and so on. I will now take up another question, *viz.*, as to how we have reacted to these influences—how much we have accepted and how much we have rejected out of these outside influences.

In dealing with this question of our reaction to these outside influences, I must first point out that there is a big gulf between our generation and the last generation. As typical exponents of the last generation, I would like to mention Tagore and Gandhi. They represent for us the last generation, and between their thoughts and ideas and the thoughts and ideas of our generation there is a big gulf.

If you study the works of Tagore and Gandhi, you will find that all along there is a conflict in their minds as to what their reaction to the western influence should be. So far as Mahatma Gandhi is concerned, he has never given us any clear solution this problem. He has left people in doubt as to what his attitude is toward the acceptance of western ideas. Generally speaking, his attitude is one of antagonism. But in actual practice he has not always acted in accordance with his own ideas, the reason being that the rest of the countrie do not share that hostility or antagonism which Mahatma Gandhi personally has toward western ideas and concepts.

You all know about Mahatma Gandhi's attitude on the question of violence of physical force. He does not advocate the use of arms, or the shedding of blood of the enemy for gaining one's freedom. This attitude towards violence or physical force is closely related to his general attitude toward foreign influence, particularly western influence.

Our generation has followed Mahatma Gandhi as the leader of a political struggle, but has not accepted his ideas on all these questions. Therefore, it would be a mistake to take Mahatma Gandhi as the exponent of the thoughts and ideas of the present generation in India.

Gandhi is in some ways a complex personality and I would like to analyze his personality, so that you may understand him better. In Gandhi, there are two aspects-Gandhi as a political leader and Gandhi as a philosopher. We have been following him in has capacity as a political leader, but we have not accepted his philosophy. Now the question arises as to how we can separate the two aspects. Why, if we do not accept his philosophy, are we following him? Though Gandhi has his own philosophy of life, he is a practical politician and therefore, he does not force his own philosophy on the people. Consequently though we are following him in our political struggle, we are free to follow our own philosophy. If Gandhi had tried to thrust his philosophy on us, we would not have accepted him as a leader. But he has kept his philosophy separate from his political struggle.

I have mentioned as representatives and exponents of the last generation Tagore and Gandhi. Now let us compare their philosophies. There are some points in which they agree, but in some other points they do not. The points on which they agree are firstly, that they would like to see the national struggle being conducted without the use of arms. In other words, on the question of physical force, they have the same views. On the question of industrialization of the country, they also have the same views. Both Tagore and Gandhi are against modern industrial civilization. But in realm of culture, their views are not same. So far as thought, art and culture are concerned, Tagore is prepared to accept foreign influence.

He believes that in the realm of culture there should be full cooperation between India and the rest of the World and there should be reciprocity. We should not be hostile or antagonistic to the culture or art or ideas of any other nation. In the realm of culture while Tagore advocates full cooperation between India and rest of the world, Gandhi's general attitude is antagonistic to foreign influence. We must however, remember that Mahatma Gandhi has nowhere given a very clear exposition of his views. I am only referring to his general attitude to this question.

I have previously remarked that there is a big gulf between the fundamental thoughts and ideas of the last generation and our generation. I will now explain what I meant thereby. As I have just said, this problem as to what our reaction should be toward foreign influence and toward industrial civilization troubled the leaders of the old generation all their lives and we see proofs of it in their actions. But, this problem does not exist for us. It does not exist for us, because our starting-point is that we want a modern India based of course on the past. We do not believe that India can achieve freedom without the use of arms. Now once you take up this attitude, that for winning freedom we have to fight and use arms, it follows that we must have modern industries. What constituted the biggest problem for the old leaders constitutes our starting point. The problem for modern India is not our attitude toward modernism or foreign influence or industrialization, but how we are to solve our present-day problems.

I believe modern Japan will understand our generation much better than modern Japan understood the last generation in India. Our stand is virtually the same. We want to build up a new and modern nation on the basis of our old culture and civilization. For that we need modern industries, modern army and all those things necessary to preserve our existence and our freedom under modern conditions.

Having dealt with the fundamental standpoint of my generation. I will go on to discuss some of the detailed problems. For the present, of course, the biggest problem is how to fight and win this war. But that is a problem of which you are aware from what you have read in the papers or heard over the radio. I will now consider some of the problems of Free India. The moment India is free, the most important problem will be organizing of our national defence in order to safe guard our freedom in future. For that we shall have to build up modern war industries, so that we may produce the arms that we shall need for self-defence. This will mean a very big programme of industrialization.

After satisfying the needs of our nation in the matter of self-defence, the next problem in the degree of importance will be that of poverty and unemployment. India today is one of the poorest countries in the world, but India was not poor before we came under the British rule. In fact, it was the wealth of India which attracted the European nations to India. One cannot say that in the matter of national wealth or resources India is poor. We are rich in natural resources, but owing to British and foreign exploitation, the country has been impoverished. So our second most important problem will be how to give employment to the millions of unemployed in India and how to relieve the appalling poverty which now exists among the masses of the

Indian people. The third problem in free India will be the problem of education. At present, under British rule, about 90% of the people are illiterate. Our problem will be to give at least an elementary education to the Indian masses as soon as possible, and along with that to give more facilities to the intellectual classes in the matter of higher education.

Connected with the question of education is another problem which is important for India and that is the question of script. In India there are principally two scripts in vogue. One is the script known as Sanskrit (or Nagri) script and the other is Arabic (or Persian) script. Up till today in all national affairs and conferences we have been using both theses scripts. I must ad that in some provinces, there are scripts in vogue which are modifications of Sanskrit script. But fundamentally there are two scripts, and in all national affairs and conferences we have to use both these two scripts.

There is now a movement to solve this problem of scripts by using the Latin script. I personally am an advocate of the Latin script. Since we have to live in the modern world, we have to be in touch with other countries and whether we like it or not, we have to learn the Latin script. If we could make the Latin script the medium of writing throughout the country, that would solve our problem. Anyway that is my own view and the view of my closest friends and collaborators.

I have refereed to three important problems in Free India: National defence, how to remove poverty and how to give education to the people. If we are to solve these three important problems, how are we going to do it? Shall we leave it to private agency and private initiative or will the State take up the responsibility of solving these problems?

Well at present, public opinion in India is that we cannot leave it to private initiative to solve these national problems, especially the economic problem. If we leave it to private initiative to solve the problem of poverty and unemployment, for instance it will probably take centuries. Therefore, public opinion in India is in favour of some sort of socialist system, in which the initiative will not be left to private individuals, but the state will take over the responsibility for solving economic questions. Whether it is a question of industrializing the country or modernizing agriculture we want the State to step in and take over the responsibility and put through reforms within a short period, so that the Indian people could be put on their legs at a very early date.

But in solving this problem we want to work in our own way. We will, naturally, study experiments made in other countries—but, after all, we have to solve our problems in an Indian way and under Indian conditions. Therefore, the system that we shall ultimately set up will be an Indian system to suit the needs of the Indian people.

Now if we do not tackle the economic question from the point of the view of the masses, the majority of who are poor, if we do not do that in India, we shall produce the same confusion or the same difficulties in our country, as we see in China today. You see in China today a split between Kuomintang and the Chinese Communist Party. Personally I do not see why this should have occurred or why, if Kuomintang Party has interests of Chinese masses at heart, there should be any need to have a separate party like the Communist Party under foreign influence.

Having learnt from experience, we do not want to repeat the mistake that China has made. We actually find today that because the nationalist movement in our generation has identified itself with the peasants who form more than 90% of the people, because we have their interests at heart, there is no raison d'etre for a separate party like the Communist Party. If the nationalists in India did not have the interests of the masses at heart, then you would have seen the same phenomenon as you see in China today.

Now we come to another question—namely, the political system or government. If we are to have an economic structure of a socialistic character, then it follows that the political system must be such as to be able to carry out that economic programme un the best possible way. You can not have a so called democratic system, if that system has to put through economic reforms on a socialistic basis. Therefore, we must have a political system-a State—of an authoritarian character. We have had some experience of democratic institutions in India and we have also studied the working of democratic institutions in countries like France, England and the United States of America. And have come to the conclusion that with a democratic system we cannot solve the problems of a Free India. Therefore, modern progressive thought in India is in favour of a State of an authoritarian character, which will work as an organ, or as the servant of the masses, and not clique or of a few rich individuals.

That is our idea with regard to the political institution in Free India. We must have a government that will function as the servant of the people and will have full powers to put through new reforms concerning industry, education, defence, etc., in Free India.

Before I pass into the next problem, I should like to mention another point, namely the attitude of Free India toward religion and caste. This is a question that is frequently asked. India has several religions. Consequently, the Government of Free India must have an absolutely neutral and impartial attitude toward all religions and leave it to the choice of every individual to profess to follow a particular faith.

With regard to caste, that is now no problem for us, because caste, as it existed in the old times, does not exist today. Now, what is caste system? The caste system means that a community is divided into certain groups on a professional or vocational basis and marriage takes place within each group.

In modern India there is no such caste distinction. A member of one caste is free to take up any other profession. So caste, in that sense does not exist today. Then there remains the question of marriage. In the old times, it was custom to marry within each caste. Nowadays, intermarriage between the different castes takes place freely. Hence caste is fast disappearing. As a matter of fact in the nationalist movement we never inquire as to what caste a man belongs to and we even do not know the caste of some of our closest collaborators, which shows that in our generation we do not think at all about caste. For Free India, therefore, caste is no problem at all. In this connection, I should like to tell you that it was the British who created the impression throughout the world that we are a people quarrelling among ourselves, especially over religion. But that is an absolutely wrong picture of India. It may be that there are certain differences among the Indian people, but such differences you will find in every other country. If we take the so called progressive countries of the world, *e.g.*, France before the outbreak of the present war, or Germany before Hitler and his Party came to power, you will find that there were acute differences among the people in these countries. Spain had even a first class civil war.

But nobody ever says that, because the people in these countries had disputes and differences, they are not fit to rule themselves. It is only in case of India that the British say that, because there are certain differences among Indian people therefore they are not fit to be free. Again, the fact is that whatever differences there are among the Indian people are largely the creation of the British Government. There are hundreds of examples to show you that throughout the history of British rule, the British have tried by every possible means to divide the Indian people. After having done so much to artificially create differences among the Indian people the British turn around and say that we are not fit to be free.

I should also point out that if you take a modern power like Soviet Russia and see how heterogeneous the composition of the Soviet Union is, you will realise that if, in spite of this heterogeneous character, so many different races professing so many different religions could be unified in one political system and become such a strong Power, there is absolutely no reason why India which has much more homogeneity than the Soviet Union, should not be united as one nation. As a matter of fact, you will find that outside India, where there is no British influence, there are no differences among the Indian people. In the Independence Movement in East Asia and in the Indian National Army there is no question of religion or caste or class. It is just in India where the British have influence and control that you will find these differences.

On the question of national unity, I should like to give you a friendly warning that British propaganda tries to give the world the impression that the Muslims of India do not support the independence movement. This is wrong. Very often you read in the papers about certain organizations like the Muslim League or the Hindu Mahasabha. The British boost these organizations, because they are in their policy pro-British and are against the Indian National Congress, and they try to make out that the Muslim League represents the Muslims of India. But that is British propaganda. The fact is that the Muslim League and its leader, Mr. Jinnah, represent only a minority of the Indian Muslims. The majority of the Indian Muslims are nationalists and they support the independence movement, as much as anyone else. The president of the Indian National Congress is a Muslim, and so are many other members of the congress, many of whom are in prison today.

These facts are not known to the outside world and the outside world gets the impression that Mr. Jinnah represents all the Muslims of India and that they are not supporting the nationalist movement. So I would like to give out this warning about British propaganda.

I have already told you about the kind of economic and political system that we would like to have in Free India. Out of this, arises the problem as to what our political philosophy is. On this question, I gave my own views in a book I wrote about 10 years ago called "The Indian Struggle". In that book I said that it would be our task in India to evolve a system that would be a synthesis of the systems in vogue in different parts of the world. For instance, if you take the conflict between Fascism (or what you might call National Socialism) on the one side and Communism on the other, I see no reason why we cannot work out a synthesis of the two systems that will embody the good points of both. It would be foolish for any one to say that any one system represents the last stage in human progress. As students of philosophy, you will admit that human progress can never stop and out of the past experience of the world we have to produce a new system. Therefore, we in India will try to work out a synthesis of the rival systems and try to embody the good points of both. Now I would like to compare some of the good points of National Socialism and Communism. You will find some things common to both. Both are called anti-democratic or totalitarian. Both are anti-capitalistic. Nevertheless, in spite of these common points, they differ on other points. When we see National Socialism in Europe today, what do we find? National Socialism has been able to create national unity and solidarity and too improve the condition of the masses. But it has not been able to radically reform the prevailing economic system which was built up on a capitalist basis.

On the other side, let us examine the Soviet experiment based on Communism. You will find one great achievement and that is planned economy. Where Communism is deficient is that it does not appreciate the value of national sentiment. What we in India would like to have is a progressive system which will fulfil the social needs of the whole people and will be based on national sentiment. In other words, it will be a synthesis of Nationalism and Socialism. This is some thing which has not been achieved by National Socialists in Germany today.

There are few points in which India does not follow Soviet Russia. Firstly, class conflict is something that is quite unnecessary in India. If the Government of free India begins to work as an organ of the masses, then there is no need for the class conflict. We can solve our problems by making the State the servant of the masses.

There is another point which has been overemphasized by Soviet Russia and that is the problem of the working classes. India being predominantly a country of peasants, the problem of the peasants will be more important than the problem of the working classes.

Another point on which we do not fully agree is that, according to Marxism, too much importance is given to the economic factor in human life. We fully appreciate the importance of the economic factor which was formerly ignored, but it is not necessary to overemphasize it.

To repeat once again our political philosophy should be a synthesis between National Socialism and Communism. The conflict between thesis and antithesis has to be resolved in a higher synthesis. This is what the law of the Dialectic demands. If this is not done, then human progress will come to an end. India will, therefore, try to move to the next stage of political and social evolution. I will now pass on the last point in my address, and that is our conception of an international order. On this point I have already spoken several times in Tokyo. I fully support the steps that have been taken through the Joint Declaration to create a new order in East Asia on the basis of freedom, justice and reciprocity. I have been personally greatly interested in international problems, having tried to work in several countries in order to get support for our movement and, in that connection; I also had the opportunity of studying the work of the League of Nations.

The experiment of the League of Nations has failed, and it is desirable and profitable for us to investigate as to why it failed. If I were to answer that I would say that it failed because the sponsor-nations were too selfish and short-sighted. The sponsor-nations were England, France and America. America dropped out of the League, so the powers that controlled the League were England and France. Now these two leading powers, instead of setting an example of unselfishness, tried to use the League of Nations for their selfish interests and for their own benefit. The only basis on which we can set up an international order is freedom, justice and reciprocity. Therefore, the work in East Asia has commenced on the right lines and on the right basis. The only task that remains for us is to see that in actual work the principles embodied in the Joint Declaration are put into effect. If they are so put into effect, then the experiment will be a success. If not, then it will again prove to be a failure.

You must have seen in my speeches and press statements that I have been very enthusiastic about this Joint Declarations. There are several reasons. Firstly, it is on the right basis and on the right lines that the work has began. Secondly, if you want to set up an international order, it has to have a beginning in a particular region. If we make it a success in one region, it can gradually be expanded all over the world.

It is very difficult to set up a world order suddenly out of nothing and make it a success. But if you begin in one region where friendship and reciprocity between the nations can be developed, and if in that region you meet with success, then that example will be emulated by other nations in other parts of the world. So the method of setting up of a regional order is the only way in which a world order can gradually be built up.

The third reason is that I have found that this idea or plan find support among the mass of the people if this country, and especially among the youths. If I had found that this new order was being sponsored by a few politicians or leaders and that the rest of the nation was apathetic or indifferent, I should certainly not be optimistic. But it is because I have found that the people as a whole, and especially the youths are vitally interested in it and support it enthusiastically, that I believe that through the cooperation of the leaders and the people and the youths, it can be made a success.

I should like to repeat that this undertaking is for the government and the people of this country a very great responsibility. As you know, your Government was responsible for sponsoring this idea, so you are the sponsor-nation. The success of this experiment will depend on the example set by the sponsor-nation. The League of Nations failed, because the sponsor-nations were selfish and short-sighted. This time if the nations that have joined together, and particularly the sponsor-nation, avoid a selfish and short-sighted policy and work on moral basis, then I see no reason why the experiment should not be a success.

I should like to emphasize again the tremendous responsibility which Japan has undertaken by becoming the sponsor-nation in this task. And when I talk of the responsibility of the nation, I want also to stress the responsibility of the youths. The youths of today will be the nation and leaders of tomorrow. An idea that is welcomed and supported by the youths will one day be supported by the whole nation. But an idea which does not find support among the youths will die a natural death. Therefore, their responsibility for making this new order a success devolves, in the last analysis, on the youths of this country. I hope and pray and trust that the youths and the students who are the future representatives of the nation will realise the tremendous moral responsibility which Japan has undertaken in initiating this new order. There may be people who doubt whether a nation can rise to a high moral level, whether a nation can be farsighted and unselfish and undertake the work of establishing a new order. I have every faith in mankind. If it is possible for one individual to be unselfish, to live one's life at a high moral level, I see no reason why an entire nation cannot also rise to that level. In the history of the world we have seen examples in which a revolution has changed the mentality of a whole nation and made it rise to a high level of morality. Therefore, if anybody has any doubt whether an entire nation can rise to that level, then I do not share that doubt.

I repeat, in conclusion, that the sponsor-nation should realize the tremendous responsibility that it has undertaken. This is a task not only for the leaders and the politicians, but for the whole nation and especially for those who are the hopes of the nation-the youths and the students.

GLIMPSES OF NETAJI

Two questions which one often asked about Netaji are, one about his personality and another about his life. The first question is, what was so exceptional in his ability which attracted and inspired those who came in touch with him? Whenever, anybody asked this question, it is reminded of the fable of "The Elephant and the blind men." Like one of those men one could not scan that great man Netaji Subhash Chandra Bose in totality. So before saying what one could perceive, let the reader allow me to look at him through the eyes of those who had better vision than one. SA Ayer, Minister for Publicity and Propaganda of Azad Hind Government had this to say in his book *Unto him a witness*. "The title of Supreme Commander, if it truly fitted any commander on the battlefields of Europe or Asia, fitted Netaji most superbly. He looked supreme, every inch of him. The way he talked and moved with the soldiers on or off the war front was one of supreme dignity and self-confidence.

The word personality assumed a meaning when Netaji, in his Supreme Commander's Uniform, stepped on to the saluting base and faced the serried ranks of the INA. And yet, the uniform itself was the simplest in the world, no medals in a row, no shining leather belt or shoulder straps, nor a sword in its scabbard hanging from his waist, nor a horse ride. Whatever, clothes he wore, he wore them smartly. Normally he wore Khaki cotton clothes except when he visited Japan. There he had to use Khaki woollens as a protection against the severe cold weather. His forage cap with two tiny well polished brass buttons in the front sat majestically on his bright and broad forehead, the face beneath the cap of a rosy wheat complexion, now inscrutable. Immobile, dignified, now wreathed in a charming smile, now reminded one of the Bengal Tiger as when he roared an inspiring exhortation to soldiers or civilians at mammoth gatherings.

It was impossible to take one's eyes of his face, whenever he ascended the platform; he held one spellbound by its compelling magnetism ....

Now let me show another glimpse of Netaji's creative qualities when he drafted the Proclamation of the Provisional Government of Azad Hind. After a long busy day, a day just earlier to 21st October 1943, it was past midnight. This is what Ayer says:

> *Then I witnessed a phenomenon. I had glimpse of the great man. He took hold of a bunch of quarter-sheets of blank paper, took pencil in hand and started writing, 'After their first defeat in the hands of the British in 1757 in Bengal ....*

He did not lift his eyes from the paper in front of him, silently handed to me the first page as soon as he finished it, and I walked out of the room and sat at the type writer. Abid and Swami went to his room in turn and brought me the Proclamation manuscript, sheet after sheet, as Netaji finished it. What amazed me was that he never even once wanted to see any earlier pages that he had written.

How he could remember every word that he had written in the preceding pages, how he could remember the sequence of the paragraphs? In the entire script there was not one word corrected or scored out, and the punctuation was complete.

That he wrote out the whole proclamation sheet after sheet without break and at one sitting was some measure of Netaji's clear thinking, remarkable memory and grasp and facile pem! The entire historic proclamation was written with the ease with which a brief letter could be penned.

The proclamation shows Netaji's extraordinary grasp of history.

Alexander Werth, one of the important Liaison Officers at the Free India Centre, in Chapter Four, "Planning for Revolution-1941-1943", in the book, *A Beacon Across Asia*, edited by Sisir K Bose, Alexander Werth and SA Ayer (published by Orient Longman) has observed (page 127):

> *Those who observed Bose during these years were all greatly impressed by the fact he succeeded so well in convincing all his co-workers-both Indian and German-about the great importance of the work they were doing and inspiring them with a sense of mission, common objectives and mutual cooperation. Whenever, there were differences of opinion or misunderstanding or even quarrels amongst his colleagues, he showed his remarkable capacity of keeping the thread of all activities of his political, military and technical co-workers in his hands so that the over all control of the whole organisation remained with him. He was the driving spirit behind all activities of the Free India Center. He succeeded in doing so much in spite of the fact that the organisation that he built up was something between an official mission and a provisional government and no so fully recognized association of a group of exiles from India.*

Earlier, after his arrival in Berlin, Netaji went under the name of Orlando Mazzota for quite some time. He intended to remain in anonymity till he could bring round the Axis Powers to declare that the Independence of India was among their war aims. He also did not wish the British to know about his whereabouts. Without going into details of how difficult his task was, let me quote HN Pandit's work-*Netaji Subhash Chandra Bose from Kabul to Battle of Imphal* (Sterling Publishers Limited-Page 38):

> *For the whole story we have to turn to the narration of MR Vyas who was one of the first four associates of Netaji in Germany when Bose was still known as Orlando Mazzotta.*

It seems an emissary of the Foreign Office went to Badgastein (where Bose was staying) with the German Government's request for cooperation. Subhash thanked the German Government for the proposal and added that the collaboration would have to be based on a very well defined agreement. His terms were:

> *For all purpose of negotiation, India should be regarded as a completely sovereign state of which he would be the representative until such time as*

the Indian people could finally constitute their own government on their own soil.

While India remained subjugation, he (Netaji) should have facilities for a separate free establishment of his own with the status of a diplomatic representative attached to the head of a sovereign state.

For the finances of such a set up, the German Government should advance an interest free loan which would be repayable by India after the termination of hostilities.

The loan so granted must be without any condition and the expenditure for the same must be subject to diplomatic immunity.

Any broadcasts, any publications or any publicity to be carried on by the establishment so contemplated, must not be subject to any German censorship even though the same may have to be carried on from territories of Germany under her occupation.

Recruitment to any National Army to be raised would be made solely by Indians or representatives duly approved by the head of the state, i.e. Subhash Chandra Bose. The oath of allegiance by the members of the Army would be to Subhash Chandra Bose who as the Head of the Sovereign State of India, would also be the Commander-in-Chief of all-India armed forces.

Though apparent from above, still it must be specially agreed that the Indian forces, while operating in any joint sub-command, must not be deployed on any front other than against the British or other troops under the British command subject to any unforeseen military entanglements.

While the free India establishment and its forces would support all anti-British actions, it would not ipso facto consider itself at war with the other allies of Great Britain.

The Nazis were flabbergasted to see the terms. Were these conditions of a powerless one-man state for cooperation with the Reich?

The man must be cut to size. The task was assigned to one of Ribbentrop's senior officers who came to meet Bose in the Foreign Office with an SS Colonel accompanying him in the mission. The following account of the conversation which took place has been given by Vyas:

Your Excellency, Ribbentrop's officer began, While we realise on many questions, don't you think that after your having come here, there could be no activity of any kind unless the German government voluntarily agrees to it?

Subhash Chandra Bose replied: "Do you mean that you could put me in prison if I do not agree to work on your terms?"

"Certainly not, Your Excellency", the SS Colonel interposed, "but you would be incapacitated and will have to remain inactive."

Bose: "If I wanted to remain inactive I would have remained in a British prison. But this war provides a unique chance for my country to be free. So I would rather go else where or even to India and fight from there, come what may."

The Foreign Office representative commented sarcastically, "But Your Excellency, even for leaving Germany, you will require our permission, isn't it?"

Apparently the officer bargained for more than he could afford, because the reply that came stunned him. : "Sir, I have heard a lot about your Gestapo. Probably the gentleman here is a representative of that body. But believe me, the British CID in India is no less efficient and ruthless. And if I have failed them and escaped, I shall do the same here. I have not come here to live the life of an exile. Gentleman, I think we shall leave it at that."

The meeting came to an end abruptly.

This happened in the second half of October 1941. For two days nothing happened. Then Ribbentrop (the Minister for Foreign affairs) had a meeting with Subhash Chandra Bose in a very friendly way. Shortly afterwards an official communication arrived that fuehrer (Hitler) had approved the civil parts of Netaji's terms from points 1 to 5.

The decision on the military points too followed in due course of time with some minor modifications. Vyas says that although there was tough bargaining in the beginning, once the agreement was signed, the Germans honoured it in letter and spirit.

The Free India Center with the status of a diplomatic mission was established with its office in Lichtensteiner Allee, opposite to the Spanish Embassy in Berlin's diplomatic enclave. After having lived in various hotels, Subhash Chandra Bose was allotted a villa in the Charlottenburg area of Berlin. Before the out break of the war, this house was occupied by the military attache to the American Embassy.

The work of the Free India Center began with a few Indian Volunteers, mainly students. To start with, they were MR Vyas, NG Gunpulay, NG Swamy, Habib-ur-Rehman, Abid Hassan Safrani and one or two more.

It can be said that more than a diplomatic mission, the Free India Center worked like the secretariat of a government to be free. India movement came to be called Azad Hind, with its emblem of Tricolour with the springing tiger and Jana Gana Mana adopted Hindi words *Subh Sukh Chain Ki Barkha Barse*—without any alteration in the tune.

Jai Hind was adopted as the greetings amongst the Indian nationals. It gave us a special identity as members of one nation irrespective of many religions and races.

Our leader Subhash Chandra Bose was addressed by the members of the Azad Hind as Netaji. This title owes its introduction to the members of the Azad Hind Free India Centre.

In Hindustani, 'Neta' means leader, the suffix 'Ji' is a common word of respect and courtesy used among equals and among the high and low alike. It sounds of closeness between the person addressed and the addresser in contrast to words like *Hazoor, Sahib, Janab, Nawab-e-Aala, Janab-e-Aali, Sahib Bahadur, Shriman, Sarkar, Alijab, Hukum*, etc.

The word Netaji became so popular that it immediately reminds one of Netaji Subhash Chandra Bose. There have been 'netas', many of them will come and go but Netaji will remain only one and one only Netaji Subhash Chandra Bose.

BOSE AND NATIONAL INTEGRATION

Netaji uttered a note of caution to his army that the partition of the country would solve no old or outstanding problem, but would give rise to fresh ones instead.

He could bear out through his INA experiment that despite disparities in religion, language and ethnicity, there was some thing of an underlying unity in the midst of diversity in our people. Bound by a common goal. A common subjectivity and action programme as it was, the INA could live down at the operational level, all manner of differences of religion, language, caste and the rest of it.

Throughout his political career Bose crusaded for unity in action and unity of faith. He never agreed to a unity of sorts for the sheer purpose of temporizing, rather he did encourage a genuine respect for all the religions and communities in his INA. He made sure that religion was treated purely a personal affair. A common greeting, a common but simple lingua franca and a National Anthem were all devised to work as cementing forces in the conduct of the INA affairs.

Not only were the INA soldiers united in their implicit allegiance to their leader and government but also they were deeply animated by a spirit of national integration. Incidentally Bose himself was a religious man in personal life, there was no place for any communal or sectarian consideration in his political ideology.

He never shied away, throughout his political life, form and insistence on complete separation of religion from the nationalist politics of the day. His ideas in regard to communal harmony found an almost complete expression and in perfect implementation in the INA.

He saw to it that INA was rendered free from all political influences which the British Raj encouraged to maintain in India as a dependency. His spirit of secularism moved and gripped the INA as a whole, much though every soldier in it had perfect liberty to practice his own religion privately. The lesson was brought home to them by Bose, that the communal divide was just a sample of British propaganda.

Nataji was quite alive to the problem of national unity since the inception of his rather short but eventful political career. His approach to this problem was both incisive and positive.

He always endeavoured to persuade the Muslims of India to join the main stream of the struggle for the emancipation of India. The Pakistan idea was never his cup of tea. Indeed through his INA and Azad Hind Government, Netaji showed us at a critical moment of our history how to forge national will in a concrete, resolute action. He fervently tried to give rise to a cultural organization in South East Asia, through which the various races and religions would be enabled to converge our Indian foundation. In his first platoon lecture to the Fauz entitled "Unity of India, past and present", he dealt with the insidious British propaganda to the world regarding our so-called manifold differences.

As early as August 1942, he raised the issue of national integration in India in the columns of a German paper. He also arranged for a committee to be set upon our national integration when the Andaman and the Nicobr Islands were occupied by the INA Government. The speech he delivered on the same subject at the Chettiar temple is one to reckon with. He facilitated the entry of men of other religions as well in the temple in the face of vehement resistance from the keepers of the temple. More than that, the pledge the INA soldiers had to sign the highlights the commitment of the army to the ideals of unity, secularism and democracy.

For the growth of a genuine national spirit in the Army, Bose waged a relentless struggle against the splitters and opportunists both in the country and outside. He made the remarkable prophecy that India freed form the British was destined to develop a strong nation. In his opinion only a truly national government could implement a meaningful programme of unity of our people and only a genuine patriotic army could bring about our unity at the barricades.

He claimed he could bring about a measure of communal unity in his ranks simply because the Britishers were not there.

Apart form this he initiated a scheme of secular and scientific education through his government and started a sustained propaganda on its behalf to fight out all divisive forces.

He felt that India must reject the Wavell plan which really meant parcel our country, a similar plan the British tried in Ireland and Palestine too. The prime item on his agenda was the removal or religious intolerance and fanaticism through intensive and ceaseless propaganda. In his famous Tokyo speech of 1944, he touched upon India's basic unity, a model which could be served to the people with in India through his INA.

For one thing the INA proved to be a living example of national unity and Gandhi was all praise for the way in which Bose infused the spirit of unity amongst his men. In fact the INA trial virtually shook the unfree and undivided Indians form their long deep slumber. Hindus, Muslims, Sikhs and Christians were evenly represented in the Government and the Army and they all unitedly posed from outside a serious challenge to the separatist forces set work in the homeland. The Indian National Army became a dramatic symbol of national unity as the trials of a Hindu, a Sikh and a Muslim INA officers proved to the hilt.

A Muslim accompanied Bose in his perilous submarine journey and another Muslim sent him off for the last time at the airport. Some of his brigades were led by Muslim officers exclusively and some were named after the living Indian nationalists leaders. The INA trials followed up by the RIN revolt represented a turning of the tide as far as the prospects of the secularism were concerned.

Netaji Subhash assembled different scattered forces in East Asia and formed an army with the help of youths of different areas and communities in India. He mobalised the a-political forces in South East Asia in order to fight the last war of liberation for a United India.

Indeed he and his INA served to hold up the dropping spirits of all sections of Indian people and example of rare unity and patriotism. He infused into his men a certain non-communal spirit, and inspired them to feel proud of their Indian identity. He inspired his men, in his own inimitable way to identify themselves not as Hindus or Muslims but as the sons and daughters of India. He succeeded in installing in them a kind of cultured sensitivity and a secular passion.

He succeeded in rousing a mighty army unified in spirit and committed ideologically to work for a free and united India. He almost fully carried out his ideas on national unity in the formation of the INA which consisted of more than sixty percent of Muslims.

He could persuade his associates to shed their religious superstitions about food and the practice of denominational faith. He forge an emotional relationship among the diverse ethnicities that came to serve in his army on their own accord. In fact the INA became a paradigm of national and emotional integration. However, it is not enough to recapitulate the INA saga but it is peremptory to take lessons form it, now more than ever, particularly when we have to tackle the problem of disintegration that threatens us today, when the whole nation is faced with a crisis of leadership of conviction and general sense of direction.

4

Mission and Leadership of Bose

Writing about Netaji Subhash Chandra Bose is a journey down memory lanes, a journey that's both painful and exhilarating: painful in the way he was taken away from us before he could see his dreams come true and I am filled with an overwhelming feeling of sadness because he is still being missed today; exhilarating in the way my admiration for this great man grows day by day.

He certainly had an extraordinary aura that was difficult to ignore. He touched the lives of thousands of Indians in the manner in which he lived. To me, Netaji has been a source of great inspiration, a way to live life sans fear. He personified the courage never to yield. He had the mettle to swim against the tide. He won people's hearts by the sheer force of his personality and he commanded energies beyond the average no one has never known anybody with his strength of will. He was formidable in so many ways: as a reformer, a revolutionary leader, and administrator, a statesman, an ambassador, a planner...How many talent is it fair for one man to have!

Netaji was a man of magnetic charm, a man of iron will, determination, dedication, discipline, immense stamina and a proclivity for hard work. He acquired the reputation of being different. And more importantly he was a man who possessed that elusive quality-strength of character. Character is about deciding the course of your life and staying by it, no matter what comes in the way. It was wellknown that he revolted against anything that was not fair to human. As a student in the Presidency College, be became involved in beating up of Professor Oaten who had apparently mishandled a student. Whether young Bose was directly involved or not is not known, but his leadership was taken for granted and he was expelled form College in 1916. This incident had an everlasting impact in the mind of this proud under graduate: in his own eyes he became a victim of racial prejudice. Racial hatred ate into his soul and he made it his mission to show himself and India superior to the white-faced foreigner.

A year later he joined the Scottish Church Collage and took to studies with a new zest. He joined the University unit of the Territorial Army and put on a soldiers uniform. His military training was to stand him in a good stead when 25 years later he led an armed revolt against the British. It can be safely said that the Scottish Church College has done much in producing a person of his calibre.

Again when he decided to give up the coveted ICS service and dedicate himself to the service of the Motherland, he knew he was taking a major decision of his lifetime. He said, "I must either chuck this rotten service and dedicate myself wholeheartedly to the country's cause, or I must bid adieu to all my ideas and aspirations." To the Under-Secretary of State of India he said, "...I did not think that one could be loyal to the British Raj and yet serve India honestly, heart and soul." The bell rang in his heart, India calling. And the rest is history.

Later in life when Netaji arrived on the Indian scene, the going was tough and those who appeared though couldn't get going. He brought in a different mind set altogether. When the whole nation was singing hosannas of Gandhiji and his doctrine of Ahimsa, Netaji was marching to the beat of a different drum-armed combat. He had a little or no faith in the idea of nonviolence. He felt that the British would understand only the language of the sword and any inaction on the part of the Indians would be inferred as weakness, as a sign of subordination. He had seen what revolution had accomplished in the other parts of the world. He sought to instil this fighting sprit among all-Indians. He was dreamy. He was unconventional. The masses sensed the mood. Scepticism turned to admiration, criticism lost out to felicitations. He no longer looked ordinary. He looked different. In Netaji there were courage and mission: he possessed one and pursued the other. That's a powerful combination. His perseverance paid of. It was the beginning of a new dawn.

Character is about staying calm in the face of adverse crisis. Whatever, the danger, Netaji was always a picture of calm and control. He missed death by inches several times and yet remained unperturbed. Once when he along with Major Abid Hassan was travelling by submarine from Germany to Japan, they were attacked by Allied submarines several times and at times the danger was great but Netaji remained a picture of calm. He coolly turned to Abid Hassan to whom he was dictating a letter and asked him, "... Hassan Sahib, what is the last word you have taken down...". Such control is indeed rare to find. Physically her was weak but his mental stamina proved to be his major strength.

Character is about hanging in there and taking your chances. He took the chance on things other people won't. This proved to be his forte. Look at the way he escaped from India in 1941. When the Second World War broke out, he decided to make his move. The long wait had been worth the while, for Netaji sent out the unequivocal message that he was indeed a man of thought and action, that he meant business which for the British implied that their days in India were numbered. The breakthroughs, the things that save countless lives and change history have never come from conventional wisdom. They have never come from playing safe. His escape was bold, daring and risky, dramatic and high voltage. Everything planned to the smallest detail. Netaji took his chance when it came and won the game.

Character is about being humane. The touchingly human side of this great man shines through small incidents. The way in which he would care for us, the INA Tokyo cadets, is still fresh in my mind. He would give us his share of food because he knew that it was in short supply and also because he thought we needed it more. In his letters to us, each word that he wrote touched a chord in our hearts and we wept with joy and love for this great leader of ours. This compassionate concern shown by Netaji drew us even closer to him, so much so that we were willing to gamble with our lives at his demand. During the war when the INA soldiers were given the option of surrendering, they embraced death with a smile and with cries of Jai Hind! There were some who wouldn't allow their wounds to be attended to because they recalled Netaji's promise, "Give me blood and I shall give you freedom…!" these men believed that by bleeding to death, they were being of service to Mother India. Such unshakable faith in their leader!

In today's times, forget following you leader, we don't even have an iota of respect for them. Our ancestors handed down a legacy of knowledge and wisdom, character and integrity, values they had imbedded form their forefathers, thinkers, sages scholars. We, the present generation, have wasted away all those primary values that are imperative for the growth of any nation. We have squandered the lessons that Netaji wanted to teach us. Lessons of valour, Lessons of self-discipline, Lessons of patriotism, Lessons of self-service. This he learnt form the great Swami Vivekananda. He was greatly influenced by the writings of the Swami who propagated salvation through service to humanity. How selflessly he did service to Mother India is evident in all his actions. Vivekananda's teachings also helped him in his years of imprisonment where he learnt to think and not to brood.

He was truly a unique phenomenon. A man who aroused thousands of Indians with his one resounding battle-cry of "Delhi Chalo". There was something in his words that went beyond mere words. There was passion. There was sincerity. There was confidence. He was the true Neta, one who was able to command the respect of his men. In his speech of the INA in Singapore of 5th July 1943, he said, "For the present, I can offer you nothing except hunger, thirst, privation, forced marches and death. But if you follow me in life and death...I shall lead you to victory and freedom." To this great man we must give due credit for he made heroes out of ordinary men, students, shopkeepers the common man. He formed the Balak Sena comprising of young boys and inculcated in them the sprit of patriotism, discipline and pride of being Indian.

His respect and belief in the womenfolk of our country led to the formation of woman's regiment—The Rani of Jhansi Regiment—and it played an active part in the war. He told them, "...When I express my confidence that you are today prepared to fight and suffer for the sake of your mother land, I do not mean only to cajole you with empty words. I know the capabilities of our womanhood well. I can, therefore, say with certainty that there is no task which our women cannot undertake and no sacrifice and suffering which our women cannot undergo...". Under him the women never lagged behind anybody and along with the men folk they also faced lathi charge by the merciless British Police and faced privations of prison life, torture and humiliations. This army did the services of Florence Nightingale and fought fearlessly like the famous Joan of Arc.

Netaji also formed the Reconstruction Brigade where he hired doctors, lawyers, administrators and engineers and involved them in all activities in the freedom movement. He made arrangements with the Japanese authorities to send students to Japan for further training. A member of Brigade writes that I was among the 45 students selected by Netaji himself for the training. Till this day I treasure the moments spent with Netaji and my souvenirs include letters written by Netaji to us. He was able to mobilize not just resources but total involvement of all-Indians. Such was his charisma. He was also able to restore the lost confidence of 40,000 demoralised soldiers who had surrendered to Japan. He found in them a wealth of conscience and in his own way prepared them for the ultimate sacrifice for the prestige of our country. They fought many heroic battle for which the present generation should be proud of.

He was very clear in his mind that the path he had adopted was strewn with difficulties and even death. He said, "...It does not matter who among us will live to see India Free. It is enough that India shall be free and that we shall give our all to make her free...". While the army could not march to Delhi victorious, it had succeeded in its intent of arousing the sentiments of the Indians in India and more important, the Indian soldiers in the British Indian Army. These men met their own countrymen in the battlefield but on opposite sides. Seeing the courage and the spirit of sacrifice of the INA men, the Indian soldiers had a change of heart. They, who so far had pledged their allegiance to the British, now rose up in revolt. When these two and a half million Indian soldiers revolted, the British Army was thrown out of gear. Netaji's giant suicide squad had done what it had set out for. While the INA had lost the war, they had won a moral victory. This revolt of the soldiers was followed by the RIN mutiny lead by courageous Punnu Khan. And then there was the public trial of the INA men at the Red Fort—an episode that spelled doom for the British. It was a disaster waiting to happen. The trial inflamed the passion of all-Indians and the British realised, albeit late, that they had lost.

Netaji is truly one of the greatest leaders that India has ever produced. He was a man who was focused. India's freedom was uppermost in his mind and nothing, absolutely nothing could come in between him and his cause. Not even his failing health or the fear of death. His single minded devotion to the cause of India's liberation is truly a lesson for all of us to learn. He said, "...Let us all stand shoulder to shoulder and say with one heart and with one voice that our motto is, as Tennyson said through Ulysses, to strive, to seek, to find and not to yield." This became his credo. And it was this faith that he was able to instil into his men. He told them, "From today you are the soldiers of the Indian National Army of Free India. You have volunteered to shoulder the responsibility of 40 crore of Indians. Form today your mind, might and money belongs to the Indian nation."

He again said, "...Your names will be written in golden letters in the history if free India. Every soldier who is martyred in this holy war will have a monument in free India. The coming generations will shower flowers on those monuments. You are very fortunate that you have got this valuable opportunity to serve the mother land..." Well this was the way Netaji thought we Indians will remember those martyrs. But no, those brave soldiers who died fighting for the freedom of our motherland are today forgotten. Their sacrifices have been sidelined. It is tragic that even our leader Netaji has not been given his due place in the history. His life has been a chronicle of continuous endeavours and relentless toil.

He was truly an extraordinary may whose only burning desire was to shake off the shackles of colonial rule. This worthy man shed his blood, suffered immensely and died for our freedom, our prosperity and our well being. It is almost as if he said to his future children: here's my gift for you. But look at the condition that India is in today. In his address to an independence day meeting in Berlin on 26th January, 1943 he said, "... And India is a country where the past has not been forgotten, but where our past history and tradition live in our blood and the marrow of our bones. It is because of this national self-consciousness that neither political domination nor economic impoverishments have been able to kill our soul..." Such sterling words form this great man. He was one leader whose style of functioning was worth imitating, whose ideas worth adopting and whose examples worth following. But today we have buried our past. We have not made use of the wisdom of the past.

Netaji's skills as a diplomat left many of his contemporaries astounded. The manner in which he dealt with Hitler—even while requesting for help from Germany he minced no words in telling Hitler that he did not approve of his treatment of Jews-leaves one with no doubt of his courage and abilities as a diplomat. The Japanese Prime Minister Tojo was so enamoured by his engaging personality and sincerity that he granted him all his requests including the formation of the Provisional Government of Free India and handing over Andaman and Nicobar Islands to the government. He maintained complete autonomy in dealings with the leaders and equalled them in more ways than one.

Much has been said and written about Netaji's conflict with Gandhiji. The conflict was only on ideology. Nonviolence was the lifelong creed of Gandhi but Netaji saw this as, a "temporary tactic, a tactic which is temporarily useful." It wasn't as if he didn't believe in the civil disobedience movement of Gandhi but as he said, "India will get freedom through an armed struggle coupled with a civil disobedience movement. But civil disobedience movement alone will not be enough .... As the British Government relies on the strength of bayonets, we too should use bayonets in order to defeat them decisively. As the enemy stands before us with the drawn sword, we should fight him only with the aid of the sword." The impossible is always absurd until it's done. Then it is possible.

The British never for a moment believed that Indians had the strength to pick up arms and fight them but Netaji made this possible. And history is a witness to the truth that India got her independence only by revolutionary stand taken by Netaji and in the words of Lord Attlee, the role of Gandhi was "minimal". When Gandhi commended his non-cooperation programme to the Indian nation at the annual session of the Congress at Nagpur on 1920 he said, "If India had the sword today, she would have drawn the sword." So it was not as if Gandhi was opposed to the armed combat but was forced to believe that his country men lacked the capacity to militarily fight the enemy, and a much better equipped one at that. Hence Satyagraha was the only viable weapon he had at hand and one that proved to be highly successful in demonstrating to the British that Indians were capable of organizing themselves into a united front.

All said and done the respect that Netaji had for Gandhi was unquestionable. It was Netaji who gave him the title of Father of the Nation. He said, "...The service which Mahatma Gandhi had rendered to India and to the cause of India's freedom is so unique and unparalleled that his name will be written in letters of gold in our national history for all time." Well, the tragic and sometimes disturbing fact is that Netaji and his contribution to India's freedom has been relegated to the background. Today a child in school is being given a very distorted picture of history. It is hoped that this situation is rectified soon for otherwise the damage done will be dreadful. But sadly, we aren't even looking in this direction. Our minds are preoccupied with other issues.

How little it takes to make our lives unbearable...the broken top button of the shirt, a traffic jam, a tyre puncture, Indian team performing badly .... Everything slightly inconvenient makes us look up to the God and complain, crib, curse. We waste time in trivialities like the protest against the Miss World pageant which was appalling to say the least. We seem to ignore larger issues that are facing us in the eye.

Issues like bride burning, child marriages, Sati, female infanticide which have debauched our society. Issues like corruption are staggering. But what is even more shocking is out total indifference to the situation. For long we have been swallowing our anger with our pride that we have begun to get used to its taste. Injustice is to us, second nature. We thrive on it and let others thrive on it.

Post independent India has been through some really rough weather. Today our hard-earned freedom for which countless men and women laid down their lives is being threatened by various foes. Why have we not been able to learn form the experiences of our past leaders, sages, thinkers and scholars? Our forefathers showed us that courage and sacrifice can triumph against overwhelming odds. Netaji said, "... I would like to remind you that a revolutionary is one who believes in the justice of a cause, and who believes that the cause is bound to prevail in the long run. He who gets depressed over failures is no revolutionary. The motto for a revolutionary is: Hope for the best, but be prepared for the worst...Hope is a quality we share with the spider. He makes us feel positive. Hope makes us forget failures. Hope brings hope. But for a leader, hope takes much more. It takes more than just waiting to make hope arrive on the horizon. He has to pledge his life. Netaji was hopeful. Still believing that his tomorrow can be bright. If the spider wouldn't give up, why should we?

The spirit of our past leaders knew no fatigue or death and by their abiding faith in India and their mission, they had shaped the destiny of future India. The optimist that he was, he said, "...And if we fail in that too (attaining independence) then there will indeed be World War III to give us another opportunity to strike for our freedom." Let us drive inspiration form the pages of his life. Fortunately for posterity, he was also a prolific writer and his own letters have survived.

For a whole section of Indians then, Netaji was a lighthouse of hope. Fifty years of Independence and we have done all that we could to extinguish that flicker of hope. We have allowed his sufferings and those countless soldiers to be diluted. Where are all those men who should have been worthy successors of our priceless heritage? Where all those modern crusaders who were are suppose to finish the task left behind by our forefathers? They paid the price for the kind of mission they had embarked upon. After all nothing can be got free, a price has to be paid for everything. With our any expectation of a miracle, this country must do all it can to see that the current scenario is corrected. Society is full of issues to fight and the least we can expect from our leaders is concrete evidence that these issues are being talked. Let our youth take charge for this is their country and they are its future.

We are not mere syncopates. We believed in Netaji. We identified with his mission. We shared his dreams. We were his partners in his fight for liberation who contributed our bit, suffered and sacrificed for our country. To the youth one seek their attention. For on their shoulders rest the future of India.

Netaji taught us to stand up and be counted for values that count-discipline, sacrifice, patriotism and good old hard work. Fifty years after independence and these fundamental values still count. His efforts are testimonials of his determination to succeed, come what may.

... He spread his wings and gave his country the opportunity to test untried waters. The results did not matter. The fact that the chance did. He made the world envious of him, envious of India and her achievements. Truly, only Netaji could have done that! Let our youth take over form where Netaji had left. We are hopefully moving into the 21st century. The young must wake up to that. And with the confidence of a winner say, *Hum honge kamayab*.

NETAJI-SYMBOL OF NATIONAL INTEGRATION

India is more than a country. It is a continent comprising of people who speak different languages, look different and dress differently. It is a country where religion has a very strong base and where followers of perhaps all known religions live and practice their faith in their respective manner. India has not only almost 850 million people but also has a great diversity of culture. For example, let us take a person from Ladak or the Kashmir Valley in the north and compare him with someone in Kanyakumari in the South or, for that matter, with someone in Rajasthan or Gujarat in the West or Nagaland and Manipur in the East.

What have they in common? They do not look alike for their climatic conditions are very different. In fact they can not even converse with one another because they speak completely different languages. Yet each is an Indian. Often they quarrel among themselves, but in time of crisis or danger, they become one. There is some thing which holds them together. It is a fine line but the bond is very strong. It is difficult to find words to describe this. It is Indianness or being an Indian-the pride of belonging to India, the land which has given them birth and where they shall return ultimately after death or where they shall return ultimately after death or where the ashes of their mortal remains will mingle and become one with the waters of the rivers which flow through the country's length and breadth.

In order to keep this vast and varied multitude of people together, the country needs a leader of the caliber of Netaji Subhash Chandra Bose. He believed passionately that all Indians, irrespective of the region they come from or language they spoke or religious faith they practiced, were members of the same family. He gave his belief practical shape and convinced all those who came in contact with him that unless this basic fact was accepted without hesitation, there was no future for India.

Netaji as Subhash Babu in his early days was a symbol of the restlessness of Indian youth, who dreamed of a great and free India. As Netaji Subhash Chandra Bose, he was the colossus who strode across East Asia and organized and led an army of liberation against the British Empire, entrenched in India for almost 200 years. In the two years when he led the Indian independence movement, he lived a dream-a dream that the dedicated and the restless youths of India had dreamt for decades and for daring to make that dream into a reality, several had gone to gallows with a smile on their faces. Netaji opened the eys so every member of Brigade so to say. He made us see Indian through the eyes of an Indian. His call was "Give me blood and I promise you freedom". Indians all over South-East Asia and Burma flocked to him in their thousands, offering all their worldly possessions and their own lives in the service of the nation.

He had the knack of getting the best of every person. There was absolutely no distinction about which part of the country he or she came from, or which religious faith he or she followed or which language he or she spoke. It was pleasure and privilege to be an Indian at that time. Many and many of us wanted to become martyrs in the service of our country for a martyr never dies; he becomes immoral and lives forever in the hearts, memory and the history of his country.

Let me now conclude by giving the Azad Hind Government National Anthem. Here the spirit of every freedom fighter of the INA is completely and adequately expressed.

National Anthem

Subh Sukh Chain ki barkha barse; Bharat bhag hai jaga
Punjab, Sind, Gujrat, Maratha, Dravid, Utkal, Banga
Chanchal Sagar Vindh Himala; Nila Jamuna Ganga
Tere nit gun gayen; tujh se jiwan paen;
Sab tan paye asha.
Suraj ban kar jag par chamke, Bharat nam subhaga
Jaya ho, Jaya ho, Jaya ho, Jaya, Jaya, Jaya, Jaya ho,
Sab ke dil men prit basae; teri mithi bani
Har sub eke rahne wale; har mazhab ke prani
Sab bhed aur farak mita ke; sab god me teri ake,
Goonthe prem ki mala
Suraj ban kar jag par chamke, Bharat nam subhaga
Jaya ho, Jaya ho, Jaya ho, Jaya, Jaya, Jaya, Jaya ho,
Bharat naam Subhaga
Subh savere pankh pakharu; tere hi gun gayen
Bas bhari bharpur hawaen; jiwan men rut layen
Sab mil kar Hind pukaren; Jai Azad Hind ke nare
Piara desh hamara
Suraj ban kar jag par chamke, Bharat nam subhaga
Jaya ho, Jaya ho, Jaya ho, Jaya, Jaya, Jaya, Jaya ho,
Bharat naam Subhaga.
Jai Hind.

HOW TRANSPARENT!

What reminds me of Netaji Subhash Chandra Bose the most are those words which he spoke to us on various occasions, when we had the good luck to wage a regular war for the Independence of India under his command from 1943 to 1945. Apart from the clarity of his vision, spontaneity of speech, serenity and uniformity of thought, with which he explained with perfect ease various problems of our struggle and his plans, was the expression on his face which served as a window through which we could see where he was leading us to. So transparent were his dealings with us! A communication with him always left us more enlightened and responsible. It gave us confidence in the righteousness of our cause, in his ability to lead us and our nation to victory and freedom. We gained so much self-confidence that we felt that the very destiny was in our hands.

"Let me show a sample of his oration when he addressed us, the soldiers of the Indian National Army, for the first time after receiving our parade at Singapore on July the 5th 1943. His concluding words were :

"I have said that today is the proudest day of my life. For an enslaved people, there can be no greater pride, no higher honour, than to be the first soldier in the Army of Liberation. But this honour carries with it a corresponding responsibility and I am deeply conscious of it. I assure you that I shall be with you in darkness and in sunshine, in sorrow and in joy, in suffering and in victory. For the present, I can offer you nothing except hunger, thirst, privation, forced marches and death. But if you follow me in life and in death, as I am confident you will, I shall lead you to victory and freedom. It does not matter who among us will live to see India free. It is enough that India shall be free and that we shall give our all to make her free. May God bless our Army and grant us victory in the coming fight.

Inquilab Zindabad!

Azad Hind Zindabad!"

Above words coming strait from the heart of the man of the splendours of Netaji Subhash went straight into our hearts. Those words left us honoured and proud of being in the INA. We felt we were important and responsible beings. Netaji's achievements and sacrifices were already so great that no further decoration could enhance his majesty. On the contrary his being first amongst us was much needed recognition for us. He placed his confidence in us. Confidence is a great morale booster. It invigorated our spirits. Our chests expanded, with heads held high and feet dug deep into ground with the battle cry—CHALO Delhi on our lips, we followed the fluttering TRICOLOUR. And we sang :

Kadam kadam Bharaey ja
Khushi Ke geet gaye ja
Ye Zindegi hai Qaum ki
Tu Waum par lutaey ja.

Within a few days of his arrival in the East, Netaji gave us Vanguard-the Rani Jhansi Regiment. We felt that the valour of the Goddess Durga had reincarnated in the daughters of Mother India. They manifested the blessings of the goddess and power of her Shakti.

With our allies the Japanese our armies advanced against the armies of Great Britain and their allies who were in occupation of the Indian Subcontinent. Some of the bloodiest battles of the Second World War were fought in the spring of 1944 on the battle fields of Akyab, Arakan, Manipur, Imphal, Nagaland, Kohima and Red Hill. India's Tricolour was planted on the liberated territory of India at Moirang in Manipur. Victory was a matter of touch and go. Then came rains. Our supply lines were cut off. Tables turned. Having lost one hundred thousand lives, we and our valiant allies the Japanese withdrew to the Irrawaddy line. Initiative passed on to opponent's hands. Delhi started getting out of our reach. The allies were winning everywhere. We had practically lost the War. When Netaji was asked, "Now what is left for us to fight for?" his prompt reply was, "To pay the price of India's Liberty."

We continued our fight on the banks of the Irrawaddy at Nyaungu and Bagan, Mount Popa and Kyauk padaung, Magwe and so on, towards Prome and Pegu on the way to Rangoon. We fought against odds. What to talk about weapons and rations, even water was scarce. So what? Wasn't it one of the things offered to us by Netaji during his very first address on 5th July.1943. His oft-repeated words, "There is no power on earth which can keep India enslaved any longer. India shall be free and before long." His prophetic words sustained our spirits. His appreciations of our actions on the battle fields kept up our morale. The fight was kept on.

Eventually we did reach Delhi—our destination—not as free persons but as prisoners. We were vanquished and the British were the victor. Dungeons of the Red Fort were our abode. Our trial was held from 5th November to 31st December 1945. The autumn of that year was one of the gloomiest the Indian nation ever had. The people did not light their homes on Diwali. The Festival of lights. The charge against us was of waging war against the King and of murder and abetment of murder. The trial was held in the dormitory of a British Barrack on the Red Fort of Delhi. According to the law death appeared to be the just punishment for us. The British Government were determined to set an example, so as to teach the Indian soldier a lesson never to dare to take up arms against the king. They had not won the World War to liquidate the British Empire. But for us it was the last chance to pay the price of India's liberty.

During the War the British had succeeded in keeping the INA actions and even the name of the Indian National Army a well guarded secret. They could not keep that secret anymore. Soldiers coming home after the War had gone through a complete psychological revolution when the brother did shed brother's blood on either side in the battlefield on lands abroad. The Indian soldier had seen the INA fight against the British guns with rifles, and tanks with bullockcarts and the aircrafts with empty stomachs in tattered uniforms. As if that was not enough, the British victorious officers and men in towns of Singapore, Malaya, Thailand and Burma, were greeted with "JAI HIND" by boys and girls of Balak Sena. Greetings of "JAI HIND" meaning "Victory to India" made soldiers of Indian Army pause and ponder as to what did they fight for? For their bread or for the British? Thus when we, the soldiers of the INA., were prisoners behind the gates of carious jails and detention camps tiny tots of Netaji's Balak Sena were still in the field shouting JAI HIND. The British had no weapon which could be used against the Balak Sena.

Under those circumstances the British Government's decision to put on trial three INA officers—a Muslim, a Hindu and a Sikh, was a blunder. The Indian public were yet in the dark about us and our actions. Actions which were noble, nationalist, according to civilized rules of International war, and for the liberation of our motherland. The British were determined to teach us a lesson and we were determined with unity and faith to sacrifice our life to pay the price for India's liberty. In a situation like that no enemy could ever favour her archenemies by providing such a grand (nor a better) stage than the historic Red Fort of Delhi. We were further favoured by our own people who united as a man to defend us during the trial. Tallest of the tall legal luminaries of India got together with Shri Bhulabhai Desai as their chief Counsel to defend the accused officers of the INA. In his historic address Mr. Desai explained, that it was the right of a subject race to wage war for their liberty. Desai's address awakened the whole nation.

How apply the British Commander in chief in India, General Sir Claud Auchinleck, who had spent all his life in the Indian Army and known the soldiers' mind well, did assess the situation then prevailing is apparent through his letter to Army Commanders dated 12th February, 1946. The letter is marked STRICTLY PERSONAL AND SECRET: NOT TO BE PASSED THROUGH ANY OFFICE.

It is a long letter in which Sir Auchinleck laboured hard to explain to his Army Commanders the effect of the action taken in respect of the first INA trial on the Indian Army as a whole. I quote just an excerpt form his letter (Published by Her Majesty's Stationary Office, in The Transfer of Power-1942-47, Volume VI, pp 939-46)

It is most important that we should study and analyse carefully these effects, as they may influence very greatly our ability, to maintain the solidarity and reliability of the Indian Army in the difficult times which undoubtedly lie ahead of us. It is for this reason that I am writing this letter to you. I have considered the desirability of making a personal public statement in explanation of my action in commuting the sentences of transportation passed by the court on the first three accused, but I have decided that this would not be in the best of interest of discipline of the maintenance of my influence and authority as Commander-in-Chief.

I feel, however, that we should do all we can to remove the feelings of doubt, resentment and even disgust which appear to exist in the minds of quite a number of British Officers, who have not the knowledge or the imagination to be able to view the situation as a whole, or to understand present state of feeling in India. As I see it, the communication of the sentences of transportation on Shah Nawaz, Dhillon and Sehgal has had the following effects in India:

(a) On the general public, moderate as well as extremist, Muslim as well Hindu. Pleasure and intense relief born of the conviction that confirmation of the Sentences would have resulted in violent internal effect.

(b) This feeling does not, in my opinion, spring universally from the idea that the convicted officers were trying to rid India of the British and therefore, to be applauded, whatever crimes they might commit, but from a generally genuine feeling that they were patriots and nationalists and that, therefore, even if they were misled they should be treated with clemency, as true sons of India. In this connection, it should be remembered, I think, that every Indian worthy of the name today a "Nationalist", though this does not mean that he is necessarily "anti-British." All the same, where India and her independence is concerned, there are no "Pro-British Indians."

Netaji's contributions in the making of India are unique. What to talk of INA, Netaji inspired not only the Indians as a whole, but also the nationals of those countries who where still not independent. The actions of the Royal Indian Navy and certain personnel of all the three Military Services at Bombay, Karachi and other places in the name of Netaji were like the last straw which broke the back of the mighty British Colonial Empire on whom the Sun never used to set. According to Netaji's oft-repeated words, "India shall be free and before long", we did attain freedom of which we are celebrating the Golden Jubilee today along with Netaji along with Netaji Subhash Chandra Bose's Birthday when he completes a century and enters the new one.

If Netaji was here today to see us free. He was the only leader who could keep India united. But when the partition of the subcontinent is an established fact, let us wish all the offsprings of Hindustan, Bangladesh and Pakistan, happiness, peace, plenty and glory.

PROCLAMATION OF THE PROVISIONAL GOVERNMENT OF AZAD HIND

After their first defeat at the hands of the British in 1757 in Bengal, the Indian people fought an uninterrupted series of hard and bitter battles over a stretch of one hundred years. The history of this period teems with examples of unparalleled heroism and self-sacrifice. And, in the pages of that history, the names of Sirajuddaula and Mohanlal of Bengal, Haider Ali, Tippu Sultan and Velu Tampi of South India, Appa Sahib Bhonsle and Peshwa Baji Rao of Maharashtra, the Begums of Oudh, Sardar Shyam Singh Atariwala of Punjab and last, but not the least, Rani Laxmibai of Jhansi, Tantia Tope, Maharaja Kunwar Singh of Dumraon and Nana Sahib—among others—the names of all these warriors are for ever engraved in letters of gold.

Unfortunately for us, our forefathers did not at first realize that the British constituted a grave threat to the whole of India, and they did not, therefore put up a united front against the enemy. Ultimately, when the Indian people were roused to the reality of the situation, they made a concerted move and under the flag of Bahadur Shah in 1857, they fought there last war as free men.

In spite of a series of brilliant victories in the early stages of this war, ill-luck and faulty leadership gradually brought about their final collapse and subjugation. Nevertheless, such heroes as the Rani of Jhansi, Tantia Tope, Kunwar Singh and Nana Sahib live like eternal stars in the nation's memory to inspire us to greater deeds of sacrifice and valour.

Forcibly disarmed by the British after 1857 and subjected to terror and brutality, the Indian people lay prostrate for a while—but with the rebirth of the Indian National Congress in 1885, there came a new awakening.

From 1885, until the end of the last World War, the Indian people in their endeavour to recover their lost liberty, tried all possible methods—namely agitation and propaganda, boycott of British goods, terrorism and sabotage—and finally armed revolution. But all these efforts failed for a time. Ultimately in 1920, when the Indian people haunted by a sense of failure, were groping for a new method, Mahatma Gandhi came forward with the new weapon of non-cooperation and civil disobedience.

For two decades thereafter, the Indian people went through a phase of intense patriotic activity. The message of freedom was carried to every Indian home. Through personal example, people were taught to suffer, to sacrifice and to die in the cause of freedom. From the centre of the remotest villages, the people were knit together into one political organization.

Thus the Indian people not only recovered their political consciousness but became a political entity once again. They could now speak with one voice and strive with one will for one common goal. From 1937 to 1939, through the work of the Congress ministers in eight provinces, they gave proof of the readiness and their capacity to administer their own affairs.

Thus, on the eve of the present World War, the stage was set for the final struggle for India's liberation. During the course of this war, Germany with the help of her allies has dealt shattering blows to our enemy in Europe-while Nippon, with the help of her allies, has inflicted a knockout blow to our enemy in East Asia. Favoured by a most happy combination of circumstances, the Indian people today have a wonderful opportunity for achieving their national emancipation.

For the first time in recent history, Indians abroad have also been politically roused and united in one organization. They are not only thinking and feeling in tune with their countrymen at home, but are also marching in step with them along the path to freedom.

In East Asia, in particular, over two million Indians are now organized as one solid phalanx, inspired by the slogan of 'Total Mobilisation'. And in front of them stand the salaried ranks of India's Army of Liberation, with the slogan 'Onward to Delhi', on their lips.

Having goaded Indians to desperation by its hypocrisy and having driven them to starvation and death by plunder and loot, British rule in India has forfeited the goodwill of the Indian people altogether and is now living a precarious existence. It needs but a flame to destroy the last vestige of that happy rule. To light that flame is the task of India's Army of Liberation. Assured of enthusiastic support of the civil population at home and also of large sections of Britain's Indian Army, and backed by gallant and invincible allies abroad-but relying in the first instance on its own strength, India's Army of Liberation is confident of fulfilling its historic role.

Now that the dawn of freedom is at hand, it is the duty of the Indian people to set up a provisional government of their own and launch the last struggle under the banner of the government. But with all the Indian leaders in prison and the people at home totally disarmed, it is not possible to set up a Provisional Government.

It is, therefore the duty of the Indian Independence League in East Asia, supported by all patriotic Indians at home and abroad, to undertake this task-the task of setting up a Provisional Government of Azad Hind (Free India) and of conducting the last fight for freedom, with the help of the Army of Liberation, (that is, the Azad Hind Fauj or the Indian National Army) organized by the League.

Having been constituted as the Provisional Government of Azad Hind by the Indian Independence League in East Asia, we enter upon our duties with full sense of responsibility that has devolved on us. We pray that the province may bless our work and struggle for the emancipation of our Motherland. And we hereby pledge our lives for our comrades in arms to the cause of her freedom, of her welfare and her exaltation among the nations of the world.

It will be the task of the Provisional Government to launch and to conduct the struggle that will bring about the expulsion of the British and their allies from the soil of India. It will then be the task of the Provisional Government to bring about the establishment of a permanent National Government of Azad Hind constituted in accordance with the will of the Indian people and enjoying their confidence.

After the British and their allies are overthrown and until a permanent National Government of Azad Hind is set up on Indian soil, the Provisional Government will administer the affairs of the country in trust for the Indian people. The provisional Government is entitled to, and hereby claims, the allegiance of every Indian. It guarantees religious liberty, as well as equal rights and equal opportunities to all its citizens. It declares its firm resolves to pursue the happiness and prosperity of the whole nation and of its parts, cherishing all the children of the nation equally and transcending all the differences cunningly fostered by an alien government in the past.

In the name of God, in the name of bygone generations who have welded the Indian people into one nation, and in the dead heroes who have bequeathed to us a tradition of heroism and self-sacrifice—we call upon the Indian people to rally round our banner and strike for India's freedom. We call upon them to launch the final struggle (against the British and all their allies in India and prosecute that struggle) with valour and perseverance in full faith in final victory-until the enemy is expelled from Indian soil and the Indian people are once again a free nation.

MODERN VIEWS OF BOSE

The INA is fondly remembered by some Japanese rightwingers, who see the Japanese efforts to support Bose as proof of their view that Japan really was fighting on behalf of the oppressed peoples of Asia. In addition, the INA is seen by some as an organisation devoid of the divisive energies of parochialism that have since plagued Indian politics.

Bose's portrait hangs in the Indian Parliament, and a statue has been erected in front of the West Bengal Legislative Assembly.

Bose was posthumously awarded the Bharat Ratna, India's highest civilian award in 1992, but it was later withdrawn in response to a Supreme Court directive following a Public Interest Litigation filed in the court against the "posthumous" nature of the award. The Award Committee could not give conclusive evidence of Bose's death and thus it invalidated the "posthumous" award. Kolkata's civil airport and a university have been named after him.

Subhash Chandra Bose

In the period between the two world wars, Gandhi was the most powerful force within the Congress, and, it's probably fair to say, in nationalist politics. By this it does not only mean that Gandhi was able to make the big decisions, or at least influence those decisions, but also that Gandhian methods had become the primary tactics of the nationalist movement. These tactics involved an emphasis on nonviolence, and a vacillation between non-cooperation and active participation.

In other wards, the Gandhi and the Congress would go for years quietly coexisting with British rule, then launch a non-cooperation campaign, gain some concessions from the British, and then go back to another period of relative quiet.

For the most part, there were few challenges to this approach outside the Congress. The terrorists carried on in certain areas of the country, especially Bengal, but they were, at the most, a nuisance. By the time of WW II, it had long become evident that elite terrorism was not going to inspire a popular revolution. After Gandhi came along and demonstrated how a popular movement might be generated, the terrorists became even less relevant.

The challenge to the predominance of Gandhi and Gandhian tactics in Indian nationalism came from within the Congress. It came from a man named Subhash Chandra Bose, who, at the height of his political influence, was one of the two or three most powerful leaders in the Congress. Gandhi certainly saw Bose as a rival and a dangerous upstart, and did his best to destroy him politically. It is focussed on Bose today not because his battles with Gandhi are particularly fascinating, but because Bose held up an alternative vision, not only of political tactics, but also of political objectives.

Whereas, Gandhi sought compromises with the British, Bose sought absolute victories. Gandhi was willing to wait a long time for independence, Bose wanted immediate action, if not immediate results. Gandhi was anti-materialistic and hostile to modern technology, Bose saw technology and mass production as essential to survival and dignity. Gandhi wanted a decentralized society and disliked the modern state; Bose wanted a strong central government and saw the modern state as the only solution to India's problems. And finally, Bose did not share Gandhi's dedication to nonviolence.

Bose came from a upperclass Bengali family. His father was a wellknown lawyer in Cuttack. He was the ninth child in a big, busy family; but his parents were aloof, and Bose grew up as a loner. He was a voracious reader, and he was especially attracted to the writings of the 19th century Hindu social reformer, Swami Vivekananda. From Vivekananda he picked up a desire to take India, especially Hindu India, back to an idealized past in which Indians had been strong, moral and free. As he grew older, and became interested in socialism, he lost this interest in mythical golden ages and his overtly Hindu outlook. But he kept his determination to do something about what he saw as social injustice towards low-caste groups, the poor, and women.

He was a brilliant student, and became active in student politics at Calcutta's Presidency College. In those wartime years, the university offered military training to students who were interested (sort of like the ROTC today), and Bose eagerly signed up. But unlike Gandhi, who also had military experience, Bose did not join because he saw it as his duty to the Empire. He joined because he believed military training was an important part of a nationalist's education. He fervently believed that India, and especially Hindus, had become politically subjugated because of their military weakness. If the nation was to be free and worthy of respect, Bose felt, its citizens must know how to fight.

Also at Presidency College, he had one of his first direct encounters with the British. He became involved in an assault by students on a British professor, and was kicked out of school. This incident has since become one of the major myths of Indian nationalism, with Bose presented as the hero and Edward Oaten, the professor, presented as a racist villain. The truth is probably not so clear-cut. What is more likely is that Oaten was tactless, and Bose was hot-headed. A sense of humour was not one of Bose's strong points; he tended to be touchy and took everything very seriously.

He eventually graduated from Scottish Church College in Calcutta (after his father pulled a few strings to get him admitted), and was then packed off to England by his family to prepare for the ICS (Indian Civil Service) exams. He arrived in England in 1919, when he was 23 years old.

It's interesting to compare Bose's English experience with Gandhi's. Bose was probably a bit less socially isolated than Gandhi had been when he had first arrived; there were more Indians around for him to spend time with. As with Gandhi, the time Bose spent in England made a deep impression on his thinking. Like Gandhi, Bose became something of a dandy in England, always wearing expensive, perfectly pressed clothes. Like Gandhi, Bose was terrified of sex, and put all his guards up when he was around English women. And like Gandhi, Bose became more conscious of his Indian identity when he was in England.

But there were some very significant differences, as well. Gandhi did not become a nationalist while he was in England. That came later. Gandhi's nationalism developed slowly over the decades, and if we had to look for pivotal movements we would have to find them in South Africa and later in Jallianwalla Bagh. Bose arrived in England as a budding nationalist, and as somebody who was very conscious, and very resentful, of the racial basis of British rule in India. In England, he wrote one of his friends: "Nothing makes me happier than to be served by the whites and to watch them clean my shoes. In England, Bose's nationalism became more clearly defined, and more militant, than it had been before.

At the same time, Bose liked England. He enjoyed the openness of English society, the freedom of expression, the debates in parliament and at the university, the fact that students weren't shadowed by the police. It made him acutely aware of how different life was in colonial India. Also, there was a lot that Bose admired about the British in England. He found them efficient and energetic, he appreciated their sense of a national interest, and what he saw as their can do attitude. These qualities-efficiency, energy, discipline, a sense of punctuality-are all central to modern industrial society, and they became central to Bose's vision of what India should be like.

He did very well in the ICS exams, and then faced a dilemma that had, by the 1920's, become common for Indian nationalists. Should he join the lAS, and participate in the administration of India, or should he keep his distance from the colonial government? Would participation constitute collaboration? Eventually Bose decided to stay away from the IAS. Quite apart from his qualms about the Indian Civil Service, there was another major factor that influenced his decision. Bose was one of those people who desperately needed a father-figure in his life. Ever since he had been a child, he had attached himself to his teachers and to various swamis, hoping to find somebody who could be a combination of spiritual advisor, political mentor, and intellectual guide. For Bose, who was already leaning towards a career in nationalist politics, one possible choice might have been Gandhi, who served those functions for Nehru. But Bose never developed this intimacy with Gandhi. He admired Gandhi, but the philosophical differences were too great.

As he resigned from the Indian Civil Service, Bose finally found his father-figure. This was C.R. Das, who was another one of those nationalist lawyer-politicians active in the Congress. In some ways, Das was a curious choice of mentor for a hot-headed extremist like Bose. Das was the ultimate machine politician. He believed in building an administrative organization within the framework of the colonial government, and then running that organization as independently as possible. He did not look for revolution; rather like Gandhi, he believed in a gradual process of piecemeal concessions. Like Gandhi, he had responded to the Rowlatt Acts by throwing himself into the non-cooperation movement. He had abandoned his legal practice and his western suits, and adopting khadi and frugality, although he was never quite as frugal as Gandhi.

Bose was drawn to C.R. Das primarily because he admired the latter's personal sacrifices. The fact that both men were Bengalis was also a factor. And perhaps, at a psychological level, Das—with his social, cultural and professional background-was sufficiently like Bose's own father.

So Bose wrote to C.R. Das, offering his services, and rather boldly outlining his own ideas of how to build a nationalist organization. Congress, he wrote, should have a permanent house. It should come up with a set of policies for all of India, including the princely states, It should have policies for improving the conditions of low-caste groups, It should have its own research and intelligence wing, and a well-organized public relations machine. These ideas are important for several reasons, For one thing, they tell us a lot about how Bose was thinking about the present and the future. Already, in 1921, he wanted the Congress to function as a parallel government, This is something that very few people inside the Congress, including Gandhi, had given much thought to, or were comfortable contemplating, For another, these ideas highlight the emphasis Bose would place on efficient organization. They reflect his conviction that society's problems could be solved not through moral persuasion—which was the Gandhian line—but through pressure exerted by powerful organizations, such as a parallel government, or an independent nation-state.

Das was impressed by Bose's ideas, and invited Bose to work with him in Calcutta. So he went, and in 1921 he plunged immediately into hectic political activity mat fully utilized his talents as an organizer. Seeing a need to develop alternatives to the colonial educational system, Bose threw himself into creating a nationalist college. He set himself up as the principal, found professors who were willing to lecture, invented courses, developed course schedules, and even planned on taking some courses himself. All this was typical of the man: he wanted to be the leader, he wanted to plan and to organize, and at the same time he wanted to learn.

When he was not working on the nationalist college, Bose was organizing strikes and demonstrations in Calcutta as part of the non-cooperation movement. The British threw him in jail, along with C.R. Das and thousands of other activists, but this was pretty much what the non-cooperation movement aimed to achieve. He was released after six months, and was immediately back at work, doing what he did best: organizing large-scale operations. There had serious flooding in parts of Bengal. Bose, working with Congress volunteers, set up relief operations that were bigger and more effective than anything the Congress had done along those lines until then. Since the colonial government didn't do much to help the flood victims, Bose's reputation as an effective political leader grew larger.

At around this time, Bose began to have his first open disagreements with Gandhi. Actually, it was Das who had the disagreement with Gandhi, and initially Bose was involved only as Das right-hand man, Das wanted the Congress to contest elections to local councils under the Montagu-Chelmsford Act of 1919, and to become actively involved in local government. Gandhi felt this would undermine non-cooperation, and refused. But Das had support within the Congress on this issue, particularly from the two Nehrus. They got together and formed the Swaraj Party. This was not really a separate party, but a group that remained within the overall Congress organization. Faced with this tension within the Congress, Gandhi compromised and allowed the Swaraj Party to participate in the elections.

In the 1924 elections to the Calcutta Municipal Corporation-*i.e.*, the city government of Calcutta-the Swaraj Party won a two-thirds majority. Bose became the Chief Executive Officer. In other words, at the age of 27, he was one of the most powerful men in the second-largest city of the British Empire. He loved the job: it allowed him to use his talent for developing and running big operations, to be innovative, and to be the boss. He took charge of all kinds of details, from designing city employees' uniforms, to creating new municipal programmes for education and public health.

In the meantime, the colonial secret service kept a close watch on him, and tried to come up with evidence that would bring him down. The colonial government had first noticed Bose during Oaten episode, and now he was seen as a particularly dangerous nationalist politician, who was becoming too powerful too fast. Eventually, in the fall of 1924, Bose was arrested on vague charges of conspiring with terrorists to kill the police commissioner of Calcutta. The charges were almost certainly false. Bose probably sympathized with the terrorists, and may have helped them find jobs, etc., but it's totally implausible that he would have jeopardized his career at that stage by trying to kill his own police chief.

In any event, the British wanted to get him out of the country, and he was sent off to jail in Burma. His health broke down in prison, and he was eventually released in 1927. He came back to India and found that a lot had changed in his political fortunes. For one thing, C.R. Das had died, and the leadership of the Swaraj Party had been taken over by Gandhi loyalists. This left Bose without a secure foothold in the political establishment. He remained active in the Congress, but his moment at the center of power had passed. He went back to being the permanent outsider. In sonic ways, this freed him up, especially when it came to being able to criticize Gandhi. Now he had less to lose.

He spoke out strongly on two issues. Firstly, he criticized Gandhi's hostility to modern technology and mass He declared: "We have to live in the present and to adapt ourselves to modern conditions. The days of the bullockcart are gone forever." And, for those of you who have been following the recent controversy over the Indian nuclear programme, he added: "Free India must arm herself for any eventuality as long as the whole world does not accept wholeheartedly the policy of disarmament."

His second point of disagreement with Gandhi was over the pace and the objectives of the nationalist movement. Gandhi tended to give the British a lot of time to respond to Congress demands, and there were long gaps between the periods of active agitation. Bose wanted immediate agitation, and could not understand why Gandhi always waited for the right moment. A true revolutionary, he felt, created the moment, rather than wait for it to arrive.

Also, Gandhi and his allies within the Congress were not, in 1928, ready to come out and demand complete independence. They preferred to define the nationalist goal as dominion status, *i.e.*, as autonomy within the British Empire. Bose found this unacceptable, and he did not hesitate to say so.

Nevertheless, he was still working closely with the Congress. During the Congress convention in Calcutta in 1928, Bose organized the ceremonies. In the process, he allowed his imagination to run wild: he put Congress volunteers in military-style uniforms, named himself General Officer Commanding, and held a military-style honour guard for Nehru senior. Once again, this was his childish delight in uniforms and smart salutes coming to the forefront. Most people didn't know whether to laugh or to cry. Gandhi, most likely, was not amused.

In 1929, Bose was elected president of the Bengal branch of the Congress, defeating Gandhi's candidate. Not long after that, he was jailed for protesting the government's treatment of revolutionaries and political prisoners. In 1930 Gandhi finally gave the call for complete independence, and launched a new campaign of civil disobedience. Bose watched the campaign from prison. While in prison, he was elected mayor of Calcutta. When he was released in the fall of 1930, he immediately went back to being the organizer of massive nationalist demonstrations. After a confrontation with the police in which he was violently assaulted, he was sent back to jail. For the time being, his career as an active politician in India came to an end.

Bose's health failed again in prison, and he went to Europe to recover. He spent most of the 1930's in Europe, shadowed by the British secret service. Nevertheless, he travelled extensively in Switzerland, Germany, Austria, Italy, Ireland and Eastern Europe. He developed extensive contacts with the European left as well as with the right, both of which had reasons to be anti-Britain, and to welcome Bose as a man who was fighting the British in India. He met Mussolini, discussed his revolutionary plans with him, and Mussolini was suitably impressed.

This period in Europe had a profound effect on Bose's politics. For one thing, his exposure to the left sharpened his faith in revolutionary socialism, and his determination to lead a socialist revolution in India. For another, his exposure to the right gave him an admiration for the techniques of organization and administration that the Nazis were trying out in Germany, and that Mussolini's fascists had been trying out in Italy.

We now have to deal with the question of Bose's political ideology at this point, especially the question of whether or not he was a fascist. Well, in a word: yes, Bose was now a fascist. He had no problems with openly admiring fascism. At the same time, he was not a Nazi, in the sense that he was not a racist, and he had no interest in theories of national purity and cultural supremacy. Bose did not seek a Hindu India, or some pure version of Indian culture. He had long outgrown his old politics of Hindu nostalgia. He welcomed Muslim participation in Indian nationalism, and he did not hesitate when it came to forming alliances with Muslim politicians.

For Bose, fascism was a technique of political organization, and a diagram for relations between government and society. Bose was not a democrat. He may have been one in the 1920's, but by the late 1930's he was quite certain that parliamentary democracy was not suitable for India. In his mind, India needed firm control by a single party, which would direct every aspect of social, political, economic and even personal life.

He believed that India's problems-such as caste discrimination, class injustice, the need for economic modernization, etc.—were so deep-rooted that mey could only be weeded out through massive state intervention. For this, Bose believed, the machinery of the state had to be in the hands of a single, powerful, reforming party organization, such as the Nazi Party in Germany or the Communist Party in the Soviet Union. At this point, he still believed that this party would be the Congress.

Bose finally returned to India in January of 1937. He was now much more radical than he had been when he had left. He was quick to reject the Government of India Act of 1935, which had allowed for greater Indian participation in the provincial governments. For Bose, the law was too little too late.

He was unhappy that the Congress had agreed to participate in the government under the Act, but this did not keep him away from Congress politics. The years in Europe had not diminished his popularity in India, and he had no trouble getting elected as the president of the Congress. He remained president for only a year, before Gandhi schemed to bring him down.

But for that one year, Bose was king, and he enjoyed himself thoroughly. As in the past, he threw himself into building Congress up as a practical parallel government. In keeping with his faith in modern technology, he set up a committee of prominent scientists to develop a viable industrial policy. He raised funds, and he campaigned tirelessly all over India. He emphasized his socialist ideals, and along with Nehru, became the recognized leader of the Congress left.

But Bose and Nehru did not become political allies. There are several reasons. There were the philosophical differences: Nehru was a democrat, Bose was authoritarian. Also Nehru, at heart, was something of an Anglophile, in the sense that he had a soft spot for India's connection with England. Bose had no such sentimental attachment. Then there were differences in temperament that played out in the way they each approached socialism and policy-making. Nehru was a visionary without much interest in the details of implementing his visions. But details mattered to Bose. And finally, there was the Gandhi factor.

In spite of his philosophical differences with Gandhi, Nehru was Gandhi's protege, and everybody knew it. Nehru would disagree with Gandhi on specific issues, but when push came to shove and a decision had to be made, he would give in and let Gandhi have his way. This was partly Out of a genuine respect for Gandhi's leadership, and partly because Nehru understood very well that his own political fortunes were linked to Gandhi's. As long as Nehru was Gandhi's boy, his own future within the Congress organization was insured. This reluctance to go up against Gandhi meant that when Gandhi turned on Bose, Nehru made no real effort to defend his fellow-socialist.

When Bose had been elected Congress president, Gandhi had accepted it. The break came in the fall of 1938, when war in Europe became a distinct possibility. Bose and the left saw the possibility of war as a tremendous political opportunity, and wanted to use this opportunity to pressure the colonial government for immediate concessions. Gandhi and the Congress right, on the other hand, wanted to issue a much weaker resolution, hoping that the British would simply do the right thing if war broke out. Bose and the left refused to give in, and Gandhi was furious. Even though Bose was the Congress president at this time, Gandhi had long enjoyed the status of the unofficial super-president of the Congress, and he did not like Bose's disobedience.

Bose was up for re-election in January of 1939, and Gandhi decided to block him. Quite apart from his personal animosity, there were real issues involved. Bose wanted the Congress to walk away from implementing the Government of India Act of 1935. He also wanted to give the colonial government an ultimatum demanding immediate independence, and to begin all-out civil disobedience if the government refused. Gandhi and the Congress right felt otherwise. In any event, Bose won his re-election, narrowly defeating P. Sitaramayya, who was Gandhi's chosen candidate.

Gandhi now worked actively to bring Bose down. The Congress constitution provided only two ways for getting rid of the president: he could be voted Out of office, or he could resign. Since Gandhi was unwilling to wait for the next election, he decided to force Bose to resign. Even though Bose was the Congress president, Gandhi's supporters controlled the party's Working Committee. Without their cooperation, the president could not operate effectively; it was a system of checks and balances similar to what we have in the US government.

Gandhi's supporters now resigned, and Bose found himself unable to form a new Working Committee against Gandhi's opposition. He tried hard to work out a compromise with Gandhi. He even offered to let Gandhi nominate the entire Working Committee, if Gandhi would only accept Bose's plan to launch an agitation for immediate independence. Gandhi politely refused, and Bose had no option except to resign, four months into his second term as president.

One of the interesting things about this whole episode is that Bose blamed Nehru more than he blamed Gandhi. He never completely cut his ties with Gandhi, and continued to try to rebuild his bridges. But he never forgave Nehru for not helping him during this crisis.

On September 3 of 1939, war finally broke out in Europe. And not just in Europe, because the Viceroy Lord Linlithgow declared war on India's behalf, without consulting a single Indian. This was a major embarrassment for the Congress, which was now faced with two choices. It could either get some significant concessions from the colonial government. Or it could resign from the ministries it controlled under the Government of India Act. So the Congress went to the government, and asked for a clear statement of its military objectives.

The government stonewalled, saying that it was too early in the war to talk about military objectives. It also refused to talk about Indian independence, saying that any such discussion would have to wait until after the war. Since there was no clearly defined military objective, it meant that the government would decide when the war was over, and when Indian independence could be discussed. Congress now resigned from its ministries. It's been suggested that the British deliberately maneuvered Congress into resigning, to have a free hand in running the government during the war. Whatever the case may be, the Congress now found itself out of office, and with nothing but moral outrage to show for it. Still Gandhi refused to launch an agitation.

Bose, meanwhile, had been busy organizing his own party, called the Forward Bloc. This was initially within the structure of the Congress. But by 1940 it had become an independent political party, mainly because the Congress had refused to tolerate its allegiance to Bose instead of to Gandhi, and had kicked its officers out of office. Things were happening very fast for Bose, as usual. In July of 1940, he was arrested and sent to prison again for planning to lead a march demanding the removal of a memorial to the victims of the Black Hole of Calcutta. He went on a hunger-strike, and in December he was released.

Then began his great adventure. Even before his last arrest, Bose had begun to think about getting himself Out of India. He felt that there was little that he could achieve in India under the circumstances. His career in the Congress had stalled, and besides, the Congress was unwilling to do what he wanted it to do. The war, he felt, was too important an opportunity to waste. So he came up with a plan. He would escape from India, get to the Soviet Union, and then go on to Germany. When he got to Germany, he would persuade the Germans to help him in his fight against the British in India.

Bose now contacted a Communist organization in Punjab. He asked if they might be able to smuggle him across the border into Afghanistan, and through Afghanistan into the USSR. They told him it was possible. In the winter of 1940-41 his journey began. Disguised as a Muslim life-insurance agent, Bose escaped from his family home in Calcutta in the middle of the night. He boarded a train at a remote rural station, and travelled to Peshawar on the border between Punjab and Afghanistan. From there, in a new disguise as a deaf-mute Pathan, and accompanied by his communist contact, he trekked across the desert to Kabul. His plan to travel across the border directly into the Soviet Union had been discarded as impractical. His current plan was to contact the Soviet embassy in Kabul.

Kabul in the 1940's was basically a truck-stop village with embassies. Bose, still posing as a deaf-mute, stayed at truck-drivers' hotel for weeks, trying to contact the Russians. He had no luck, the Russians suspected that he was a British agent trying to infiltrate the Soviet Union. Next Bose contacted the Germans.

They heard him out, and were intrigued by his ideas, but dragged their feet. Eventually it was the Italians who rescued him. The Italian diplomat in Kabul was fascinated by Bose's plans. He gave Bose an Italian passport and the name Orlando Mazzotta, and persuaded the Germans and the Soviets to help him. Finally, in March of 1941, Bose travelled to the Soviet border in a diplomatic car, took a train to Moscow, and then flew to Berlin.

Bose remained in Germany for the next two years. He offered the Germans a deal. If they helped him, he said, he could trigger a revolution in India. Having to deal with a revolutionary situation in India would distract British forces from the war against Germany. In the process, Britain would lose the war with Germany, and lose India simultaneously. This was the big picture. To bring all this about, Bose put forward several ideas. Some of these he accomplished; in others areas he was frustrated. Let's look at his political objectives first.

Bose wanted facilities for broadcasting radio messages into India. This the Germans readily provided, and he made regular speeches directed at the Indian public. In his broadcasts, Bose urged people to use the war as an opportunity to break free. Germany would win the war, and the British should not be allowed to hang on in India. The first broadcasts created a sensation in India, largely because Bose's disappearance had generated a lot of public interest. But it didn't go much further than that. This was because in spite of Bose's presence in Berlin, to most Indians the war with Germany was still far away, and people couldn't really visualize the German army sweeping through the Caucasus to liberate India. Also, by this time, Gandhi and the Congress had finally launched the Quit India Movement, and a violent revolutionary situation already existed in India.

Bose's other major accomplishment in Germany was organizing the Indian Legion. In the course of the fighting in North Africa, the Germans had taken thousands of Indian POWs. Bose went to the POW camps, and asked the Indian soldiers to join him to fight against the British. This idea was not entirely new. An expatriate Indian named Mohammed Iqbal Shedai had already made a start organizing Indian POWs captured by the Italians. For a while, Bose and Shedai ran parallel efforts with the POWs. Then the Indian soldiers in Shedai's camp mutinied, This discredited Shedai, and left Bose as the only Indian organizing an army to fight on the side of the Axis.

Ultimately, the Indian Legion that Bose organized in Germany numbered about 3000 soldiers. It was not easy putting this force together. Initially, when Bose visited the POW camps to talk to the soldiers, he got a hostile reception. The British Indian Army may have been an army without a nationalist ideology, but it would be a mistake to think of it as a purely mercenary force. The colonial army had its own ideology, which was a combination of loyalty to the British throne, loyalty to the commanding officer, loyalty to the regiment, and a tradition of service in which the same family or same village sent many generations of soldiers into the Army.

But Bose persisted. He had the men separated from their officers, and talked to them one on one. Eventually, he got through. He promised them proper treatment from the Germans, appropriate rank, pay and benefits, and he promised them victory. The British, he told them, were certain to lose the war; they were like a dead snake that people continue to fear. If only they shook off this fear, Bose said, victory and freedom would be theirs. Bose had planned that when the German swing through the Southern USSR and the Middle East reached India, the Indian Legion would spearhead the attack on India. He anticipated that this would have two results. One was that when the soldiers of the colonial Indian Army faced the Indian Legion, they would refuse to continue to fight for the British and desert en masse to Bose's side. The other was that an invasion of India by Indian Legion would galvanize the Indian population into rising up against the British, and make Bose's task easier.

As things turned out, however, the Indian Legion came to a rather sad end. First, the Russians stopped the German advance at the battle of Stalingrad. This, combined with the defeat at El Alamein, meant that the Germans would be unlikely to get anywhere near India.

Second, after Bose left Germany in 1943, the Legion was left without an effective leader to look Out for them. They were absorbed into the German army and deployed in France. Now they knew they weren't going to be fighting for India's freedom, and their morale and discipline disintegrated. Many deserted, some joined the French resistance, and the rest disappeared in the chaos of the German retreat.

Bose's biggest frustration in Germany had to do with diplomatic recognition. He wanted Germany to officially recognize India as independent, and him as the leader of a government in exile. This the Germans refused to give him. The reasons lay partly in apathy, partly in the Master Race mentality, and partly in the peculiarities of Hitler's vision of the post-war world.

Hitler was not entirely comfortable with the idea of helping Indians—whom he saw as racially inferior—to defeat the British. The British were Aryans, after all.

In his own way, Hitler admired the English, and through much of the war he continued to hope that he could come to some kind of an understanding with Britain: essentially, that Germany would get a free hand in Europe, and England would get to keep most of its empire. He was perfectly willing to use Bose to make trouble for the British, but he had no long-term interest in India's future, one way or another.

Bose knew this, of course. He wanted to use the Germans for his own purposes. But eventually, as things turned out, neither was able to do very much for the other side. But by the middle of 1942, Bose was already looking beyond Germany, to Japan.

The string of Japanese victories after Pearl Harbor had achieved two things. One was that Singapore, which was a major British military stronghold, had fallen to the Japanese.

This placed tens of thousands of Indian soldiers in Japanese hands. What Bose had tried to do with the Indian Legion in Germany, he could try in South-East Asia on a much larger scale. The other thing that encouraged Bose was the fact that Japanese forces had come all the way to the Indian border with Burma. In other words, if he could organize an army in Japanese-occupied territory, and attack on India would be a relatively practical idea.

So, in February of 1943, the Germans did Bose one last favour: they helped him get to Japan. He travelled in a German submarine to the coast of Mozambique, where he transferred to a Japanese submarine. This submarine took him to South-East Asia.

The former British colonies of South-East Asia-Burma, Malaya, and Singapore-had large Indian populations, and Bose was welcomed as a conquering hero. In a sense, they had been waiting for him; in spite of all efforts to keep his plans secret, rumours had been circulating that he would come. The Japanese welcomed him also, and were far more enthusiastic about working with him than the Germans had been.

I'll give you an example of the difference in attitude: when Bose was on the German sub, he ate bread that tasted like it had been dipped in diesel. On the Japanese sub, the crew had brought along Indian spices especially for him, and cooked him Indian curries until he protested about the frequent meals. After he reached Asia, Bose travelled widely in the Japanese-help territories: to Burma, Malaya, Singapore, the Philippines, Vietnam, occupied China, and of course Japan. Unlike his uneasy relationship with Hitler, he quickly developed an excellent relationship with Tojo.

The Japanese gave Bose two things which he had wanted very badly: diplomatic recognition as the premier of free India, and a real army. Let's talk about his political status first.

He didn't have a territory, but he had a people: the Indian population of South-East Asia was placed under his jurisdiction. Bose got all the privileges and trappings of a head of state: the motorcade, the official aircraft, the honour guards, the works, He enjoyed it. In part, this was sheer megalomania: his old love of playing the great leader was resurfacing with a vengeance. In part, however, Bose recognized that it was necessary for him to play this role if was to deal effectively with the Japanese. He did not have any illusions about how the Japanese treated subject peoples. He knew that if he, and the Indians of South-East Asia, were to be taken seriously as allies, he had to insist upon his own status as an important political leader.

Bose did in fact run a real government in South-East Asia. I'm referring not to his status as leader of the government-in-exile of India, but to his status as leader of the local Indians. The regime Bose put together in Singapore, with the help of people who came forward to work with him, had the power to make and enforce laws, to collect taxes, and to recruit soldiers for the army. This people who paid the taxes and obeyed the laws did so willingly at first. Towards the end of the war, this cooperation became strained. As the Japanese collapsed and Tokyo's funding for Bose's army dried up, Bose pressed the local Indians for higher war taxes, and punished people who tried to hold back. This cost him some of his local popularity.

The army, to some extent, already existed when Bose arrived in Asia. After the fall of Singapore, an Indian officer named Mohan Singh had created the Indian National Army, or the INA as it came to be known, from Indian POWs.

This force was much larger than the Indian Legion in Germany. As such, it was a viable military and political resource. Mohan Singh himself had rather an unhappy career with the INA. Soldiers had joined the INA on the understanding that they would fight only on the Indian front. When the Japanese tried to send the INA to fight in other parts of South-East Asia, several units mutinied. These units were disbanded, and Mohan Singh ended up in a Japanese prison.

This was, in a way, a parallel of what had happened in Europe with Shedai's army. When Bose came to Asia, he quickly assumed command of what was left of Mohan Singh's old INA. At this time, this force had only 13,000 soldiers. But Bose had big plans. He wanted to expand the INA in two phases, first to 50,000 soldiers, and then to a force of 3 million. The men would come from the colonial Indian Army as well as from the South-East Asian Indian community.

The Japanese were shocked at such an ambitious plan, and told Bose that they would be able to arm a much smaller force, of about 30,000. Eventually, the INA reached a peak strength of around 50,000. It was an interesting social experiment in more ways than one.

The colonial Indian Army had organized its units around ethnicity and religion, so that the British could play off one group of Indians against another if necessary. In contrast, the INA had fully integrated units. It also had a regiment of female troops: this was the Rani of Jhansi Brigade, named after the queen who had died fighting the British in the Rebellion of 1857.

For Bose, the big numbers were necessary for their political effect. It didn't matter if most of the 3 million weren't equipped with adequate weapons. He saw the INA as a psychological force as well as a military asset.

He knew that if people in India became aware that a nationalist army of 3 million was waiting just across the border, ready to invade, it would have a tremendous effect on the way Indians related to the British. It would inspire pride and confidence, it would take away the fear of British power, and it would make it impossible for the British to maintain control.

In fact, Bose's whole strategy for using the INA depended upon this psychological factor. He wanted the force to spearhead a Japanese invasion, expecting that this would totally demoralize and dissolve the colonial Indian army, drawing its soldiers into the INA. He expected also that the general public would respond with overwhelming support.

It turned out that he was half right. The INA lost the war, but won the peace. In the summer of 1944, the Japanese were finally ready to begin their invasion of India.

They attacked from Burma in a two-pronged approach, hoping to capture the town of Imphal. This would then become the base for the rest of the invasion. But, at this critical point in Bose's plan, everything that could go wrong went wrong, The monsoon came early, and the Japanese assault became bogged down in the rain and the mud.

Also, by this point, the war in the Pacific was going very badly for the Japanese. Therefore, the Japanese had allocated most of their air power to the Pacific theatre, leaving their forces in the Burma-India theatre without any air cover. This gave the British a crucial advantage.

Then there were other factors. Food rations became exhausted. Allied air strikes cut the supply lines. Japanese and INA units found themselves eating grass and jungle flowers to stay alive.

Japanese commanders on the ground made some serious tactical errors. Normally, when things are going well, a few mistakes don't have to be fatal. But by 1944 the Japanese had overreached their capabilities. The attack on Imphal failed, and the counterattack was devastatingly effective.

The INA became caught up in this disaster, and never recovered. The INA's coordination with Japanese units was poor to begin with. Once things began to go badly for the Japanese, INA units became stranded. Some units fought well and there were plenty of individual heroics to go around, but it made no difference to the overall failure.

The biggest failure was the INA's inability to break up the morale of the colonial Indian Army, which did most of the fighting at Imphal, and which played a major role in the Allied counterattack.

Bose had expected that when the INA met the British Indian Army, colonial troops would immediately desert to the nationalist side. This did not happen. Bose had seriously underestimated the ideological strength of the colonial military. In fact, what often happened was the reverse.

Starving and out of ammunition in the jungle, shocked by the failure of the Japanese offensive, many INA troops were eager to return to their old units and their old comrades in the colonial army. There were over 700 desertions, and eventually Bose had to give orders that deserters would be shot on suspicion.

After the Imphal defeat, the Japanese retreated steadily through Burma and into Malaya, pursued by British and colonial Indian troops. The INA retreated with them. This retreat, ironically, brought Out Bose's best qualities as a leader. On the long trek from Burma to Bankok, followed closely by British tanks and under frequent attack from the air, he marched for days on end, refusing the offer of a car while his men had to walk. Throughout the march, he made sure that INA troops had proper food and medical care. In the chaos of the retreat, Bose was their best protection, and everybody knew it. Without him, the Japanese would have been only too eager to abandon the INA.

Bose returned to Singapore and tried for a while to rebuild the INA. This was the period when he demanded ten percent of the value of peoples assets to pay for military expenses, and made himself unpopular with the wealthier Indians in Malaya. But for Japan, the war was almost over. After the nuclear bombing of Hiroshima and Nagasaki, there was nothing left for Bose in working with Tokyo.

He now made a political gamble. The Soviets had been an ally of the British during the war, and an enemy of his allies, the Germans and the Japanese. But Bose correctly foresaw that the Soviet alliance with the west would not last. He decided to travel to Manchuria, which had just been overrun by the USSR. He planned to continue his fight against the British, but from Russia this time.

On 16th August, a day after the Japanese surrendered, Bose boarded a Japanese bomber in Saigon, on his way to Darien, in China. On the 18th of August, after a refueling stop in Taipei, the bomber crashed. Bose was still alive, but badly burned. He died in a Japanese military hospital in Taipei, soon afterwards.

The story didn't end there, During the war, the British had carefully suppressed all news about the INA. This news now finally broke in India. Bose immediately became a hero of mythical proportions. People refused to believe he was dead; in fact, people refused to believe it for decades.

Also, Bose's predictions about the psychological value of his army were finally vindicated. The British played into his hands by making a series of miscalculations about how to deal with 25,000 captured INA soldiers. Misreading the public mood, the British decided to stage a series of highly publicized trials of INA officers in New Delhi.

Incredibly, they believed that since the INA had taken up arms against Indians in the colonial army, the Indian public would want them to be severely punished.

Exactly the opposite happened. When three INA officers-Shah Nawaz Khan, G.S. Dhillon and Prem Kumar Sahgal—were put on trial for treason and murder in the Red Fort, the public quickly grasped the symbolism of the affair.

The three officers included a Hindu, a Muslim and a Sikh. In other words, all three of India's major religious communities were seen as being on trial for having come together to fight for their country. The fact that the trials were being held at the Red Fort, where the last independent Indian regime had been based, was seen as an added insult.

Even before the trials began, celebrations honouring the INA were held all over India. When the trials did begin, anti-British crowds besieged the Red Fort, and more than a hundred people were killed or injured by police firing.

In Calcutta, Hindus and Muslims, flying the flags of the Congress as well as the Muslim League, attacked British and American military bases. Scores of military vehicles were damaged or destroyed. Over 200 military personnel were injured, and 32 Indians were killed. The violence soon spread across much of Northern India, all the way to Bombay and Karachi.

Congress leaders like Gandhi and Nehru, who had been uncomfortable with Bose while he was alive, now eagerly jumped on the INA bandwagon. Nehru put on his old lawyer's robes and participated in the defense of the officers on trial. Gandhi made speeches praising Bose.

Confronted by this public hostility, the British found themselves unable to punish the INA prisoners as severely as they would have liked. Most got commuted sentences, or short prison terms. Nevertheless, the British persisted with the trials, and the violence continued to grow. Early in 1946, martial law had to be declared in Calcutta.

At around the same time, Indian troops in the colonial navy and air force mutinied, citing sympathy for the INA as well as unhappiness about their conditions of service. Within days, 78 warships had pulled down the Union Jack. Fierce battles erupted in the streets of Karachi and Bombay, in which tanks and machineguns were used. In Bombay, the mutineers were supported by the working class. 600,000 textile workers went on strike, and joined the sailors in street battles against British forces.

The rebels eventually failed, in part because they didn't have the firepower that the British were able to call in, and in part because the Congress panicked and told them to stop fighting.

The mutineers had looked to the Congress and the Muslim League to lead them. By the spring of 1946, however, the Congress and the League were too deeply implicated in the government of the country to see any good in this kind of unrest. Leaders like Nehru and Jinnah knew that independence was now at the most only a couple of years away.

As such, they did not want to encourage something as messy, as volatile and as dangerous as an armed rebellion. They had no experience and no stomach for leading this kind of movement, and they quietly supported the British efforts to crush the rebels.

But Bose's predictions about what would happen when the INA entered India had, to a considerable degree, come true, He had predicted a public uprising and sympathy from colonial troops, and now he was proved right. This is what I meant when I said that the INA lost the war but won the peace. But if Bose was right, where did he go wrong?

Well, as I've argued, that Bose misread the nature of the colonial army. On the battlefield, when everything was at stake, the colonial army retained its loyalties. It was only after the war that sections of it mutinied.

It can also be argued that Bose misread the political situation in India in the 1940's. Being away in Germany and South-East Asia had isolated him from the political realities of wartime India, and he had missed some crucial changes in the way the wind was blowing.

By 1942, the British were willing to discuss independence for India when the war ended. By 1945, there was no doubt that negotiations would soon begin. Yet Bose continued to fight a military battle, instead of rejoining the political process.

Was this unnecessary, and a mistake? Not if you were in Bose's shoes. He had taken up arms against the British, and his relations with the Congress had collapsed. He had reason to believe that if he returned to India while it was controlled by the British or the Congress, he would be treated as a war criminal.

Also, although India was clearly on its way to independence by the mid-40's, this was not the kind of independence that Bose had wanted. For Bose, the revolution at home was as important as throwing out the British, and for this he needed to be completely in charge. He did not believe that the replacement of British rule by a conservative parliamentary democracy would not bring about fundamental changes in the structure of Indian society.

This brings us some of the most basic questions about Bose, the nationalist and the politician. What are we to make of the fact that he wanted to invite the Germans and the Japanese to invade India? And how do we reconcile his heroic status with the fact that he aligned himself with Nazi Germany, and that he openly advocated dictatorship as the best form of government for India?

Perhaps the biggest weakness in Bose's plan was his belief that even after bringing the Japanese into India, he could maintain effective control of the country. At a diplomatic level, he had grounds for believing he could pull this off.

He refused to take India into the Japanese Co-Prosperity Sphere, which was the euphemism the Japanese used for their new empire in Asia, The Japanese accepted Bose's decision on this. Still, if the invasion of India had succeeded, it is difficult to see how he could have remained fully independent of Japanese control.

Bose felt that since the people of India would be with him, he would be able to resist Japanese demands. He knew that India was a long way from Japan, and that the Japanese were already at the limits of their capabilities. He also pointed out that the American revolutionaries had accepted assistance from France, and this didn't make the US a French colony. He may have had a point. But this analogy has its limits. Given the fact the INA was completely dependent on Japan for arms and ammunition, and that it would take time to develop an industrial infrastructure in India, Japan would probably have had a lot of leverage.

There is no getting away from the fact that Bose deliberately ignored the moral evil that Nazi Germany represented. He had lived in Germany for much of the 1930s and the early 40s. He must have known something of what was going on.

He had the courage to speak out against some of the racist aspects of the Nazi ideology, and even speak his mind to Hitler himself. But he was not sufficiently disturbed by Nazism to reject Hitler's help. Similarly, his alliance with Japan ignored the atrocities that the Japanese had perpetrated against people in the countries they had occupied.

Unlike Gandhi and Nehru, Bose believed that the end justified the means. He wanted freedom for India, and to some extent, he didn't care who he had to approach for assistance. But this explanation, is too kind to Bose. At some basic level, Bose had an ideological affinity for fascism, and he was a little too comfortable with using the state to crush dissent and ideological diversity.

Indians who refused to believe that Bose was dead, and who continued to believe for decades that he was alive somewhere in the Soviet Union, hoped he would just surface again some day like a messiah, and solve all of India's problems. Yet these people misunderstand Bose, and what he stood for. Had the INA and Bose succeeded on the battlefield, a free India would have been a totalitarian society.

Bose was passionate in his patriotism, and genuinely well-intentioned. He was genuine in his desire to help the disadvantaged segments of Indian society. But good intentions are not enough. Some of the greatest tyrants of the 20th century had good intentions: Lenin, Mao, Pol Pot. (You'll notice that these are all tyrants of the left. Tyrants of the right like Hitler, Franco, or the Shah of Iran, don't get credit for good intentions.)

Bose didn't seem to realize that the methods you choose do matter in the final analysis. Totalitarian institutions inevitably corrupt even the best-intentioned people. Even if it hadn't corrupted Bose himself, even if he had remained a so called benevolent dictator, there would have been no guarantees that his successor would have been benevolent. Ultimately, dying at the end of the war was the best thing Bose could have done for India.

5

Political Work, Ideology and Views of Bose

Second, his radical political ideology was shaped by a consuming frustration with the unsuccessful efforts of others to gain independence for India. His "fascist" outlook did not come from a drive for personal power or social elevation. While he was ambitious, and clearly enjoyed the devotion of his followers, his obsession was not adulation or power, but rather freedom for his beloved Motherland—a goal for which he was willing to suffer and sacrifice, even at the cost of his life.

Bose was favourably impressed with the discipline and organizational strength of fascism as early as 1930, when he first expressed support for a synthesis of fascism and socialism. During his stays in Europe during the 1930s, he was deeply moved by the dynamism of the two major "fascist" powers, Italy and Germany. After observing these regimes first-hand, he developed a political ideology of his own that, he was convinced, could bring about the liberation of India and the total reconstruction of Indian society along vaguely authoritarian-socialist lines.

Bose's lack of success in his lifelong effort to liberate India from alien rule was certainly not due to any lack of effort. From 1921, when he became the first Indian to resign formally from the Indian Civil Service, until his death in 1945 as leader of an Indian government in exile, Subhash Chandra Bose struggled ceaselessly to achieve freedom and prosperity for his beloved homeland.

Tripuri Congress Redux

The purpose of this essay is not to belittle Mahatma Gandhi. The reader will notice that nowhere has Gandhi's campaign to oust Bose been termed as immoral or unethical. At the same time it is not possible to know the truth by imposing divinity on Gandhi.

The Tripuri Congress session of 1939 is a crucial event in the history of the Indian National Congress. The united resistance and non-cooperation of the conservative leadership cleared the way for the removal of the recently re-elected Congress president Subhash Chandra Bose.

Bose was compelled to resign very soon. It won't be an exaggeration to say that the Tripuri session was the theatre of the demise of Bose's political career. Mahatma Gandhi was not present in the Tripuri session, but later when Bose repeatedly sought his intervention to end the stalemate, his stubborn refusal only hastened Bose's resignation. Even today Tripuri remains in the collective memory of Bengalis as a gross injustice done by Gandhi to Bose and Bengal. The consequent loss of Gandhi's image continues till today. On re-evaluating the incident after almost 65 years, certain questions arise which have never been answered squarely. This essay raises those little-discussed issues.

Was Gandhi Afraid of Bose?

Gandhi himself proposed Bose's name as the president of Congress in the Haripura Session of 1938. But within a year he literally became desperate to remove Bose and did not hesitate to take recourse to any sort of tactics to serve the purpose. His only objective at that time was Bose's removal by any means. No opinion regarding whether Gandhi's move was ethical or not can be objective, but at the same time it is pertinent to ask if he was afraid of Bose. Blind followers of Gandhi will of course laugh away such a question.

They will argue that at that the national level Gandhi's status and influence was supreme, whereas the sphere of Bose's influence was limited. In that case, the question that begs answer is why was Gandhi so worried? It was clear as daylight to the whole country that he did not want Bose to continue. Despite such explicit opposition from Gandhi how did Bose get re-elected? Certainly not by rigging the election! Perhaps Gandhi was not perturbed even by the British government to the extent as he was by Bose. If he was confident of himself, what was the reason for Gandhi not to confront Bose directly rather than reverting to political trickery?

It is important to be clear about one thing regarding this issue. Many intellectuals, despite having high regards for Bose, cannot consider the Bose-Gandhi feud objectively. It almost amounts to sin for them even to think that Gandhi can do something unethical.

They meticulously desist from associating Gandhi with any sort of Machiavellian politics since they consider him as much above petty politics. Furthermore, they present the accounts of many contemporary revolutionaries who could not see any wrong in Gandhi's actions in spite of being Bose's followers. It is now time to show clearly how both schools of arguments do not hold ground.

Firstly, overwhelming evidence has come to light showing Gandhi directly involved in the conspiracy to remove Bose. Gandhi's statements, letters, etc. of those days are now available with the publication of his complete works. However, it was not possible for the revolutionaries during the Tripuri session to understand Gandhi's intentions, which he did not share even with his closest associates. Thus, it was virtually impossible for those revolutionaries, who despite being followers of Bose respected Gandhi, to assess Gandhi's true character. Therefore, even as they were pained by the anti-Bose actions of Gandhi, they failed to realize the Machiavellian tactics adopted by him.

Secondly, the question of right or wrong is in once sense irrelevant here since Machiavellian strategies are to some extent required in realpolitik. If Gandhi was determined to get rid of Bose for the sake of his own power and influence then his actions can be regarded as the most unethical. On the other hand, if he was moved by the consideration that removing Bose was necessary for the good of the country then his actions cannot be labelled unethical, since the interest of the country is always larger than the individual. It is not easy to resolve this debate.

It can however be resolved easily if Gandhi is seen as a clever politician instead of placing him in the high pedestal as a divine personality, without going into the question of right or wrong. It is abundantly evident that Gandhi was bothered by the rise of Bose and that he took recourse to a confrontation by proxy rather than facing him in a direct way. It was almost a nonviolent guerilla war. From Gandhi's point of view he was right. It is foolish to expect that he would give up to his biggest political challenger. Rather it is expected that he would resist fiercely with his entire prowess.

Even if Gandhians are upset, it will have to be admitted that only when one is pushed to the wall one becomes as desperate to fight back as Gandhi was. From that perspective Bose emerged victorious at Tripuri. Gandhi's statement that Sitaramayya's defeat was an indirect defeat for him was true in essence. To wash off the bitter taste of defeat, Gandhi threw away his principle of means being more important than the goal. It was possible to see such an astonishing U-turn of Gandhism only due to Bose's victory.

Tripuri and the subsequent flow of events prove beyond any doubt that Gandhi jettisoned his cherished ideals and instead adopted a totally un-Gandhian approach. It can be said that changing strategies or positions in politics is not unethical. Therefore, it will suffice to say, without raising the issue of ethics, that Gandhi became desperate and broke out of his own value system since he acutely felt an existential crisis. From that perspective, Tripuri saw the defeat of the conventional Gandhism and the emergence of a new Machiavellian Gandhism. The events of Tripuri provide the burning proof that Gandhiism is not based on eternal ideals and values.

POLITICAL WORKS AND VIEWS

Subhash Chandra Bose advocated complete freedom for India at the earliest, whereas most of the Congress Committee wanted it in phases, through a Dominion status. Even though Bose and Gandhi had differing ideologies, the latter called Bose the *"Prince among the Patriots"* in 1942.

Bose admired Gandhi, recognising his importance as a symbol of Indian Nationalism; he called him "The Father of Our Nation" in a radio broadcast from Rangoon in 1944, in which he stated that "I am convinced that if we do desire freedom we must be prepared to wade through blood", a statement somewhat at odds with Gandhi's philosophy of nonviolence. Thus, although they shared the goal of an Independent India, by 1939 the two had become divided over the strategy which should be used to achieve Indian Independence, and to some degree the form which the post-Independence state should take: Gandhi was hostile to industrialisation, whilst Bose saw it as the only route to making India strong and self-sufficient (in this he may have been influenced, like many other Indian intellectuals of the time, by reports of the success of the Soviet five-year plans). Nehru disagreed with Gandhi on this point as well, though not over the tactics of protest.

At the time the Second World War began, great divisions existed in the Indian independence movement about whether to exploit the weakness of the British to achieve independence. Some felt that any distinctions between the political allegiances and ideologies of the warring factions of Europe were inconsequential in the face of the possibility of Indian independence, given the fact that the British themselves showed so little respect for democracy or democratic reforms in India. Others felt that it was inappropriate to seek concessions when Britain itself was in peril, or else that pressure was better applied within India and in peaceful fashion, and found that their distaste for Nazi Germany and Japan outweighed any possibility that an alliance with them would bring India's independence closer.

Bose, in particular, was accused of 'collaborating' with the Axis, after he fled to Germany in 1941 and offered Hitler an alliance. He criticized the British during World War II, saying that while Britain was allegedly fighting for the freedom of the European nations under Nazi control, it would not grant independence to its own colonies, including India. It may be observed that along with Nehru, Bose had organized and led protest marches against the Japanese invasion of Manchuria in 1931, and of China itself in 1938, when he was Congress president. In 1937 he published an article attacking Japanese Imperialism in the Far East, although he betrayed some admiration for other aspects of the Japanese regime. Bose's earlier correspondence (prior to 1939) also reflects his deep disapproval of the racist practices of, and annulment of democratic institutions in Nazi Germany. He also, however, expressed admiration for the authoritarian methods (though not the racial ideologies) which he saw in Italy and Germany during the 1930s, and thought they could be used in building an independent India. Nevertheless, Bose's tenure as Congress Party President (1938-39) did not reflect any particular anti-democratic or authoritarian attributes. Nirad C. Chaudhuri, Anton Pelinka and Leonard Gordon have remarked that Bose's skills were best illustrated at the negotiating table, rather than on the battlefield.

That Bose eventually changed his political stance reflects his deep discontent with the nature of the British rule, and a growing belief that the formation of an Indian free state was too far into the future on the British political roadmap to be acceptable. At the Tripura Congress session of 1939, he made his views quite explicit-he demanded for a programme of immediately giving the British Government a six-months ultimatum to grant the national demand of independence and of launching a mass civil disobedience movement if it failed to do so. He believed that "... the country was internally more ripe for a revolution than ever before and that the coming international crisis would give India an opportunity for achieving her emancipation, which is rare in human history.". Bose's judgment in allying with the Japanese has been questioned, as many argue that he would have been unable to ensure an independent India had he ridden to power on Japanese bayonets, and was in danger of being turned into a puppet ruler like Pu-yi, the last Chinese Emperor in Manchukuo. In 1943 Rash Behari Bose had urged this on him during his last visit to Subhash Bose in Singapore, pointing out that the Japanese had claimed right of conquest in Manchuria and would do so in India, whilst Quit India had shown that this would not be accepted by the Indian Nation.

Nevertheless, given the INA's overwhelming dependence on Japanese military support, he would have been in a very weak position. Bose also seems to have ignored the appalling treatment meted out by the Japanese to the Asian inhabitants of the lands they conquered as part of the Greater East Asian Co-prosperity sphere, which included the forcible recruitment of labour from the overseas Indian population to build projects such as the Burma Railway, and massacres of Malayan Chinese in Singapore where he spent most of the War.

Bose has been branded as a fascist in some quarters. Others believe that Bose had clearly expressed his belief that democracy was the best option for India. The pro-Bose thinkers believe that his authoritarian control of the Indian National Army was based on political pragmatism and a post-colonial recovery doctrine rather than any anti-democratic belief.. However, during the war (and possibly as early as the 1930s) Bose seems to have decided that no democratic system could be adequate to overcome India's poverty and social inequalities, and he wrote that an authoritarian state, similar to that of Soviet Russia (which he had also seen and admired) would be needed for the process of national rebuilding. Accordingly some suggest that Bose's alliance with the Axis during the war was based on more than just pragmatism, and that Bose may have been a Fascist, though not a Nazi; alternatively, others consider he might have been using populist methods of mobilization common to many postcolonial leaders.

Had either of the alliances he forged during the war resulted in Indian independence in the manner he envisaged, it would have been at the cost of an Allied defeat in the Second World War, a price that some Indians would argue is too high: Gandhi himself, in the immediate aftermath of the war, said that Bose had been "foolish in imagining, that by allying himself with the Japanese and the Germans, who were not only aggressive Powers, but also dangerous Powers, he could get Indian freedom". The alternative of nonviolent protest within India espoused by Gandhi and the rest of Congress ultimately led to British withdrawal, albeit at the expense of the partition of the country along communal lines. Even before 1939, Congress had secured political concessions from the British in the form of elected Provincial Assemblies, and an agreement that the British taxpayer would foot the bill for Indian re-armament. Although it was rejected by Congress at the time, the 1942 Cripps mission's offer of full independence after the war could be considered the point at which the British departure became inevitable. Britain's weakness after the war, and domestic political pressure on the Labour Government also made British withdrawal more likely. Publicly at least, Bose never believed that this would happen unless they were driven out by force: as late as 1944, three years prior to Independence, he announced that "I am honestly convinced that the British Government will never recognise India's demand for independence".. Nirad Chaudhuri considered it a backhanded tribute to Bose that the Congress tricolor and the Muslim League green flag flew together for the last time during the mutiny of the Indian navy in Bombay unleashed in 1946 partly at anger within the Navy at the trial of INA officers by the British.

Judith Brown argues that the Mutiny of the Indian Navy was a minor factor in the British decision to leave compared to domestic political pressure, American hostility to any continuation of the *Raj*, and the breakdown of almost all networks of support and collaboration brought about by thirty years of Congress agitation. By 1946 over 50% of the members of the Indian Civil Service were Indians, and even Churchill recognised that the offer of independence made by the Cripps Mission in 1942 could not now be withdrawn. In this interpretation concerns over the loyalty of the military were only one factor amongst many amidst the general breakdown in authority: nor, it could be argued, did all this necessarily stem from the activities of Bose and the INA. The prospect of communalism infecting the armed forces worried the British just as much.

There is no doubt that Bose was considered a great patriot, and was considered as such even by his rivals in the Congress. Gandhi himself wrote that Bose's "... patriotism is second to none", and he was moved to proclaim after Bose's disappearance that he was a "prince among patriots"-a reference, in particular, to Bose's achievement in integrating women and men from all the regions and religions of India in the Indian National Army. Bose wanted freedom for India at the earliest opportunity, and to some extent, he didn't care who he had to approach for assistance. It is thus quite understandable that he remains a controversial figure to this day.

MASS MOBILIZATION

Bose was, nonetheless, a consistent advocate of total mobilization: the mustering of national resources on a scale normally associated with military-like action. Realizing that manpower was easily India's greatest resource (and arguably the only one available to the independence movement), he proclaimed that all Indians—male and female, urban and rural, rich and poor—should actively participate in the fight for freedom. From his earliest days in politics to his death in 1945, he sought to rouse the great Indian masses, and involve them directly in the political struggle. Their support for representatives at the provincial or national levels was not enough; they must themselves rise up and win independence.

During the 1930s, however, his political position was never strong enough to call for other resources than manpower, nor was India—under British control—able to offer other resources. Additionally, total mobilization during peacetime, without an impending war or revolution in the awareness of the masses, had never been achieved (not even by the Nazis) and, arguably, never could be achieved.

Bose, an astute man, no doubt realized this. With the formation of the Provisional Government of Azad Hind, he was at last in a position to appeal directly for total mobilization to the mass of Indians—at least in South-East Asia, and, less directly to those in India itself. Along with his call for mass mobilization, he demanded that all available resources be provided for the cause of freedom. For example, he told a mass meeting in Singapore in July 9, 1943:

> *Friends! You will now realize that the time has come for the three million Indians living in East Asia to mobilize all their available resources, including money and manpower. Half-hearted measures will not do. I want Total Mobilization and nothing less, for we have been told repeatedly, even by our enemies, that this is a total war... Out of this total mobilization I expect at least three hundred thousand soldiers and three crores of dollars [$ 30,000,000]. I want also a unit of brave women to form a death-defying regiment who will wield the sword which the brave Rani of Jhansi wielded...*

Of course, Bose demanded not only the total mobilization of Indian resources in South Asia, but of Indian resources everywhere. He called for mass mobilization not only in support of his army, but also for his dynamic new government, the various branches of which required financing and manpower.

WOMEN'S EQUALITY

As can be seen from the passage quoted above, Bose called on both men and women for total support. Unlike the German National Socialists and the Italian Fascists, who stressed the masculine in almost all spheres of social and political activity, Bose believed that women were the equals of men, and should, therefore be likewise prepared to fight and sacrifice for India's liberation.

Throughout the 1920s and 1930s he had campaigned in India to bring women more fully into the life of the nation. After his return to Asia in 1943, he called on women to serve as soldiers in the Indian National Army—at the time a most radical view. "When I express my confidence that you are today prepared to fight and suffer for the sake of your motherland," he told the women's section of the Independence League in July 1943,

> *I do not mean only to cajole you with empty words. I know the capabilities of our womanhood well. I can, therefore, say with certainty that there is no task which our women cannot undertake and no sacrifice and suffering which our women cannot undergo... To those who say that it will not be proper for*

> *our women to carry guns, my only request is that they look into the pages of our history. What brave deeds the Rani of Jhansi performed during the First War of Independence in 1857... Indians—both common people and members of the British Indian army—who are on the border areas of India, will, on seeing you march with guns on your shoulders, voluntarily come forward to receive the guns from you and carry on the struggle started by you.*

A women's regiment was formed in 1943, and came to number about 1,000 women. It was named, appropriately, the "Rani of Jhansi Regiment," after a heroine of the Indian rebellion of 1857-58 against British rule. While those less suited to combat duties were employed as nurses and in other support roles, the majority were trained as soldiers.

When the INA attacked British forces from Burma in East India in mid-1944, the women of the Jhansi Regiment fought alongside the men, suffering equally heavy casualties. When the army was forced to withdraw, the women were given no privileges. Along with the men, they marched for more than a thousand kilometres.

COMMITMENT TO YOUTH

Lastly, Bose was also deeply committed to the youth movement, a devotion that featured prominently in his political ideology. Convinced that young people were by nature idealistic, restless and open to new ideas —such his own radical and militant outlook—Bose accordingly devoted a great deal of time and effort to the new Youth Leagues that were formed in a number of provinces during the 1920s.

Throughout his career he presided over far more youth conferences than any other all-India political figure, and his speeches to younger people he steadfastly urged a spirit of activism that contrasted sharply with the passivism preached by Gandhi and many of the older politicians. "One of the most hopeful signs of the time," he claimed at the 1928 Maharashtra Provincial Conference, "is the awakening among the youth of this country...

Friends! I would implore you to assist in the awakening of youth and in the organization of the youth movement. Self-conscious youth will not only act, but will also dream; will not only destroy, but will also build. It will succeed where even you may fail; it will create for you a new India—and a free India—out of the failures, trials and experiences of the past."

India's liberation would be achieved not by Gandhi and the leading politicians of his generation, whose conservative, reformist policies bred passivity and inactivity. It would, Bose believed, be achieved only through the efforts and sacrifices of the militant, revolutionary and politically-conscious younger generation.

Economic Views

In contrast to the copious record of Bose's political ideology and actions, much less is available about other important elements of his outlook, such as his economic views and policies. For example, while he condemned capitalism and extolled socialism in the pages of *The Indian Struggle,* Bose was very vague about just what monetary or credit systems he foresaw in a free India. They would be set up, he simply wrote, "in the light of the theories and the experiments that have been and are current in the modern world." Throughout his career he never wrote or said anything more specific about such matters. He appears to have had no precise ideas about political economy, save that economics was not important in itself but must be subordinated to national political considerations. Any discussion here of what economic systems he favoured, and when and how he intended to implement them, would thus be merely speculative.

Gandhi as an Avatar of Machiavelli

The name of the famous Italian intellectual Nicolo Machiavelli has been associated with all sorts of unethical means for achieving political goals. Machiavelli laid more importance on the goal than on the means and advocated the dissociation of religion from politics. In the second sense Gandhi was not Machiavellian since he advocated just the opposite, which is, associating religion with politics. In the first sense he did follow the Machiavellian way to remove Bose out of his way. Bose was ready to follow any path for the attainment of independence for India, but never adopted Machiavellian ways in case of internal politics of Congress. This is where he is different from Gandhi.

Although Bose understood perfectly the nature of the British Raj, he dangerously failed to understand Gandhi. It has been rightly said by Amalesh Tripathi that Bose did not realize that his real conflict was with Gandhi himself. In his letter to Jawaharlal Nehru on 28 August 1939 he complained, "If the old guard wanted to fight why did they not do so in a straightforward manner? Why did they bring Mahatma Gandhi between us?" On 4 April 1939 Sarat Chandra Bose, Bose's elder brother had written to Nehru along the same lines, "I believe I shall not be unjust if I say that the members of the Working Committee would have shown greater courage and straightforwardness if they had decided to act on their own and not used Mahatmaji as their cover.

Their plain duty was to keep Mahatmaji above all controversy as he should be in our political life." Both put on the dock Gandhi's followers like Sardar Patel, Bhulabhai Desai, etc.

Sarat Bose expressed his displeasure in a sharp letter written to Gandhi on 21 March 1939. He wrote, "Tripuri was an eye opener to me. The exhibition of truth and nonviolence of your chosen disciples stunk in my nostrils. The election of Subhash was not a defeat for yourself, but of the high command of which Sardar Patel is the shining light." In fact the conservative leadership comprising of Patel, Desai and others kicked up a vilification campaign against Bose at Tripuri after calling his illness a 'political fever.' Bose wrote about this painful experience in his essay "My strange Illness." Patel was the focus of his wrath in his letter of 28 March too. Bose wrote to Nehru, "Was there nothing wrong in Sardar Patel making full use of the name and authority of Mahatma Gandhi for electioneering purposes?" He failed to understand that his true opponent was Gandhi who was actually controlling the unfolding of events from behind the curtain. In that sense Patel and others did not take recourse to any trickery and confronted Bose openly. The allegations that Bose brought agains them should have been raised against Gandhi. Why was he fighting a proxy war instead of playing a frontal role?

Gandhi wrote to his secretary Mahadev Desai on 29 January 1939 that he might not attend the Tripuri session if Bose wins the election. On 3 February 1939 he wrote to Nehru that he will serve the country although he will not attend the Congress session. He left for Rajkot on 27 February and the infamous Pant resolution was proposed on 8 March 1939: a classic example of pure Machiavellian politics.

Gandhi knew well that the Pant resolution will be proposed in his absence, but then he will be able to deny any responsibility for the proposal. At a time when Bose was repeatedly asking for Gandhi's opinion and seeking his intervention, all he could say was that he did not want to impose his choice on Bose. He wrote on 10 April 1939 that the more he read the Pant proposal the worse he feels, but he can't explain. Today many intellectuals who have high regard for both Gandhi and Bose can't see any dishonesty in Gandhi's action.

They, however cannot be blamed since Bose himself failed to see any dishonesty in Gandhi. He even rebuked Narendra Narayan Chakrabarty when he suggested so. The question that now arises is whether Gandhi would have felt it necessary to carry on with his programme of fast at Rajkot if Bose was defeated. Secondly, if Gandhi was unhappy with the Pant proposal why did he not ask for an amendment? Thirdly, while advising Bose to constitute his cabinet of similar thinking leaders, was Gandhi not aware of its impossibility at that point of time? It would be over simplification to say that Gandhi was revengeful, but the fact remains that such a crafty politician has rarely been seen in this country.

That was one area where Bose could not equal Gandhi as he was a staunch opponent of the trend of politicking in Congress. The British Raj, however knew Gandhi as a clever Machiavellian politician. Although Bose opposed Gandhi's politics, he had high regards for him. Perhaps that is why he could not comprehend the true nature of Gandhi's politics. Now the question is, did Gandhi play this game of war by proxy to maintain his image? If that was the case, it was a terrible miscalculation because the Tripuri events pained even many of his followers. In general his image suffered a blow. His true intentions were clear as daylight.

When he described Bose's victory as his own defeat, there was no deception. Rather such straight talk is laudable. Had be provided the leadership to the conservative politicians in opposing Bose then surely his image would have gained a new high and he would have been praised. But instead he chose a path which was murky. He gained a victory which was but temporary. It was impossible for Gandhi to suppress Bose. The evidence of that has been written in golden letters in future history.

Did Bose have a Weakness for Gandhi?

Bose started making efforts to bring an end to his conflict with Gandhi after the Tripuri session. Manabendra Nath Roy rightly advised him in a letter written on 1 February 1939 to accept Gandhi's challenge and constitute a cabinet of his liking. However, Bose did not accept the advice. This was one reason of losing the support of the leftists. Revolutionary of the Juagantar group told the writer that Bose's seeking of Gandhi's support, who had meted him such undignified treatment, also led to anger in certain sections of the revolutionary groups. Late Manohar Mukhopadhyay, another revolutionary of the Jugantar group, also told the writer that Bose was hesitant act against Gandhi. Perhaps there is some truth in such opinion, but if Bose showed any soft attitude in certain situations towards Gandhi it was due to strategic reasons, not due to any weakness. The former Prime Minister Morarji Desai has made a laughable statement in his autobiography that Gandhi accepted Bose as the president in the Haripura Congress only after Bose promised that he will go by Gandhi's directions. Those familiar with Bose's character know well that he was not one to submit to Gandhi in such a way, but might have just restrained his extreme revolutionary identity for the time being.

Rajendra Prasad has written in his autobiography that if Bose had expressed his willingness to be re-elected to Gandhi perhaps the Tripuri conflict could have been avoided. How strange! Would Bose beg Gandhi for his democratic rights? He did not compromise on this issue because with all his respect for Gandhi he was not prepared to take his words as the final. And if he had withdrawn himself from the contest in accordance with Gandhi's wishes, he could not have held his head high in future. This would have not only set a bad precedent, but would have stifled democracy in Congress.

Of course democracy was ultimately stifled in Congress due to Gandhi and his followers, but Bose was not involved with that. He did not sign the death warrant of democracy in Congress. It can of course be asked that why did Bose allow Pant resolution to be raised knowing that it was unconstitutional and undemocratic? He explained to Gandhi in a letter written on 25 March 1939 that he could have vetoed this proposal but did not do so because his democratic outlook had the priority over the issue of constitutional validity. He also wrote, "I felt it would be unmanly to take shelter behind the constitution at a time when I felt that there was the possibility of an adverse vote."

This is where Bose committed a blunder since it made easy for Gandhi to write on 30 March 1939, "Since you think that Pant's resolution was out of order and the clause relating to the Working Committee is clearly unconstitutional, and were ultra vires your course is absolutely clear. Your choice of the committee should be unfettered." Even if this might appear to be transparent, so certain questions are bound to arise. Firstly, why didn't Gandhi clearly comment on the Pant resolution? Gandhi asked Bose to form the cabinet of his choice only because Bose thought that the proposal was unconstitutional. In other words, Gandhi himself did not think that the proposal was unconstitutional. He told Bose on 10 April 1939, "The framers meant well. But it does not answer the present difficulty. You should, therefore give it your own interpretation." By talking about the good intention of the proposal Gandhi supported it indirectly, but never spelt it out clearly. It would have been manly if he had stated his opinion clearly, but instead he created a situation where there was no other way for Bose than to resign.

It is true that Bose sought Gandhi's intervention repeatedly at that time, but that was not from his weakness for him. He hoped against hope that Gandhi will resolve the internal conflict of Congress in the larger interest of the country. He wrote to Gandhi on 31 March 1939, "We are not vindictive and we do not nurse grievances. There is no doubt that today there is a wide gulf between the two main blocs or parties in the Congress. But the gulf can be bridged – that by you." In another letter he wrote, "I am temperamentally not a vindictive person and I do not nurse grievances. I have the mentality of a boxer that is to shake hands smilingly when the boxing bout is over and take the revolt in a sporting spirit." Bose could never imagine that his sportsman spirit will have no impact on Gandhi's mind. Gandhi was so disturbed by him that he had already thought up his course of action. Usually action agenda in politics is determined according to time and expediency, but in this case it was determined much earlier in what can be called fait accompli. Gandhi can be asked if he had started considering himself as weak. His innovativeness shows through the methods he adopted to remove Bose from his position. It is unfortunate that instead of applying such political methods against the British Raj, he used it against a great son of India.

Bose was a staunch anti-imperialist, but due to irony of fate he became a victim to both imperialist oppression and subversive internal politics of Congress. He wanted a compromise with Gandhi in the interest of the larger interest of the country. The British Raj always wanted to split India by its divide and rule policy. Bose wanted to rise above personal grievances realizing that the internal conflict will only strengthen the British policy of divide and rule. But Gandhi was immovable from his position and thus all efforts of Bose failed. It must be remembered that despite all this Bose kept the path of cooperation with Gandhi open. He also joined the special session of Congress on Gandhi's invitation at Wardha after being expelled from Congress. Bose baiters might see an effort of appeasement in this but if Bose truly had any weakness for Gandhi he wouldn't have searched for an alternative to the Gandhian way.

Probably he had hoped that he would be able to convince Gandhi to accept the relevance and importance of his plan of action. When he realized that he was only chasing a mirage, he decided to leave the country. Whether the country gained or suffered a loss will be judged by history but the fact remains that Bose was the only leader who showed the courage of proposing an alternative to the Gandhian way. The main source of his conflict with Gandhi can be found in his unique nature.

NETAJI'S EARLIER ACTIVITIES

His religious tendency and service to the poor and down-trodden were apparent, when he was about twelve years of age. They had a small Ashram for this purpose and held schools for "harijan" boys. They helped the poor and needy and nursed and gave medical aid to the sick and diseased.

He had the opportunity of living in the same house at Puri, Orissa, with Swami Brahmananda, president, Ramkrishna Mission and his brother Swamijis on a few occasions and in some respects Swami Vivekananda was his ideal. He started Durgah Pujah in a mess, in which some of his schoolmates lived at Cuttack, Orissa, and he was instrumental in introducing the same in almost all the jails in India and Burma, where he was incarcerated, at times against the vehement opposition of the British administrators.

When cholera was raging fiercely in a remote part of the district of Cuttack, he took training in its treatment under Dr. Debendra Nath Mukherji, who was similarly inclined. As his parents were away from Cuttack and as his guardian did not permit him to go to the cholera-affected area, he was not found in the house the next morning. As both he and his ashramites were of a secretive nature, two strong young men were despatched to bring him back forcibly and who, after wandering about a lot, managed to trace him in an out-of-the-place cholera-infected village, but they were unable to bring him back. He returned later on of his own accord, after he had finished his work there.

During the latter part of 1922, he went to the flood-stricken areas of North Bengal and did relief work there under the guidance of the renowned Professor and Philanthropist, Dr. P. C. Ray. When he was a student of the Presidency College, Calcutta, he left his Calcutta residence, without informing anybody, not even his mother and there was no news from him for about a month. He returned home suddenly in a bad state of health and it transpired that he was in search of a Guru, (religious preceptor) and had trekked widely and in some portions of the Himalayan regions. Whatever he did was without any fuss or publicity and some of his activities were of a secretive nature.

As he grew up, politics, mainly, liberation of India from British yoke, was added to his existing mental outlook and this was practically the only goal of his life thereafter. To this end, he resigned from the Indian Civil Service and on his return to India, his first duty was to meet Shri M. K. Gandhi and to place himself under his command.

On reaching Calcutta, he became the right-hand man of Shri C. R. Das, who had sacrificed his extensive lucrative practice as a Barrister-at-Law in the High Court and had started working for the independence of India. During the course of such activities, Netaji suffered humiliation at the hands of the British rulers and their stooges and was imprisoned several times for prolonged periods, generally under Regulation III of 1818.

Though it was said, that he had connection with revolutionary activities, he was not hauled up under any such specific charge, probably due to his intense secretive nature of work. For gaining experience in this line, he underwent military training in the Calcutta University Corps and carrying this into practice, he gave similar training to the Indian National Congress volunteers. It was unique in the annals of the Congress, when in 1928, he arranged a mile long procession for the president, Pandit Motilal Nehru, on his arrival in Calcutta and led his volunteers on horseback, as General Officer Commanding, in military formation through the streets of Calcutta.

He was intensely patriotic and could never brook any dishonour to his country or to his countrymen. In this connection, he was said to have been implicated in an affair against a British Professor, for which he was rusticated by the University. Two other outstanding achievements of his, among others, were the complete boycott of the Prince of Wales' visit to Calcutta and in getting rid of the Britishers from the administration and from the contracts in the Calcutta Municipal Corporation and in running the same on purely nationalistic lines.

It is also wellknown how in January, 1941, he gave the slip to the British rulers, whose about 250 Police staff kept a day and night watch over him, and, after travelling through the whole of Northern India, entered Afghanistan, with Germany as his destination.

This was planned and executed in an exceedingly secret manner and his only confidants were, probably, only one of his brothers, three nephews and a niece, who were under strict oaths of secrecy to him.

His aged mother, who was occupying an adjoining room, and all others, including members of his family and his political associates, had no knowledge of this. As pre-arranged, the public as well as the other members of his family, came to know that he had left home, only when his confidants broke the news after about ten days of his actual departure and after he was reported to have crossed the Indian frontier and had entered Afghanistan safely.

His secret and hazardous mission and dare-devil enterprise in coming all the way to the Far East from Germany in 1943 to hasten his work for the Independence of India, first in a German and subsequently in a Japanese submarine, risking the Allied naval blockade and mines, is too well known, as also the fact that during his military operations against them in Burma, he was quite oblivious to aerial bombing by them and took shelter on rare occasion; and only, when compelled to do so by his followers and that, after he had seer that all others had been safely lodged.

He was an arch secret service man, with a dogged determination in carrying out his plans, always unmindful of the difficulties and consequences that the] would entail. In such matters, he confided in the minimum few, devised his plans and movements secretly and in the furtherance of or in the execution of the same, there was nothing in the world, including his own self, that he could not risk or sacrifice. All these characteristics of his were revealed to the world in greater prominence in his activities in the Far East during the years 1943 to 1945 and for which, the people there of all nationalities had the highest admiration and regard for him.

For this, credit is due to his countrymen there for their intense and all-out sacrifice, to the Japanese Government and that great nation for their unstinted help to and cooperation with him in his struggle for the liberation of India from foreign yoke and to the heads of all the States there and their citizens for the facilities and help rendered by them. It is my humble opinion, that it is mainly due to them that his achievement there could be so brilliant.

This is the person, who inspired his countrymen, living in foreign lands in East Asia, into volunteering their lives for fighting with arms against the British rulers for the independence of their country, who, with such support and sacrifice, inaugurated the Provisional Government of Azad Hind with all the usual requisites and paraphernalia of a Government, that was recognised by no less than nine free nations of the world, who organised the Azad Hind Fauj (Indian National Army), manned, trained and officered by his countrymen and who led that army as a separate entity against the British rulers with the great and mighty Japanese Army by his side.

Though physically unsuccessful in the end against them, final victory was his, as his demand for the independence of India by force against force, permeated the ranks of the British Indian Army, Navy and Air Force Services and which expedited the departure of the British rulers from India.

Colleagues Accept Netaji's Plan Partly

Undaunted by superior enemy forces, he was determined to carry on his struggle for the liberation of India and not depressed by failure in his pilgrimage to Delhi, via Imphal and Kohima, he closed that chapter there, and secretly planned his next move, *viz.* that the "Next road to Delhi would be via Moscow."

In furtherance of this new plan, he was fortunate enough in securing the whole hearted support of the Japanese Government, who in spite of utter depression and confusion in their ranks, due to their surrender to the Anglo-Americans, were magnanimous enough in taking him away from the clutches of their common enemy.

Regarding this new plan, some details of which have been given earlier, the Japanese Government were giving protection to their friend and ally and were removing him to a safe zone, as the Anglo-Americans were naturally expected to wreak their vengeance on him.

While removing him in a brand—new bomber plane from his centre of activities, with only one of his trusted followers, *viz.* Col. Habibur Rahman, and whom probably they were reluctant to allow and who, therefore, was probably allowed to travel only up to a portion of the journey, his plane is alleged to have met with an accident, resulting in his death.

It has been stated above, that not only in my opinion, but also in that of my colleagues, this plan, agreed upon both by the Japanese as well as by Netaji, was prearranged and the last and the most significant portion of it was, that after Netaji had found himself in a safe place, the Japanese Government would announce that he had died and that is actually what they subsequently did.

This was just in keeping with what he had previously planned in Calcutta in January, 1941, and that is what his collaborating nephews actually did, *viz.*, that they announced, after reports had been received that he had safely crossed the Indian frontier and had entered Afghanistan, that Netaji had left the house and which consequently was about ten days after his actual departure from Calcutta. I fully realise that this, however, does not take away the possibility of a plane crash, as after all an accident is an accident and is in most cases beyond human control.

Therefore, up to the time of Netaji's arrival at Saigon and his subsequent boarding the plane there for an "unknown destination," which has been stated by many eminent persons, there has been more or less unanimity of opinion among all the three members of the committee.

Events immediately following this, are of vital importance and the evidence on record has, therefore got to be considered very carefully and the conclusions should be arrived at after mature deliberation and irrespective of any consideration, whatsoever, especially when these conclusions are not only eagerly awaited by our countrymen, but are of exceptional interest to millions of persons of different nationalities throughout the world.

It may be considered by the most critical and sceptic reader that the foregoing pages may have been written with some bias or prejudice on my part and which, unfortunately for me, may have suggested itself to him from the fact that I happen to be a very close relation of Netaji Subhash Chandra Bose, but I assure him with all sincerity, that it is not so.

On the other hand, I take this as an opportunity to place before him for his most careful consideration that the facts, circumstances and manipulations, some of which have lately gained so much in volume, as to have overflown the normal bounds and found expression in newspaper reports, correspondence and interviews with some of the highest officials of the land, would go to show that the findings arrived at by my learned colleagues were preconceived and prearranged and for being in accordance with the confirmed opinion of the Prime Minister and of his Government. Instead of prejudicing him by telling him what the correct finding of the evidence on record should be, I would in all earnestness, request him, my government and my countrymen to peruse, not only the conflicting reports submitted by the members of the committee, but also the evidence on which, reports submitted by the Committee have been based and thereby form their respective individual opinion regarding the subject-matter of this enquiry.

Terms of Reference

Now to come to the subject-matter of this enquiry, it would be necessary, in the first instance, to consider the TERMS of REFERENCE, which are as follows: "To enquire into and to report to the Government of India on the circumstances concerning the departure of Netaji Subhash Chandra Bose from Bangkok about the 16th August, 1945, his alleged death as result of an aircraft accident and subsequent developments connected therewith."

The points necessary to be considered may, therefore, be classified as follows:

I. Circumstances Concerning the Departure, which may be subdivided into, (a) Circumstances and (b) Departure.

II. Alleged death as a result of an Aircraft Accident.

In this connection, it may be said that the wording of the "Terms of Reference" is such as to give the impression that the aircraft accident has been accepted as a settled fact. In my humble opinion, it should not be so, as the truth or otherwise of this point is an important subject-matter for decision in this enquiry.

The points that may arise subsequent to this alleged accident, hinge to a great extent on the finding on this point. So, before making a decision on this crucial point, it would be indispensably necessary to consider carefully, the whole of the evidence on all the other connected points. If after such careful consideration, the finding be that the aircraft accident did not take place, then only would that finding be a very definite, conclusive and irrevocable one. With such a finding the remaining subject-matter of this enquiry would automatically simplify be itself considerably.

Therefore, it has got to be decided first, (a) as to whether the aircraft accident took place or not, and then, (b) if it be held, that such accident did not take place, whether the remaining evidence on record would justify and confirm that finding, and (c) that if it be held, on the contrary, that such accident did take place, then it has got to be decided further, whether, (d) death took place, or, (e) death did not take place.

III. Subsequent developments connected therewith

The points to be considered here, depend, mainly, on the findings on points II (a), (b), (c), (d) & (e) above.

If according to point II (b), the definite finding be that the aircraft accident did not take place, then it would automatically follow that Netaji did not die.

The subsequent developments arising there—from would therefore, be as to where Netaji went after leaving Saigon. As no steps were taken for making enquiries on these lines, it would suffice to say here that, as it has been held that the aircraft accident did not take place, so Netaji did not die and there is no knowledge of his subsequent whereabouts. If, however, according to II (c), it be held that aircraft accident took place, then such accident may or may not have caused death to Netaji, and so the next finding would be in accordance with either II (b) or II (e). If the finding be in accordance with II (e), *viz.*, that Netaji did not die, then the subsequent developments arising therefrom, would more or less, be similar to those of II (b) stated above.

If, however, the finding be in accordance with II(d), *viz.*, that Netaji died as a result of that aircraft accident, then the subsequent developments would not only be as to how his body was disposed of, but it would also be very important and necessary to account for the baggage, including treasure, he was carrying, the dress he was wearing, the articles he was wearing or carrying on his person, *e.g.*, his wrist watch, his spectacles, his rings, fountain pen, cigarette case, cigarette lighter, religious books, Gita & Chandi, purse, magnifying glass, insignia as Supreme Commander, INA & 1.1. L. badges, etc. and, as stated by Shri Das, witness No. 2, his revolver also.

As regards treasure, it is my humble opinion, that so much of the evidence on record regarding it, as is necessary for the correct decision of the subject-matter of this enquiry, as embodied in the TERMS of REFERENCE and its clarification noted above, may only be taken into consideration for the purposes of this enquiry and as, by itself, it is a very important and complicated matter, it should, if considered necessary, form the subject-matter of a separate enquiry, which should go into full details, commencing from the various sources from and the different descriptions in which they were obtained and ending with the small fraction of the same now in deposit in the National Museum, Rashtrapati Bhawan, New Delhi and after considering carefully all the intermediate stages.

(a) *Circumstances:* It has been discussed, considered and held under the heading, NETAJI'S PLAN, recorded above, that due to the surrender of the Japanese nation and consequently that of the Indian National Army, formed and organised by Netaji in the Far East, that a plan was agreed upon both by the Japanese as well as by Netaji, that the Japanese would move Netaji to a safe zone, *viz.*, Manchuria, where the Anglo-Americans would no longer be able to arrest him, with the ultimate object of entering Russian territory, where he would continue his struggle for the liberation of India and in pursuance of that plan, Netaji left Bangkok on the morning of 17-8-45 and Saigon the same afternoon with Manchuria, as his destination under the auspices of the Japanese.

With regard to this plan and up to Netaji's departure by a Japanese plane from Saigon on 17-8-45, there has been more or less unanimity of opinion among all the three members of the committee.

It is, unfortunately, not possible for me to make a definite statement on this matter, as in spite of repeated requests, no one was furnished with the complete draft report and all other important and relevant papers, exhibits, photographs etc., that are on the record.

All of Netaji's associates in the Far East, who have been examined before us, have stated about Netaji's plan of going to Manchuria, when he parted company from them in a plane from Saigon on 17-8-45 for an "unknown destination."

Though Col. Habibur Rahman had admittedly more secret consultations with Netaji than the rest of his Indian brethren there and though he was the only Indian to proceed with him beyond Saigon, there can be no douninew that Netaji's destination was Dairen in Manchuria and he also knew more of Netaji's secrets than any of the others.

The fact that Col. Rahman states that Netaji's destination was Tokyo with intention to return to Singapore soon and that he does not state Dairen or Manchuria or Russia, is enough to suggest, as stated by Shri Dwijendranath Bose and Shri Arabinda Bose, witnesses Nos. 22 & 24 respectively, that he did so intentionally, on the lines he was tutored by Netaji, and not to mention the names of these places, but Tokyo instead, so as to give a wrong scent about Netaji's whereabouts and also to save the Japanese Government from embarrassment and also to narrate the story of the plane crash, etc., as was announced by the Japanese in consultation with Netaji and which he did to the best of his abilities.

Both of them state that Col. Rahman must have been under strict oath of secrecy to Netaji not to divulge his plans or secrets. They are those nephews of Netaji and two out of his only five confidants, who helped him to get out of Calcutta secretly in January, 1941 and who were also instructed by him to make such statements, which he had tutored them to say and who were also under similar oaths of secrecy to him, regarding his escape from Calcutta.

Netaji started contacting the Russian Ambassador in Tokyo as early as 1944, because he was under the impression at that time that the Japanese would lose the war and he along with them and because he considered Russsia to be a suitable country for carrying on his future struggle for the independence of India. With the gradual lapse of time, this took more definite shape. Shri A. M. Sahay, witness No. 30, and some others have stated that Netaji made attempts at contacting the Chinese Communists through Mr. Ho Chi Minh's party and also the Russians through Mr. M. Shigemitsu, the Foreign Minister of Japan and others. Shri Debnath Das, witness No. 2, also stated that one of Netaji's plans was to go to Yenan, the headquarters of Mr. Mao Tse Tung and that Netaji had asked Shri lyer, witness No. 6, his Minister for Information and Broadcasting, in May, 1945 to write to Mr. Shigemitsu and enquire whether the Japanese Government would contact the Russians on his behalf and provide other facilities to him and to a few members of his staff for going to Russia. A reply to this was received from the Japanese Government in June, 1945.

Shri Das further stated that on more than one occasion, Netaji requested General Isoda, witness No. 35, to continue letting him know the position of the Japanese in Manchuria and North China. Witness No. 5, Col. Pritam Singh, deposed that Netaji had told him that he (Netaji) had contacted the Russians through Mr. Shigemitsu and he wished that he and some of his party should move to Russian territory and operate from there and he also said that the ideology of the Russians was so different from that of the Anglo-Americans, that sooner or later and in about ten years' time, they would come to a clash, when it would be an opportune moment for them to go into action again for the independence of India.

All these would go a long way to show and prove that Netaji's plan of going to Russia via Manchuria, after his failure in his armed struggle against the Anglo-Americans in South-East Asia, was not a cursory suggestion, but was a carefully-thought—of well-matured plan, which, as a matter of fact, was the only alternative left to him, as he did not want to surrender himself to the Anglo-Americans and thereby be instrumental in not only finishing himself, but also bringing to an end, his only cherished goal in life, *viz.*, the independence of his mother country.

He was naturally very sincere in having his plan executed. It is also proved that though the Japanese Government were in utter distress and confusion, due to their surrender to the Anglo-Americans, they were magnanimous enough "in respecting Mr. Chandra Bose's last wishes" and were also, with all sincerity, giving effect to the same plan, by taking him in a plane to Manchuria and had deputed one of their topmost and renowned generals, who knew that territory well and who, according to Mr. T. Negishi, witness No. 20, was considered to be a key man for negotiations with Russia, with instructions to remain with him there and to help him in crossing over into the adjoining Russian territory.

The Japanese Government were keen for the quick execution of their plan and their instructions were, that the plane should make a detour to Dairen in Manchuria, and after dropping only Netaji and General Shidei there, the plane would then come back to Japan and alight the remaining passengers there.

The keenness and sincerity on the part of both the Japanese as well as Netaji for the proper and prompt execution of the plan, naturally gives additional importance to it and as the main idea underlying it, was to remove Netaji to a safe place, so that the Anglo-Americans would not be in a position to get hold of him, it would be a natural sequence for the Japanese to announce that Netaji had died, after they were sure that Netaji was safely lodged in a place that was not under the control of the Anglo-Americans.

It will be of interest to mention here, that, according to the statements of Shri Dwijendra Nath Bose and Shri Arabinda Bose, witnesses Nos. 22 and 24 respectively, a similar announcement was made by them, when Netaji secretly left Calcutta in January, 1941 and it was made ten days after his actual departure from Calcutta and after information had been received that he had crossed the Indian frontier and was safe in Afghanistan and beyond the clutches of the British rulers of India.

From the evidence on record on this point and which is practically free from discrepancies, though the statements have been made by persons of different nationalities, it can, therefore, definitely be said that the aforesaid plan has been proved very convincingly and without the shadow of a doubt.

It has been stated earlier that both the British as well as the Americans had made thorough and on-the-spot enquiries under different auspices soon after the surrender of the Japanese and had also tried to arrest Netaji under the Enemy Agents' Ordinance and also as he was considered to be an "International War Criminal" and because they doubted the truth of the announcement made by the Japanese that Netaji had died in a plane crash accident and as they considered it to be a hoax and believed that he was alive and was hiding somewhere.

Being the victorious party, they had all the facilities and opportunities of making thorough enquiries in all the areas, where they thought Netaji could possibly have been living or hiding. In one of their reports, it transpires that Netaji wanted to shift a nucleus of his Government to Yunan Province in China and through the Communists there, to get into touch with Soviet Russia. Another report states that in July, 1945, Netaji sought permission to enter U.S.S.R. via Manchuria, with a few selected members of his movement, but the same source contends that there was no need for the Japanese to ask the Russians for Netaji's entry, because he wanted to go to Manchuria, from where he thought he would be able to get into touch with the Russian forces.

The same report also states that it is beyond doubt that Netaji had plans to go underground together with a number of his selected friends. This report contains the final conclusion arrived at as a result of the enquiry, and it is to the effect that in the absence of substantial proof, it is still difficult to state conclusively the fate of Bose.

This finding, to say the least, carries great weight and, having been contrary to the expectations of the Anglo-Americans, maximum efforts must have been made by them to find out Netaji's whereabouts and also to arrest him for purposes of taking action against him, as he was not only an arch enemy of theirs, because, being a British Indian subject, he waged war against his King and Emperor, but was also a top-ranking "International War Criminal", against which persons, after the last war, the maximum penalty was generally inflicted. It must have been with great reluctance and sorrow that the British and American enquiring officers were compelled to come to the finding that it was difficult to state conclusively the fate of Netaji Bose, which finding, however, should be considered to carry great weight.

6

Mutiny in the British Indian Army

The defence based its argument on the host of precedents, old and new, which supported the right of subject countries to fight for their freedom. But, for all Desai's eloquence, as far as the court-martial was concerned he was arguing a lost cause-one they were incapable of appreciating, let alone accepting. The predictable verdict was that all three of officers were guilty of waging war against the King. Dhillon and Sehgal were acquitted of the charge of murder and abetment of murder; Shah Nawaz was found guilty of abetting murder. All three were sentenced to transportation for life, cashiering and forfeiture of arrears of pay and allowances.

INDIAN NATIONAL ARMY OF LIBERATION IN THE EAST

On 15 February 1942, Singapore fell to the Japanese army advancing southward from the Malayan peninsula. Two days later, in an impressive ceremony held at Farrar Park in the heart of the town, Indian troops were handed over to the Japanese as prisoners-of-war by their commanding officer, Colonel Hunt.

Major Fujiwara took them over on behalf of the victorious Japanese, and then announced that he was handing them over to Captain Mohan Singh of the Indian contingents, who should be obeyed by them as their Supreme Commander. Mohan Singh then spoke to the Indian POWs, expressing his intention of raising an Indian National Army out of them to fight for India's freedom.

He held a preliminary discussion with some prominent Indians in Malay and Burma in a meeting in Singapore on 9 and 10 March, which was attended by Rashbehari Bose, a veteran Indian revolutionary exile living in Japan for the last quarter of a century. Bose then called a conference in Tokyo, which was held 28-30 March.

The delegates representing several East and South-East Asian countries present at the conference, decided to form the Indian Independence League to organize an Indian independence movement in East Asia. Bose was recognized as head of the organization. The conference further resolved that "militay action against the British in India will be taken only by the INA and under Indian command, together with such military, naval and air cooperation and assistance as may be requested from the Japanese by the Council of Action" and further, "after the liberation of India, the framing of the future Constitution of India will be left entirely to the representatives of the people of India."

On 15 June 1942, a Conference opened in Bangkok with over a hundred delegates of the IIL attending from all over Asia. By the close of the nine-day conference a resolution was unanimously adopted setting forth the policies of the independence movement in East Asia. The III, was proclaimed the organization to work for India's freedom; the Indian National Army was declared the military arm of the movement with Mohan Singh as the Commander-in-chief and Rashbehari Bose was elected president of the Council of Action.

It was further decided that Singapore would be the headquarters of the IIL. Netaji had stated in a message to the conference that his personal experience had convinced him that Japan, Italy and Germany were sworn enemies of British imperialism; yet, independence could come only through the efforts of Indians themselves. India's freedom would mean the rout of British imperialism. The Indian National Army was officially inaugurated in September 1942.

Unfortunately, at this point a distrust began to grow within the Indian group against Rashbehari Bose's leadership. Some thought that having been long associated with Japan, he gave precedence to the Japanese interests over Indian interests. According to Japanese records:

Some even thought that he was just the protege of the Japanese, and that the latter was exploiting Indians for their own ends. Such resentment finally resulted in a revolt of a group of leaders headed by Captain Mohan Singh within the INA in November 1942. As a consequence, Mohan Singh and his associate, Colonel Gill were both arrested by the Japanese and the Indian Army was disbanded. However, in 1943 a new Indian Army was organized, put under the command of Lt. Col. Bhonsle, who held this post until the final dissolution of the army.

Describing the revived INA. Joyce Lebra writes:

On 15 February 1943, the INA was reorganized and former ranks and badges revived. The Director of the Military Bureau, Lieutenant-Colonel Bhonsle, was clearly placed under the authority of the III. to avoid any repetition of III ANA rivalry. Under Bhonsle was Lt. Col. Shah Nawaz Khan as Chief of General Staff-, Major P.K. Sahgal as Military Secretary; Major Habibur Rahman as commandant of the Officers' Training School; and Lt. Col. A.C. Chatterji, and later Major A.D. Jehangir, as head of enlightenment and culture. Apart from this policy-forming body was the Army itself, under the command of Lt. Col. M.Z. Kiani. This was the organization which held the INA together until the arrival of Subhash Chandra Bose from Berlin, six months later.

In February, the Japanese military officer Iwakuro had called a meeting of about three hundred officers of the INA at Bidadri camp in Singapore and spoke to them about the advisability of joining the army, but with no effect. According to Ghosh, "Later on, in a 'Heart to heart talk' with some officers, it emerged that a large number of officers and men would be willing to continue in the INA on the express condition that Netaji would be coming to Singapore."

The story of Netaji's exploits in Germany and the history of the Indian Legion was known to Indian revolutionaries of the IIL in East Asia for some time now, and they awaited his arrival eagerly. As the first INA wavered, faltered and was finally disbanded, and as its successor merely continued to exist, the need for Netaji's leadership began to be felt more keenly. Mohan Singh had mentioned his name to General Fujiwara as early as 1941. In all conferences the need of his guidance had been emphasized by the delegates. While Netaji and Abid Hasan continued to push toward the East making a wide sweep out into the Atlantic, by pre-arrangement, a Japanese submarine left Penang Island on 20 April for the tip of Africa, under strict orders not to attack or risk detection. The two submarines had a rendevous four hundred miles south-southwest of Madagascar on 26 April. After sighting each other and confirming their identity, the submarines waited for a day for the sea to become calm.

Then on 28 April, in what was known to be the only known submarine-to-submarine transfer of passengers (in the annals of World War II) in an area dominated by the enemy's air and naval strength, Netaji and Abid Hasan were transhipped into the Japanese submarine via a rubber raft. Travelling across the ocean, the Japanese 1-29 reached Sabang on 6 May, 1943. It was an isolated offshore islet north of Sumatra.

There, Netaji was welcomed by Colonel Yamamoto, who was the head of the Hikari Kikan, the Japanese-Indian liaison group. From Sabang, Netaji and Yamamoto left for Tokyo by plane, stopping en route at Penang, Manila,

Saigon and Taiwan. The plane landed in Tokyo on 16 May. All throughout his submarine voyage from Germany and for about a month after his arrival in Tokyo, Netaji's identity and presence was kept a secret. He was supposed to be a Japanese VIP named Matsuda.

Although he remained incognito during the first few weeks in Japan, Netaji did not waste any time by just waiting. From 17 May onwards, he met Japanese Army and Navy Chiefs-of-Staff, Navy Minister and Foreign Minister in rapid succession. However, he had to wait for nearly three weeks before Japanese Prime Minister Tojo granted him an interview.

But Tojo was so impressed with Netaji's personality that he offered to meet him again after four days. Two days later, on 16 June, Netaji was invited to visit the Diet (the Japanese Parliament) where Tojo surprised him with his historic declaration on India:

> *We are indignant about the fact that India is still under the ruthless suppression of Britain and are in full sympathy with her desperate struggle for independence. We are determined to extend every possible assistance to the cause of India's independence. It is our belief that the day is not far off when India will enjoy freedom and prosperity after winning independence.*

It was not until 18 June that Tokyo Radio announced Netaji's arrival. The news was reported in the Tokyo press the following day. At this announcement, the atmosphere was electrified overnight. The Axis press and radio stressed the significance of the event.

The INA and the Indian independence movement suddenly assumed far greater importance in the eyes of all. On 19 June, Netaji held a press conference. This was followed by two broadcasts to publicize further his presence in East Asia, and during the course of these he unfolded his plan of action.

As Ghosh describes, Bose's plan stood for the coordination of the nationalist forces within India and abroad to make it a gigantic movement powerful enough to overthrow the British rulers of India. The assumption on which Bose seemed to have based his grand scheme was that the internal conditions in India were ripe for a revolt. The no-cooperation movement must turn into an active revolt.

And to quote Netaji's own words during the press conference: "Civil Disobedience must develop into armed struggle. And only when the Indian people have received the baptism of fire on a large scale would they be qualified to achieve freedom." Netaji then embarked upon a series of meetings, press conferences radio broadcasts and lectures in order to explain his immediate task to the people concerned, and the world.

Accompanied by Rasbehari Bose, Netaji arrived at Singapore from Tokyo on 27 June. He was given a tumultuous welcome by the resident Indians and was profusely 'garlanded', wherever he went. His speeches kept the listeners spellbound. By now, a legend had grown around him, and its magic infected his audiences. Addressing representatives of the Indian communities in East Asia on 4 July he said:

> *Not content with a civil disobedience campaign, Indian people are now morally prepared to employ other means for achieving their liberation. The time has therefore come to pass on to the next stage of our campaign. All organizations whether inside India or outside, must now transform themselves into a disciplined fighting organization under one leadership. The aim and purpose of this organization should be to take up arms against British imperialism when the time is ripe and signal is given.*

At a public meeting where Netaji spoke these words, Rashbehari Bose formally handed over to Subhash Chandra Bose the leadership of the III, and command of the INA. The hall was packed to capacity. In his last speech as leader of the movement Rasbehari Bose said:

> *Friends! This is one of the happiest moments in my life. I have brought you one of the most outstanding personalities of our great Motherland to participate in our campaign. In your presence today, I resign my office as president of the Indian Independence League in East Asia. From now on, Subhash Chandra Bose is your president, your leader in the fight for India's independence, and I am confident that under his leadership, you will march on to battle and to victory.*

In that meeting Netaji announced his plan to organize a Provisional Government of Free India.

It will be the task of this provisional government to lead the Indian Revolution to its successful conclusion ... The Provisional Government will have to prepare the Indian people, inside and outside India, for an armed struggle which will be the culmination of all our national efforts since 1883. We have a grim fight ahead of us. In this final march to freedom, you will have to face danger, thirst, privation, forced marches—and death. Only when you pass this test will freedom be yours.

The next day, on 5 July, Netaji took over the command of the Indian National Army, now christened Azad Hind Fauj (Free India Army). Tojo arrived from Manila in time to review the parade of troops standing alongside with Bose. Addressing the soldiers, Nctaji said:

> *Throughout my pubic career, I have always felt that, though India is otherwise ripe for independence in every way, she has lacked one thing, namely, an army*

of liberation. George Washington of America could fight and win freedom, because he had his army. Garibaldi could liberate Italy because he had his armed volunteers behind him. It is your privilege and honour to be the first to come forward and organize India's national army.

By doing so you have removed the last obstacle in our path to freedom... When France declared war on Germany in 1939 and the campaign began, there was but one cry which rose from the lips of German soldiers-"To Paris! To Paris!" When the brave soldiers of Nippon set out on their march in December 1941, there was but one cry which rose from their lips-"To Singapore! To Singapore!" Comrades! My soldiers! Let your battle-cry be-"To Delhi! To Delhil"

How many of us will individually survive this war of freedom, I do not know. But I do know this, that we shall ultimately win and our task will not end until our surviving heroes hold the victory parade on another graveyard of the British Empire—Lal Kila or the Red Fortress of ancient Delhi.

On 27 July, Netaji left Singapore for a 17-day, tour of the East Asian and South-East Asian countries. The prime objective of this tour was to enlist moral and monetary support for his movement from other countries, as well as the resident Indian communities. He was given a rousing reception in Rangoon, where he attended the Burmese independence on 1 August; from Rangoon Netaji went to Bangkok and met Thai Prime Minister Pilbulsongram.

He won the moral support of Thailand and tumultuous ovation from the Indian community. He then flew to Saigon and addressed Indians there. Returning to Singapore for a brief rest, he flew to Penang to address a rally of 15,000 Indians. Everywhere, he held his audience spellbound for hours with his superb oratory, and at the conclusion of his speech the people raced to reach the platform and pile up all they had before him-a total of two million dollars. This scene was repeated over and over in towns and cities all over South-East Asia, when Netaji stood before thousands of people like a prophet, addressing them for the cause of India's freedom. Merchants, traders, businessmen and women came forward everywhere and donated their wealth and ornaments in abundance, to enable their leader to fulfil his mission. In his plan for total mobilization, Netaji had outlined a grandiose scheme for an army of three million men. However, the immediate target was set at 50,000. The Major part of this number would be from the Indian POWs and the rest from civilian volunteers.

According to Bose's plan there would be three divisions from thirty thousand regulars and another unit of twenty thousand mainly from civilian volunteers. The Japanese authorities informea Netaji at that time that it could provide arms for thirty thousand men only. However, by 1945, it was authoritatively known that the actual strength of the INA rose to not less than 45,000 men.

After completing the task of reorganizing the Indian Independence League and launching preparations for revolutionizing the army, and after conducting a successful campaign to mobilize the support of the Indian communities throughout South-East Asia—a phase which lasted from July to October Netaji turned toward formation of the Provisional Government of Azad Hind (Free India).

This had to be done before the army could be sent for action in the battlefield. This government was officially proclaimed in Singapore at a mass rally on 21 October 1943 where Netaji was unanimously elected as the Head of the State and The Supreme Commander of the Indian National Army. While taking the oath he said:

> *In the name of God, I take this sacred oath that to liberate India and the three hundred eighty million of my countrymen, L Subhash Chandra Bose, will continue the sacred war of freedom till the last breath of my life. I shall remain always a servant of India, and to look after the welfare of three hundred eighty million of Indian brothers and sisters shall be for me my highest duty. Even after winning freedom, I will always be prepared to shed even the last drop of my blood for the preservation of India's freedom.*

The Provisional Government of Free India had five ministers with Netaji as the Head of the State, Prime Minister and Minister for War and advisers representing the Indian communities in East Asia. The first momentous decision which the new government took was its declaration of war on Britain and the United States, which was decided on the night of 22-23 October. Toye writes: "The Cabinet had not been unanimous about the inclusion of the U.S.A. Bose had shown impatience and displeasure—there was never any question then or later of his absolute authority: the cabinet had no responsibility and could only tender advice.

Recognition of the Provisional Government came quickly from nine countries-the Axis powers and their allies. They were: Japan, Burma, Croatia, Germany, the Philippines, Nanking China, Manchuto, Italy and Siam (Thailand), but for some unknown reasons, Vichy France withheld its recognition. The Japanese Army promised allout support for the provisional government.

Toward the end of October, Netaji flew to Tokyo again to meet Tojo and to attend the greater East Asia Conference. Since India technically did not fall within this sphere, he attended as an observer. He made an impressive speech at the conference, stressing the creation of a new Asia where all vestiges of colonialism and imperialism would be eliminated.

The Japanese navy had captured the Andaman and Nicober islands in the Bay of Bengal during the early months of war. As a result of Netaji's requests, Prime Minister Tojo announced at the conference that Japan had decided to place the two islands under the jurisdiction of the Provisional Government of Free India, thereby giving it its first sovereignty over a territory.

The ceremonial transfer took place in December, and Netaji named Lieutenant-Colonel Loganathan, an officer in the Medical Services, as the chief commissioner in charge of the civil administration of the islands. Soon thereafter, preparations began for sending the army to the front and moving the provisional government headquarters to Rangoon, in Burma. In the meantime, Netaji announced the formation of a women's brigade within the INA, and named it "Rani of Jhansi Regiment," after the celebrated queen of Jhansi, Laxmibai, who had led her soldiers against the British in an uprising during the First War of Independence in 1857.

Coincidentially, another Laxmi, Lieutenant-Col. Laxmi, was placed in charge of this regiment by Netaji. In November it was agreed between Netaji and the Japanese militay headquarters, that the INA first division and the civil and military headquarters would move to Burma in January 1944.

BRITISH MILITARY

However, the British military authorities had become painfully aware of the consequences of the trial. Even before it had opened, INA. days had been organised in various parts of the country. The day the proceedings got under way the police had to open fire on a protesting crowd at Madura in south India.

Then, as the trial proceeded, the Red Fort itself was besieged; more than a hundred were killed or injured by police firing. Between 21 and 26 November Calcutta was strike-bound. In a rare gesture of communal amity, Hindus and Muslims-their trucks flying both Congress and Muslim League flags—jointly took over the city, attacking American and British military establishments and shouting the slogans of freedom and nationalism coined by Bose. Some forty-nine military vehicles were destroyed and ninety-seven damaged, and about 200 military personnel injured: thirty-two Indians lost their lives and 200 were wounded. The violence soon spread along the Gangetic plain to Patna, Allahabad and Benares, and eventually places as far apart as Karachi and Bombay were affected.

Claude Auchinleck was no longer the confident Commander-in-Chief who had ordered the trial, and even as it was proceeding he wrote to the Viceroy expressing his doubts:

> *I know from my long experience of Indian troops how hard it is even for the best and most sympathetic British officer to gauge the inner feelings of the Indian soldier, and history supports me in this view. I do not think any senior British officer today knows what is the real feeling among the Indian ranks regarding the 'INA'. I myself feel, from my own instinct largely, but also from the information I have had from various sources, that there is a growing feeling of sympathy for the 'INA' and an increasing tendency to disregard the brutalities committed by some of its members as well as the forswearing by all of them of their original allegiance. It is impossible to apply our standards of ethics to this problem or to shape our policy as we would, had the 'I N A' been of our own race.*

Not wishing to be caught napping again, Auchinleck set up a special organisation in his military headquarters 'to find out the real feelings of Indian ranks on this subject'. He also decided that no more INA personnel would be tried on the major charge of waging war against the King, and that only those who had committed 'acts of gross brutality' would be brought before the courts—at most between twenty and fifty men. Later Mason, joint secretary in the War Department of the Government of India, declared that the INA's 'patriotic motive would be taken at its face value and its members would be treated as though prisoners of war'.

A week before the trial ended the Viceroy empowered Auchinleck to commute sentences of death or transportation for life, and when, as required, Auchinleck came to confirm the sentences of the three men, he only agreed to the verdict of cashiering and forfeiture of pay: the transportation decision was quashed and, taking into account 'the prevailing circumstances', the men were set free.

INA accused released and welcomed as heroes Shah Nawaz, Sahgal and Dhillon were welcomed like the heroes of a conquering army and their tales were carried back to the remotest villages of India to be told, retold and eventually mythologised. For a time the INA seemed to have become India—even for Gandhi. Now, in his weekly Harijan column, he invariably referred to Bose as 'Netaji', and conceded that 'the hypnotism of the INA has cast its spell upon us. Netaji's name is one to conjure with. His patriotism is second to none (I use the present tense intentionally). His bravery shines through all his actions.'

He, too, believed Netaji was alive.

The British, however, continued with the selective trials, and on 4 February 1946 Captain Abdul Rashid was sentenced to seven years, imprisonment for certain acts of brutality. Rashid was a Muslim, and now the Muslim League came into the picture. For four days between 11 and 14 February the streets of Calcutta Bombay and Delhi witnessed unique political demonstrations in which Hindus and Muslims forgot their differences and came together to fight the INA's battles. Four days of strict martial law were required to bring Calcutta back to normal; by then nearly fifty were dead and over five hundred injured.

In January, too, some 5,200 Royal Indian Air Force personnel had gone on strike to protest over their conditions and as an expression of sympathy for the INA. cause. And on 18 February a revolt began on HMS Talwar, a training ship of the Indian navy moored off Bombay.

By nightfall on the 20th virtually the whole of the Royal Indian Navy was in open rebellion: seventy-eight ships in the various ports of India—Bombay, Karachi, Madras, Vizagapatanam, Calcutta and Cochin, and even in the Andamans—and nearly all the shore establishments had hauled down the Union Jack. Only ten ships and two shore establishments still remained with the British.

Other units of the armed forces were quickly affected. Between 22 and 25 February the R. I. A. F. in Bombay and Madras went on strike and on the 27th Indian soldiers in Jabalpur followed. In Bombay and Karachi, the main naval centres, ratings were able to generate impressive mass support.

In Karachi gun battles had ensued which continued for two days before heavy British reinforcements finally defeated the men. In Bombay there had been what even the British owned *Times of India* was forced to call 'mass uprising. .. in sympathy with the naval mutiny. .. unparalleled in the city's history'. The communists and the Congress Left had called for sympathy strikes and over 600,000 workers from the textile mills of Bombay had responded. For almost three days they had fought running, unequal battles with British troops in the streets and lanes of Bombay.

The British had tanks and machineguns, the workers had improvised weapons and even at times stones from dug-up roads. But for a few days some of Bombay's teeming working class slums had become 'no-go areas', and the British had to call in white troops to quell the uprising. In the end 270 had died and 1,300 had been injured (the government's official figures were lower: 187 and 1,002).

Attlee quick to understand implications and negotiate 'independence'... Undoubtedly a revolutionary situation had been created. But now, suddenly, the ratings found there were no leaders. They knew their navy but they had been horribly wrong about the Indian political parties. The naval ratings had virtually given the politicians a whole unit of the British Indian armed forces; they had even started calling it the Indian National Navy. For the politicians, however, this was too alarming a prospect.

Jinnah advised the men to go back and assured them that, if they did so, he would use constitutional means to remedy their complaints of bad food and service conditions. The Congress leaders were plainly frightened by the prospect of leading a revolution; Nehru came to Bombay and deplored the revolt. And as the ratings wondered what might have happened if there had been a leader prepared to lead them-Bose perhaps—the British re-took their ships.

But if the Indian politicians had no use for revolutionary situations, the Labour government had been quick to understand the implications.

On 4 December 1945 Herbert Morrison announced in the House of Commons that a ten-member parliamentary delegation would visit India to study the situation. The five-week visit took place in January and February 1946 and by the end of it nearly all the visiting MPs were convinced that India was in a dangerous state.

The February disturbances convinced Attlee that the imperial tide had at last ebbed. India could be held by force of arms for a few years more, but the cost for a Britain devastated by war would be too high.

The British government announced in February 1946 that a Cabinet mission of three ministers would visit India. That mission, in fact, failed in its purpose, the situation required another intervention by Attlee; it was his speech in the House of Commons on 20 February 1947—when he pledged the British government to transfer power to Indian hands, if necessary as two separate nations, 'not later than June 1948'—that finally led to the emergence of the two nations of India and Pakistan on 15 August 1947.

That such a situation existed in 1945 owed a great deal to Subhash Bose. He did not precisely visualise the extent of the post war turmoil; his wildest dreams could not have matched the fervour the INA trials produced. But he had told his men in Burma to fraternise with the Indians in the British Indian Army, and till the end he was confident that if Indians kept up their resolve, Britain-in an increasingly hostile postwar world-would have to concede independence.

True, his army did not parade as victors in the Red Fort; but their trial as vanquished had proved that his belief in a revolutionary consciousness that was grounded in a deeper understanding of the Indian people than his enemies credited him with, or even his most fervent friends believed in. The vision had been genuine: he just did not have the means, while alive, to translate it into a reality. Even Dilip, so sceptical of worldly struggles, recognised that the romance of Subhas' army had finally breached the dyke that separated Indians from the other army maintained to enslave them.

Through 1946 and 1947, as Indian leaders bartered with the British and among themselves to produce a divided India, they appeared to be constantly looking over their shoulders to reassure themselves that Bose's ghost was not like Hamlet's father, turning into flesh and blood. The years of struggle had wearied them, they did not have the stomach for another fight and they were relieved to get what crumbs they could from the imperial table. When the Congress finally accepted the partition plan Nehru had only this consolation to offer for the sudden abandonment of a lifetime's principles:

> *But of one thing I am convinced, that ultimately there will be a united and strong India. We have often to go through the valley of the shadow before we reach the sunlit mountain-tops.*

It was poor comfort for the holocaust that partition produced, and even today, for many Indians, the sunlit mountain-tops are still obscured by the shadows.

Had Bose returned to India....

> *Had Bose returned to India after the war he might well have prevented the tragedy. He was not a tired politician ready to accept office under any terms. Although his uncompromising hostility to Jinnah and Pakistan might have led to a civil war, the cost of that could not have been greater than the senseless waste of partition.*

Certainly Bose's often repeated warning that the Congress would pay dearly for the acceptance of 'office mentality' was historically acute. It came when in the late thirties the Congress was struggling to cope with the consequences of the 1935 Government of India Act, and the blandishments it offered. In the 1936 elections, the Congress reaped the rewards of nearly two decades of unceasing mass struggle against the British and totally vanquished the Muslim League.

But by 1945, after a decade of negotiations and some power-sharing with the British, the Congress was reduced to the level of the Muslim League; just another group, albeit powerful, seeking the rewards of office. And by placing such faith in the negotiating chamber the Congress had played into the hands of Jinnah, the master lawyer and negotiator. As Bose had foreseen, the Congress had thrown away the trump card of its power-mass struggle-for the dubious delights of the round table.

But could Indians have lived with Bose? An extreme man, he produced extreme reactions: total adulation or permanent rejection. Certainly the India of Bose would have been very different from the India of Nehru. Bose had often said that India needed at least twenty years of iron dictatorial rule, and he would most certainly have rejected the type of parliamentary democracy that has developed. This opens up the whole question of whether it is better for people to have food or to have freedom to change their political rulers every five years. The argument can never be resolved—though, given the recent adulation of the West for China, some of the oldest democracies in the world seem to think food is more important.

Surely Bose's rule would have degenerated into autocracy, like that of Mrs. Gandhi between 1975 and 1977? Though the analogy is not quite accurate (Mrs. Gandhi's rule degenerated long before the events of June 1975), for conclusive evidence Bose's critics point to his behaviour in Germany and with the Japanese during the war. In a climate that brooked no dissent and where the leader was always right, he too came to believe that he could do no wrong.

Part of the possible reason for this change of personality-if there was a change—may lie in the fact that at that stage, particularly in South-East Asia, he found himself a king without any worthwhile courtiers. The people who surrounded him there were political innocents, thrust into the wider world by events beyond their control: they could only applaud, never interject. Bose was, as the official Japanese history puts it, 'a bright morning star amidst them'. There is also evidence to suggest that Subhash Bose was not quite the dictator a simple reading of his speeches makes him out to be. No doubt there was an authoritarian streak in him, but his actions often belied his dictatorial postures in 1939, as Congress president, he behaved—against Gandhi's wishesless like an autocrat and more like a negotiator who had won one round and expected to reap some benefit from it. Throughout his political career he was always loyal to colleagues even at the risk of damaging his own chances: hardly the mark of a man of iron.

Almost alone among Indian leaders, Bose offered solutions that were both visionary and practical. Nehru's socialism may have been more rounded; rigorously logical and free of Bose's celebrated eclecticism. But its strain of romanticism divorced it from the realities of India, and the Nehru years resulted, almost inevitably, in a country with the most progressive socialist legislation outside the Soviet bloc which happily allowed the most unbridled capitalism to grow and flourish on a feudal structure that had changed little, if at all, since the British days. The cynicism this produced has bitten so deep that every government since has had to struggle against it and no combination in Indian politics looks likely to counteract the years of wasted opportunities and lost hopes.

This may seem hard, given the undoubted economic progress India has made in the last thirty years. When the British left, India had little or no industrial capacity; now she is the tenth industrial power in the world, exporting machinery to the West and capable of producing her own nuclear weapons. But the rapid industrialisation has been uneven and ill-directed, with the beneficiaries limited to a small, if growing, sector of the country.

Bose had the capacity to inspire total love and dedication, and produce gold from dross. He was hated by many, but those he 'touched' loved him with an almost overpowering sense of completeness. And this, combined with his rigorous, matter-of-fact manner and an instinctive feel for ancient Indian loyalties, might well have produced the revolution that India needed-and still lacks.

The ideological development that Bose sought has never materialised...

Like Turkey's Kemal Ataturk-a man he admired-Bose might well have produced a nation at once new, yet full of old virtues. This is best illustrated in his approach to women: he was not one for making strident feminist statements but, even on that submarine bringing him from Germany to Japan, he was busily telling Abid Hasan of the need to get Indian women to join the I.N.A., and how they would have to abandon their beloved sarees in order to do so. In South Asia he did get many immigrant women to join the I.N.A.-demonstrating that Indian feminism could be happily blended with the exigency of war.

The ideological development that Bose sought has never materialised. Like all national-liberation movements, the independent Congress was a coalition: of business seeking to oust British capital, of rural kulaks confident that native rulers would do more for them than alien ones, of various interest groups and of socialists aware that the Congress was the only party capable of furthering their ideas. Gandhi did suggest that the Congress should disband after independence, but this was clearly impossible: self-interest, if nothing else, ruled it out. Today almost all the major political groups in India—Communists, socialists, free-enterprise capitalists, Gandhian socialists-trace their ancestry to the Congress: only the right-wing Hindu Jan Sangh can claim a different parentage.

The absence of ideological development has meant the politics of banter, with interest groups perpetually feuding amongst themselves, extraordinary alliances—as between Marxists and religious obscurantists—and, above all, comical political defections. Once, in a northern state, a single individual's change of support from Congress to opposition parties led to the fall of two state governments in a single day.

The most valid criticism of Bose is related to the nature of the nationalist movement itself. For Bose's faults—and there were many—were inevitable in a nationalist fighting a colonial-imperial power that both fanned nationalism, and denied it legitimate expression. The Raj, as Marx penetratingly observed, did unwittingly bring modern ideas into India-but the nationalist reaction it produced in India was distorted by the British presence.

Pre-British India was seen as a land of milk and honey in which there had been no problems, no caste system and no evils, only Indian harmony and peace. And it is a measure of the failure of Indian nationalism that what in most countries would be dismissed as delicious nonsense is still taken seriously.

Today P.N. Oak, ADC to Major-General Bhonsle of the I.N.A., can claim respectable reviews in Indian papers by writing books asserting that 5,000 years ago India had an empire which included Britain. If the world has not appreciated this, it is, argues Oak, because the relevant chapters of world history have been 'lost'. Bose was aware of India's ills, but he often came close to endorsing the delicious nonsense of pre-British bliss, if only for rhetorical purposes.

Though he bravely maintained his independence from both the Germans and the Japanese-no mean feat—he deliberately avoided the wider implications of their awful philosophies. However, his argument that foreign help was required in order to drive the British out was justified by the events of 1945-46, and has been the bedrock of nearly all successful national-liberation movements since the war. In this, at least, Bose was probably far ahead of his time. In our age, when a national-liberation movement's accepting foreign help from all and sundry is a common fact of life, the idea may seem of no great significance. In the early forties, for a subject non-white race even to think of any such thing was revolutionary indeed.

....'t is our duty,' Bose told his INA, 'to pay for our liberty with our own blood. The freedom that we shall win through our sacrifice and exertions, we shall be able to preserve with our own strength.' .....

Subhash Chandra Bose, the Indian National Army, and the War of India's Liberation- Ranjan Borra, Journal of Historical Review, no. 3, 4 (Winter 1982)

"The arrival of Subhash Chandra Bose in Germany in 1941 (during the turbulent period of World War II) and his anti-British activities in that country in cooperation with the German government, culminated in the formation of an Indian legion. This marks perhaps the most significant event in the annals of India's fight for independence. This event not only can be regarded as a historical link-up with what Bose himself chose to describe as "The Great Revolution of 1857," and which (in his words) "has been incorrectly called by English historians 'the Sepoy Mutiny,' but which is regarded by the Indian people as the First War of Independence."

It also represents the historical fact that, by that time persuasive methods conducted through a nonviolent struggle under the leadership of Gandhi, had failed. An armed assault on the citadel of the British Empire in India was the only alternative left to deliver the country from bondage.

While other leaders of the Indian National Congress fell short of realizing this fact and thus betrayed a lack of pragmatic approach to the turn of world events that provided India with a golden opportunity to strike at the British by a force of arms, Bose rose to the needs of the hour and was quick to seize that opportunity.

While Bose's compatriots in India remained totally wedded to an ideological creed (nonviolence), which at that time could only serve the British and postpone the advent of independence, and while their ideological interpretations of the new revolutionary regimes in Europe—again largely influenced by British propaganda-prevented them from even harboring any thought of seeking their alliance and cooperation in the struggle against a common enemy, Subhash Chandra Bose alone had the courage to take the great plunge, thus risking his own life and reputation, solely in the interest and cause of his country. In January 1941, while under both house arrest, and strict British surveillance, he escaped.

After an arduous trek through the rugged terrains of several countries, with an Italian passport under the assumed name of Orlando Mazzota (in which he was aided by underground revolutionaries and foreign diplomatic agents)—Bose appeared in Berlin, via Moscow, on 28 March 1941.

Bose was welcome in Germany, although the news of his arrival there was kept a secret for some time for political reasons. The German Foreign Office, which was assigned the primary responsibility of dealing with Bose and taking care of him, had been well informed of the background and political status of the Indian leader through its pre-war Consulate-General at Calcutta and also by its representative in Kabul.

Bose himself, naturally some what impatient for getting into action soon after his arrival in Berlin, submitted a memorandum to the German government on 9 April 1941 which outlined a plan for cooperation between the Axis powers and India.

Among other things, it called for the setting up of a "Free India Government" in Europe, preferably in Berlin; establishment of a Free India broadcasting station calling upon the Indian people to assert their independence and rise up in revolt against the British authorities; underground work in Afghanistan (Kabul) involving independent tribal territories lying between Afghanistan and India and within India itself for fostering and aiding the revolution; provision of finances by Germany in the form of a loan to the Free India government-in-exile; and deployment of German military contingents to smash the British army in India.

In a supplementary memorandum bearing the same date, Bose requested that an early pronouncement be made regarding the freedom of India and the Arab countries.

It is significant to note that the memorandum did not mention the need for formation of an Indian legion. Evidently the idea of recruiting the Indian prisoners of war for the purpose of establishing a nucleus of an Indian National Army did not occur to him during his early days in Berlin.

At that time the German government was in the process of formulating its own plan for dealing with Subhash Chandra Bose in the best possible manner.

The Foreign Office felt itself inadequate to discharge this awesome responsibility without referring the whole matter to Hitler. While this issue was being considered at the highest level of the government, Bose's own requests as set forth in the submitted memorandum, made it far too complicated and involved to be resolved at an early date.

There was a long wait for Bose, during which period he often tended to become frustrated. Nevertheless, through several sympathetic officers of the Foreign Office, he continued to press his requests and put forth new ideas.

Finally, after months of waiting and many moments of disappointment often bordering on despair for Bose, Germany agreed to give him unconditional and all-out help.

The two immediate results of this decision were the establishment of a Free India Center and inauguration of a Free India Radio, both beginning their operations in November 1941.

These two organizations played vital and significant roles in projecting Bose's increasing activities in Germany, but a detailed account of their operation lies outside the purview of this paper. It should suffice to say that the German government put at Bose's disposal adequate funds to run these two organizations, and he was allowed complete freedom to run them the way he liked at his own discretion.

In its first official meeting on 2 November 1941, the Free India Center adopted four historical resolutions that would serve as guidelines for the entire movement in subsequent months and years in Europe and Asia.

First, Jai Hind or Victory to India, would be the official form of salutation; secondly, Nobel laureate poet Rabindranath Tagore's famous patriotic song *Jana Gana Mana* was to be the national anthem for the free India Bose was fighting for; thirdly, in a multilingual state like India, the most widely-spoken language, Hindustani, was to be the national language; and fourthly, Subhash Chandra Bose would hereafter be known and addressed as Netaji, the Indian equivalent of the "leader" or the "Führer."

In November 1941, Azad Hind Radio (or the Free India Radio) opened its programme with an announcing speech by Netaji himself, which, in fact, was a disclosure of his identity that had been kept officially secret for so long. The radio programmes were broadcast in several Indian languages on a regular basis. During this long period of "hibernation," the period between Netaji's arrival in Berlin and the beginning of operations of the two organizations, it can be reasonably assumed that the idea of forming an Indian legion that could be developed into an Indian Army of Liberation in the West, crossed Bose's mind.

He might even have discussed this matter with his colleagues—the Indian compatriots in Germany who had joined him—as to how best to implement the idea. However, as mentioned earlier, his first memorandum submitted to the German Government did not include any such plan. According to N.G. Ganpuley, who was his associate in Berlin, Netaji himself, when he left India, could not have, by any stretch of imagination, thought of forming a national army unit outside the country, and therefore he had no definite plans chalked out for its realization. Even while in Berlin, he could not think of it during the first few months of his stay there.

When and how, therefore, did he come to conceive such a plan? Mr. Ganpuley relates an interesting episode in this regard. To quote again from his book:

> *It was all due to a brain wave of Netaji which started working by a simple incident. He read one day about some half a dozen Indian prisoners-of-war who were brought to Berlin by the Radio Department to listen to the BBC and other stations which sent out their programmes in Hindustani. He saw them there going about, not as free Indians, but as prisoners-of-war. They were brought to the Radio Office every day to listen to and translate the Hindustani programmes, and were sent back to their quarters escorted by a sentry ... After he had a talk with them about war, about their captivity*

and their present life, his active mind started working... He pondered over it for sometime and decided to form a small national military unit ... No sooner was this decision taken by him ... he started negotiating with that section of the German Foreign Office with which he was in constant touch. He put before them his plans for training Indian youths from the prisoners' camps for a national militia.

Although somewhat skeptical and hesitant at the beginning, the German response to the plans was encouraging. It was a time psychologically well-chosen by Netaji.

The allied forces had been defeated on the continent, and the Wehrmacht was marching ahead successfully in the Soviet Union. It was also a historical coincidence that a large number of British Indian prisoners-of war, captured during Rommel's blitzkrieg in North Africa, lay in German hands.

Netaji's first idea was to form small parachute parties to spread propaganda in, and transmit intelligence from, the North-West Frontier in India. The reaction of some selected prisoners who were brought to Berlin from the camp of Lamsdorf in Germany and Cyrenaica was so encouraging that he asked for all-Indian prisoners held in North Africa to be brought over to Germany at once.

The Germans complied with this request, and the prisoners began to be concentrated at Annaburg camp near Dresden. The recruitment efforts, however, at the onset met with some opposition from the prisoners, who evidently had misgivings about Netaji's intentions and motivations. In this regard Hugh Toye writes:

When Bose himself visited the camp in December there was still marked hostility. His speech was interrupted, and much of what he had to say went unheard. But private interviews were more encouraging; the men's questions showed interest-what rank would they receive? What credit would be given for Indian Army seniority? How would the Legionary stand in relation to the German soldier? Bose refused to bargain, and some who might have been influential recruits were turned away. On the other hand, many of the men paid him homage as a distinguished Indian, several professed themselves ready to join the Legion unconditionally.

Netaji sought and got agreement from the Germans that the Wehrmacht would train the Indians in the strictest military discipline, and they were to be trained in all branches of infantry in using weapons and motorized units the same way a German formation is trained; the Indian legionaries were not to be mixed up with any of the German formations; that they were not to be sent to any front other than in India for fighting against the British, but would be allowed to fight in self-defense at any other place if surprised by any enemy formation; that in all other respects the Legion members would enjoy the same facilities and amenities regarding pay, clothing, food, leave, etc., as a German unit.

By December 1941 all arrangements were complete and the next important task was to persuade men to come forward and form the nucleus. It appeared that the POWs needed to be convinced that there were civilian Indian youth as well, studying, well placed in life and responsible to their families at home, who were ready to give up everything to join the Legion.

Ten of the forty young Indians then residing in Berlin, came forward. They were quickly joined by five POWs who were already in Berlin in connection with the German radio propaganda, and the first group of fifteen people was thus formed.

On 25 December 1941 a meeting of Indian residents in Berlin was called in the office of the Free India Center, to give a send-off to the first fifteen who were to leave the following day for Frankenburg, the first training camp and headquarters for the Legion. The brief ceremony was simple and solemn. Netaji blessed the Legion, the first of its kind in the history of the struggle for Indian independence. He christened it Azad Hind Fauj (Indian National Army). The Indian Army of Liberation in the West thus had a humble and modest birth.

The strength of the Legion grew steadily, as the task of recruitment continued unabated. Once trained to a certain level and discipline, the members of the first batch were assigned the additional responsibility of visiting the Annaberg camp and aiding in the recruitment process. While the Legion was sent to Frankenburg in Saxony, another group was taken to Meseritz in Brandenburg to be trained in tactical warfare. Abid Hasan and N.G. Swamy, the two original recruiters whom Netaji had sent to the Annaberg camp in 1941, had become *defacto* foundermembers of the Legion at Frankenburg and the irregular Company at Meseritz respectively.

At Meseritz, the Indians were placed under the command of Hauptmarm Harbig, whose first object was to make them forget that they had been prisoners. There were Tajiks, Uzbeks and Persians as well under training for operational roles similar to that envisaged for the Indians.

In due course the trainees went on to tactical operational training, such as wireless operating, demolitions and riding, and also undertook special mountain and parachute courses. According to Toye, "Morale, discipline and Indo-German relations were excellent, the German officers first-rate."

Netaji visited the camps from time to time and watched progress of the trainees. Since he himself was inclined toward military training and discipline, he followed the German training methods with great interest. It is understood that while in Germany Netaji himself underwent the rigours of such training, although authoritative documents on this subject are yet to be located by this writer.

While in India, he was a member of the University Training Corps at school and commanded the volunteers at an annual session of the Indian National Congress, but he never had a formal military education prior to his arrival in Germany in 1941. As Joyce Lebra writes: "Though Bose was without any previous military experience, he got his training and discipline German-style, along with the soldiers of the Indian Legion."

To him, formation of a legion was more positive, more nationalistic and more gratifying than mere radio propaganda. Unlike his ex-compatriots in the Indian National Congress, including Gandhi, Nehru and Patel, he would rather seek confrontation with the British-with an army-than to work out a compromise with them on a conference table, on the issue of India's freedom.

A firm believer in discipline and organization, nothing perhaps could be more satisfying to him than to see his men being trained by the German Command, with officers of the highest calibre. In four months, the number of trainees rose to three hundred. In another six months a further three hundred were added. By December 1942, exactly a year after the recruitment of the Legion was inaugurated, it attained the strength of four battalions. At the beginning of 1943 the Legion would be 2000 strong, well on its way up to the culminating point of 3500 men. But let us step back to early 1942, almost a year after Netaji's arrival in Berlin.

After the inauguration of the Free India Center, Free India Radio, and the sending of the first fifteen legionaries to the Frankenburg training camp, Netaji's activities in Germany began in full swing. His presence in Germany was not yet officially admitted-he was still being referred to as Signor Orlando Mazzota or His Excellency Mazzota—but he began to be known to more and more people in Berlin. Josef Goebbels wrote in his diary on 1 March:

> *We have succeeded in prevailing upon the Indian nationalist leader, Bose, to issue an imposing declaration of war against England. It will be published most prominently in the German press and commented upon. In that way we shall now begin our official fight on behalf of India, even though we don't as yet admit it openly.*

On 14 March, he remarked of Bose, "He is an excellent worker." The fall of Singapore was a signal for Netaji to broadcast his first official speech over the Free India Radio, repeating his vow to fight British imperialism until the end. This he followed with a declaration of war against England, although at that stage such a pronouncement could only be symbolic. Netaji had not yet obtained an Axis declaration in support of the freedom of India that he pressed for in the supplement of his first memorandum to the German government. That government was of the opinion that the time was not ripe yet for such a declaration and unless a pronouncement of this nature could be supported by military action, it would not be of much value.

Meanwhile, Japan proposed a tripartite declaration on India. Encouraged by this, Bose met Mussolini in Rome on 5 May, and persuaded him to obtain such a declaration in favour of Indian independence. Mussolini telegraphed the Germans, proposing proceeding at once with the declaration. To back his new proposal Mussolini told the Germans that he had urged Bose to set up a "counter-government" and to appear more conspicuously. The German reaction, which still remained guarded, is recorded by Dr. Goebbels in his diary on 11 May:

> *We don't like this idea very much, since we do not think the time has yet come for such a political manoeuvre. It does appear though that the Japanese are very eager for some such step. However, emigre governments must not live too long in a vacuum. Unless they have some actuality to support them, they only exist in the realm of theory.*

Netaji apparently was of the opinion that a tripartite declaration on Indian independence, followed up by a government-in-exile, would give some credibility to his declaration of war on England, push over the brink the imminent revolution in India, and legitimize the Indian legion. However, Hitler held a different view. During an interview at the Führer's field headquarters on 29 May, he told Netaii that a well-equipped army of a few thousand could control millions of unarmed revolutionaries, and there could be no political change in India until an external power knocked at her door. Germany could not yet do this.

To convince Netaji, he took him to a wall map, pointed to the German positions in Russia and to India. The immense distances were yet to be bridged before such a declaration could be made. The world would consider it premature, even coming from him, at this stage. Hitler was perhaps being realistic, but nevertheless it must have come as some sort of disappointment for Netaji.

In July 1942, the Germans suggested that a contingent of the Irregular Company be sent for front-line propaganda against Indian troops at El Alamein; but Rommel, who did not like battlefields turned into proving grounds for

Foreign Office ideas, opposed the move. However, at the Lehrregiment manoeuvers in September, and on field exercises in October, the Indian performance won high praise.

By January 1943, it was realized that maintenance of the irregulars as a separate entity was not of much practical use, and the ninety Indian men, (excepting four under N.G. Swamy who were being trained for work within Indiaj were absorbed into the Legion. Since the supply of recruits from the Annaburg camp was fast being depleted, it was decided to hasten the shipment of prisoners of war from Italy.

According to an agreement between Italy and Germany, all Indian POWs were to be sent directly to Germany without being held in Italian camps. But, in the meanwhile, an unforseen impediment stood in the way. A long-time Indian resident in Rome, Iqbal Shedai, formed an Indian unit under the Italians, and began broadcasting from Rome with the aid of a few Indian prisoners.

It is understood that he had conferred with Netaji a few times, but obviously had no intention of co-operating with him. From radio broadcasting, he advanced into forming an Indian military unit, although it was in clear violation of the Italo-German agreement. The unit was named the Centro Militare India, but existed only from April to November 1942.

During its brief period of existence, however, Shedai succeeded in diverting several hundred volunteers to Italian camps, who would normally have gone to Germany. In November the unit was three hundred and fifty strong, having been trained by Italian officers. On 9 November, after the Allied landing in North Africa, it was learnt that the men were being sent to fight in Libya, contrary to Shedai's promises. When they refused to go and mutinied, Shedai refused to intervene. Consequently, the Centro Militare India was disbanded. It was never revived, and thus a barrier that stood in Netaji's way toward recruitment was removed.

In August 1942, the Legion was moved to Koenigsbrueck, a large military training center in Saxony. This had been a regular training ground for the German infantry and motorized units for decades. Here the first contingents paraded before Netaji's eyes in October, and the growth was rapid. However, the rapid expansion of the Legion also posed the problem of finances.

Hitherto, payment to soldiers was being made from the monthly grants to the Free India Center and its office. As the number of Legionaries grew, that source became insufficient. For this problem there could be but one solution: direct payment to the Legion by the Germans.

This would mean hereafter that the Legionaries would receive promotions and precedence as soldiers of national socialist Germany, and would become, in fact, a regiment of the German army, while retaining its separate name and distinction. This was agreed upon between Netaji and the German government, necessitating the taking of a formal oath of loyalty to Adolph Hitler on the part of the Legionaries. Describing the ceremony, Hugh Toye writes:

> *Five hundred Legionaries were assembled. Their German commander, Lieutenant-Colonel Krappe, addressed them, and the oath was administered by German officers to six men at a time. All was done with solemnity, the soldiers touching their officer's sword as they spoke the German words: 'I swear by God this holy oath, that I will obey the leader of the German State and people, Adolph Hitler, as commander of the German Armed Forces, in the fight for freedom of India, in which fight the leader is Subhash Chandra Bose, and that as a brave soldier, I am willing to lay down my life for this oath.' Bose presented to the Legion its standard, a tricolor in the green, white and saffron of the Indian National Congress, superimposed with the figure of a springing tiger in place of the Congress spinning wheel. "Our names," he said, "will be written in gold letters in the history of free India; every martyr in this holy war will have a monument there." It was a brave, colorful show, and for Bose, a moment of pride and emotion. "I shall lead the army," he said, "when we march to India together." The Legionaries looked well in their new uniforms, the silken banner gleaming in their midst; their drill did them credit.*

What was Netaji's plan for leading this army to India? When the Germans launched out beyond Stalingrad into Central Asia, the Indian irregulars, trained at Messeritz, would accompany their Tajik and Uzbek counterparts along with the German Troops.

After Uzbekistan and Afghanistan were reached the Indian Company would leap ahead of the German advance to disrupt the British-Indian defenses in Northwestern India. Netaji spoke of dropping parachute brigades, calling on the Indian peasantry to assist them. Through radio he issued warnings to British Indian soldiers and police to the effect that unless they assisted the liberation forces they would one day have to answer to the free Indian government for their criminal support of the British.

The effect of the Indian army of liberation marching into India along with the German forces would be such that the entire British Indian Army morale would collapse, coinciding with a revolutionary uprising against the British. The Legion would then be the nucleus of an expanding army of free India.

Netaji's plan, largely dependent on German Military successes in the Soviet Union, undoubtedly had a setback when the Wehrmacht was halted at Stalingrad. After the German retreat from that city, the plan for marching into India from the West had to be abandoned. The tide of war was turning swiftly, calling for devising new strategies on the part of Netaji.

While the German army's second thrust into Russia encountered an unexpected counter-offensive at Stalingrad and thus was forced to turn back, in another part of the world the forces of another Axis partner were forging ahead, nearer and nearer to India.

Japan was achieving spectacular successes in the Far East and was ready to welcome Netaji as the leader of millions of Indians who lived in the countries of East and South-East Asia. To Netaji, the Japanese attitude was extremely encouraging. Tolo, the Prime Minister, had issued statements in the Diet about Indian freedom early in 1942, and by March there was a Japanese proposal for a tripartite declaration on India.

A small band of Indian National Army legionaires had already been in existence in the Southeast under Japanese patronage, although a few of its leaders, including Mohan Singh, had fallen out with the Japanese. Netaji would have no difficulty in reorganizing and expanding this organization.

He would get the active support of millions of overseas Indians, and the many thousands of British Indian prisoners-of-war would provide him a greater opportunity for recruitment, and for thus organizing a formidable army of liberation that could immediately be deployed in forward positions as the Imperial Japanese Army kept on advancing through the steaming jungles of the Malayan peninsula and Burma. During his meeting with Hitler on 29 May, the Führer had also suggested that in view of the prevalent world situation, Netaji should shift the center of his activities from Germany to the Far East.

Netaji could look back at his two years work in Germany with a sense of pride and accomplishment. Broadcasting, publications and propaganda were all extended. Azad Hind Radio had extended programmes in several languages, and reports indicated that they were being listened to with interest in target areas; Azad Hind, a bilingual journal, was being published regularly.

There were other papers for the Legion besides; the Free India Center had attained an acknowledged status in Germany. It was treated as a foreign mission, entitling its members to a higher scale of rations, and exemption from some of the Aliens' regulations. Netaji himself was given a good villa, a car and special rations for entertainment purposes. His personal allowance amounted to about eight hundred pounds a month.

The monthly grant for the Free India Center rose from 1,200 pounds in 1941 to 3,200 pounds in 1944. All these Netaji stipulated as a loan from the

German government, to be returned after India gained independence with the Axis assistance. However, the turn of events now demanded his presence in a different theatre-of-war.

What would happen to the Legion in Netaji's absence? It was now 3,500 strong, well trained and equipped, ready for action. Netaii consulted with his aides in Berlin. A.C.N. Nambiar, an Indian journalist who had been in Europe for some eighteen years prior to Netaji's arrival in Germany, was his right-hand man. While preparing for his journey to the Asian theatre-of-war, Netaji passed on to Nambiar his policy and instructions. As Hugh Toye writes:

> *There were plans for new branches of the Free India Center, for broadcasting, for Indians to study German police methods, and for the training of Indian seamen and airmen. As for the legion, it must be used actively as soon as possible, the German officers and NCOs must be quickly replaced by Indians, there must be no communalism. Legionaries were to be trained on all the most modern German equipment, including heavy artillery and tanks; Bose would send further instructions as opportunity offered.*

A few words must be added regarding the Indo-German cooperation and comradeship during the critical days of World War II when the Legion was formed. None could describe it better than Adalbert Seifriz, who was a German Officer in the training camp of the Legionaries. He writes:

> *Agreeing to the proposal of Bose was a magnificient concession and consideration shown to the great personality of Bose by the German Government in those critical times when all German efforts were concentrated on the war ... The mutual understanding and respect between Indians and Germans and the increasing contact between them in the interest of the common task made it possible for the Indian Legion to sustain and keep up discipline right up to the German capitulation in 1945. During the period of training and even afterwards the comradeship between Indians and Germans could not be destroyed ... A meeting with Subhash Bose was a special event for the German training staff.-We spent many evenings with him, discussing the future of India. He lives in the minds of the training staff members as an idealistic and fighting personality, never sparing himself in the service of his people and his country ... The most rewarding fact was the real comradeship which grew between Indians and Germans, which proved true in dangerous hours, and exists still today in numerous cases. The Indian Legion was a precious instrument in strengthening and consolidating Indo-German friendship.*

A report of Hitler's visit to the Indian Legion headquarters in Dresden was given by Shantaram Vishnu Samanta (one of the Legionaries) during a press interview in India, after his release from an internment camp. According to his statement, Hitler addressed the soldiers of the Legion after Netaji had left for East Asia. He spoke in German and his speech was translated into Hindustani by an interpreter. He said:

> *You are fortunate having been born in a country of glorious cultural traditions and a colossal manpower. I am impressed by the burning passion with which you and your Netaji seek to liberate your country from foreign domination. Your Netaji's status is even greater than mine. While I am the leader of eighty million Germans, he is the leader of 400 million Indians. In all respects he is a greater leader and a greater general than myself. I salute him, and Germany salutes him. It is the duty of all Indians to accept him as their führer and obey him implicitly. I have no doubt that if you do this, his guidance will lead India very soon to freedom.*

A statement by another soldier of the Indian Legion, who remains anonymous, has a somewhat different version. It stated that both Netaji and Hitler took a joint salute of the Indian Legion and a German infantry. In addition to comments cited earlier, Hitler was reported to have made these remarks as well:

> *German civilians, soldiers and free Indians! I take this opportunity to welcome your acting Führer, Herr Subhash Chandra Bose. He has come here to guide all those free Indians who love their country and are determined to free it from foreign yoke. It is too much for me to dare to give you any instructions or advice because you are sons of a free country, and you would naturally like to obey implicitly the accredited leader of your own land.*

However, reports of Hitler's visit and address to the Indian Legionaries are not confirmed from any other source. Netaji would be leaving Germany on 8 February 1943. On 26 January, "Independence Day for India," there was a great party in Berlin where hundreds of guests drank his health. On 28 January, which was set aside for observance as the "Legion Day" in honour of the Indian Legion, he addressed the Legion for the last time. It is believed that his departure was kept secret from his army.

So, there were no visible emotions among the men; no gesture of a farewell. The impression Netaji was leaving at the Free India Center, was that he was going on a prolonged tour. So there were no signs of any anxiety. Except for a few top-ranking German officers and his closest aides, hardly anybody was aware that within a week-and-a-half he would be embarking on the most perilous journey ever undertaken by man; a submarine voyage through mine-infested waters to the other side of the world. In his absence, Nambiar settled down in his job as his successor and soon gained respect of the legionaries.

Two months after Netaii's departure, as a result of discussion between the German Army Command and the Free India Center, it was decided to transfer the Legion from Koenigsbrueck to a coastal region in Holland, to involve it in a practical coastal defense training. It was also in accordance with Netaji's Wishes. He had often expressed a desire to give his troops, whenever possible, some training in coastal defence.

After the first battalion was given a hearty send-off, an untoward incident happened within the legion; two companies of the second battalion refused to move. It was soon found out that there were three main reasons for staging this minor rebellion.

Some legionaries were unhappy that they were not promoted, but their names had to be put on the waiting list; some simply did not want to leave Koenigsbrueck; some were influenced by a rumor that Netaji had abandoned them and had gone off leaving them entirely in German hands, who were now going to use them in the Western Front, instead of sending them to the East to fight for India's liberation.

However, the rebellion was soon quelled after a team of NCOs visited the officials of the Free India Center in Berlin and obtained clarification regarding the rebel Legionaries' grievances.

The team went back to the camp and assured the men that they were not being sent to fight a war but were there purely for practical training purposes according to Netaji's wishes; that the promotions were not being passed up, they would follow in due course; and that Netaji had not abandoned them, and they would be informed about his whereabouts and plans as soon as possible. In pursuance of military discipline, the ringleaders of this act of insubordination were sent to prison camps for a specified period.

The Legion was stationed in the coastal areas of Holland for five months. Afterwards, there was a decision to move it to the coastal area of Bordeaux in France from the mouth of the Girond, opposite the fortification of Foyan to the Bay of Arcachon.

The Legion was taking charge here. The stay in France was utilized to give the Legionaries a thorough training in the weaponry required for the defense of the Atlantic Wall. In the spring of 1944, the first batch of twelve Indians were promoted to officers. Field Marshal Rommel, who took charge of the Atlantic Wall, once visited the area where the Indian contingent was located. Ganpulay writes:

> *... after having seen the work carried out by the Indians,, he exclaimed: "I am pleasantly surprised to find that in spite of very little training in coastal defense, the work done here is fairly satisfactory." While departing, he said*

to the Indian soldiers: "I am glad to see you have done good work; I wish you and your leader all the good luck!"

In the spring of 1944, one company of the Legion was sent to North Italy at the request of some officers who were seeking an opportunity to confront the British forces. After the Normandy invasion by the Allied forces in June 1944, the military situation in Europe began to deteriorate. It eventually became so critical that the German High Command decided to order the Indian Legion to return to Germany.

So after about ten months of stay in the coastal region of Lacanau in France, the Indian Legion started its road back. It is to be understood at this point that with the landing of the Allied troops in France and their gradual advance through the French countryside, the French Maquis (underground) guerrillas had become very active, and along with the German troops they made the Legionaries as well the target of their attacks.

After travelling a certain distance, the first battalion of the Legion was temporarily located in the area of Mansle near Poitiers, while the second and the third battalion were stationed in Angouleme and Poitiers respectively. After a rest for ten days in this region, during which period they had to ward off sporadic attacks by the French underground, the Legionaries took to the road once again. In this long march back to Germany, the Legion demonstrated exemplary courage and fortitude, and underwent rigours and hardships of battlefield with equanimity.

At this time, British propaganda was directed to these men which was full of empty promises; some material was dropped from the air, while agents infiltrated into the ranks to persuade the men to desert. The propaganda promised the would be deserters reinstatement in the British Indian army with full retroactive pay and pension, but the British hypocrisy was once again manifest in the fact that a few of the soldiers who had fallen victim to this bait were shot later by the French publicly in a market place in Poitiers without any trial, along with some German prisoners-of-war.

In following the saga of the Indian Army of Liberation in the West, one has to remember that its fate was indissolubly linked with that of the Axis powers in Europe, especially Germany. The overpowering of the new revolutionary regimes of Europe by forces representing an alliance of capitalism and Marxism was an international tragedy which engulfed the Indian Legion in Europe as well.

During its retreat into Germany, it encountered the enemy forces on several occasions and fought rearguard action with British and French forces, displaying exemplary bravery. The German military training had converted the regiment not only into a highly disciplined body, but a hard-core fighting unit as well.

It is indeed a historical irony that this superb force could not be utilized for the purpose and way its creator and leader, Subhash Chandra Bose, had dreamt of. Nevertheless, the 950th Indian Regiment, as the Legion was officially designated, left its footprints in the battlefields of France and Germany, as their many other gallant comrades of the German Army.

In the fall of 1944 until Christmas, the Indian Legion spent its time in the quiet villages of Southern Germany. Between Christmas and the New Year 1945, the unit was ordered to move into the military camp at the garrison town of Heuberg. In the spring of 1945 the Allied forces crossed the Rhine. The Russians entered the East German provinces murdering and plundering cities, townships and villages. Heavy bomber formations began destroying German cities.

Transport systems became completely disorganized and paralyzed. The end was near, and there was no point in remaining in the barracks. The Legion, therefore, left its winter quarters at Heuberg in March 1945, and headed for the Alpine passes. By that time all communications with the Free India Center in Berlin had been cut off. The Legion commanders took decisions independently.

The Legion had already reached the Alpine regions east of Bodensee. However, with the surrender of the German forces on 7 May, all hopes also ended for the Free India Army. While attempting to cross over to Switzerland, the legionaries were overwhelmed by American and French units and were made prisoners. Those who fell into the hands of the French had to suffer very cruel treatment. Several were shot, while others died in prison camps in miserable conditions. The rest were eventually handed over to the British.

Although thus swept into the maelstrom of the Axis disintegration in Europe, Netaji's army of liberation in the west had carved for itself a niche in history; for, indeed, it was a nucleus which would eventually precipitate a much larger fighting force elsewhere.

Inspired by its leader, that force would march into India to set in motion a process that would eventually deliver the country from an alien bondage. One, therefore, must not regard the saga of the Indian National Army in Europe as an isolated event that ended tragically.

While its dream of crossing the Caucasus along with its allies, the German Armed Forces, and entering India from the Northwest, did not materialize in reality, its extension and successor, India's army of liberation in the east, did enter the country from the opposite direction, thus fulfilling the cherished dream of Netaji and his soldiers. Not only that, as we shall see subsequently, but that army made the mightiest contribution toward finally ending an imperialist rule in India.

During his interview with Netaji, Hitler had suggested to him that since it would take at least another one or two years before Germany could gain direct influence in India, and while Japan's influence, in view of its spectacular successes in South-East Asia, could come in a few months, Bose should negotiate with the Japanese.

The Führer warned Bose against an air journey which could compel him to a forced landing in British territory. He thought Bose was too important a personality to let his life be endangered by such an experiment. Hitler suggested that he could place a German submarine at his disposal which would take him to Bangkok on a journey around the Cape of Good Hope.

However, despite Hitler's suggestions, it is believed that the German Foreign Office showed some reluctance in the matter of Netaji's leaving Germany and going to Japan. Col. Yamamoto Bin, Japanese military attache in Berlin (and a good personal friend of Netaji) along with the Japanese ambassador Lieutenant-General Oshima Hiroshi, had met Netaji as early as October 1941 when the latter expressed hopes for enlisting Japanese aid in his plan for wresting Indian independence. This was the beginning of a series of such meetings.

After the entry of Japan in World War II in December, Netaji was more eager to go as soon as possible to East Asia and fight beside Japan for India's liberation. He reportedly urged Oshima to use his good offices to secure his passage to Asia. It was about at this point that both Oshima and Yamamoto encountered a feeling of reluctance in the matter on the part of the German Foreign Office.

They had the feeling that Germany was not to willing to let Japan lead India to independence. Bose was already a useful ally as an Indian patriot, and his propaganda broadcasts were effective in both India and Britain. The Indian Legion was already having a psychological impact in India and worrying the Allies. For these reasons, "they were guarding Bose like a tiger cub."

In the meantime, Ambassador Oshima had also met with Hitler and explained Bose's plan to him. According to Japanese records.

The Führer readily agreed with Oshima that it was better for Bose to shift his activities to South-East Asia now that his country's (Japan's) armies had overrun the area. The second problem was whether Bose would get enough support in Tokyo for his activities. On this, Oshima had contacted Tokyo many times but had not received any firm answer. Finally, Tokyo replied to Oshima that in principle it had no objection to Bose's visit to Japan. The third problem was to provide Bose with a safe means of transport to Japan. Communication between Germany and Japan was impossible during those days. Passage by boat was ruled out; and it was decided to use a plane belonging to the Lufthansa Company to airlift Bose from Germany to Japan via the Soviet Union. Tojo (Japanese Prime Minister) objected to this on the grounds that this would amount to a breach of trust with the Soviet Union. An attempt was made by both Yamamoto and Bose to get an Italian plane, but this also did not work. Finally the choice fell on a submarine. Germany agreed to carry Bose up to a certain unknown point in the east and asked that a Japanese submarine be pressed into service thence forward. After a series of exchanges with his government, Oshima finally obtained Tokyo's approval of the plan and communicated it to Bose.

7

Bose, Forward Bloc and Imphal Campaign

The All India Forward Bloc is a leftwing nationalist political party in India. It emerged as a faction within the Indian National Congress in 1939, led by Subhas Chandra Bose. The party re-established as an independent political party after the independence of India. It has its main stronghold in West Bengal.

FORMATION OF THE FORWARD BLOC

The Forward Bloc of the Indian National Congress was formed on 3 May 1939 by Netaji Subhash Chandra Bose, who had resigned from the presidency of the Indian National Congress on April 29 after being outmaneuvered by Mohandas K. Gandhi. The formation of the Forward Bloc was announced to the public at a rally in Calcutta. Bose said that who all were joining, they had to never turn their back to the British and must fill the pledge form by cutting their finger and signing it with their blood. First of all, seventeen young girls came up and signed the pledge form. Initially the aim of the Forward Bloc was to rally all the leftwing sections within the Congress and develop an alternative leadership inside the Congress. Bose became the president of the Forward Bloc and S.S. Cavesheer its vice-president. A Forward Bloc Conference was held in Bombay in the end of June. At that conference the constitution and programme of the Forward Bloc were approved. In July 1939 Subhas Chandra Bose announced the Committee of the Forward Bloc. It had Subhas Chandra Bose as president, S.S. Cavesheer from Punjab as its vice-president, Lal Shankarlal from Delhi, as its general secretary and Pandit B Tripathi and Khurshed Nariman from Bombay as secretaries. Other prominent members were Annapurniah from Andhra Pradesh, Senapati Bapat, Hari Vishnu Kamnath from Bombay, Pasumpon U. Muthuramalingam Thevar from Tamil

Nadu and Sheel Bhadra Yajee from Bihar. Satya Ranjan Bakshi, was appointed as the secretary of the Bengal Provincial Forward Bloc.

In August the same year Bose began publishing a newspaper titled *Forward Bloc*. He travelled around the country, rallying support for his new political project.

Nagpur Conference

The following year, on June 20–22, 1940, the Forward Bloc held its first All India Conference in Nagpur. The conference declared the Forward Bloc to be a socialist political party, and the date of June 22 is considered as the founding date of the party by the Forward Bloc itself. The conference passed a resolution titled 'All Power to the Indian People', urging militant action for struggle against British colonial rule. Subhas Chandra Bose was elected as the president of the party and H.V. Kamath the general secretary.

Arrest and Exile of Bose

Soon thereafter, on July 2, Bose was arrested and detained in Presidency Jail, Calcutta. In January 1941 he escaped from house arrest, and clandestinely went into exile. He travelled to the Soviet Union via Afghanistan, seeking Soviet support for the Indian independence struggle. Stalin declined Bose's request, and he then travelled to Germany. In Berlin he set up the Free India Centre, and rallied the Indian Legion.

In August 1942 the British authorities banned the Forward Bloc. Its offices around the country were ransacked. In 1943 Bose was transported to Asia, where he took over the leadership of the Indian National Army. During the final phase of the war the INA fought alongside the Japanese against the British army. Inside India, local activists of the Forward Bloc continued the anti-British activities without central coordination. For example, in Bihar members were involved in the Azad Dasta resistance groups, and distributed propaganda in support of Bose and INA. They did not have, however, any organic link neither with Bose nor the INA.

Post-war Reorganization

At the end of the war, the Forward Bloc was reorganized. In February 1946 R.S. Ruiker organised an All India Active Workers Conference at Jabalpur, Madhya Pradesh. The conference declared the formation of the 'FB Workers Assembly', in practice the legal cover of the still illegal Forward Bloc. Notably some leading communists from Bombay, like K.N. Joglekar and Soli Batliwalli, joined the 'FB Workers Assembly'. The Workers Assembly Conference declared that the "Forward Bloc is a Socialist Party, accepting the theory of class struggle in its fullest implications and a programme of revolutionary mass action for the attainment of Socialism leading to a Classless Society."

The Ahead of the 1946 assembly elections the ban on the Bloc was lifted in June that year. The Working Committee of the Forward Bloc met on June 10.

Elections to the Constituent Assembly and to Provincial Legislatures were held in December 1946. The Forward Bloc contested the elections. H.V. Kamath won a seat in the Constituent Assembly and Jyotish Chandra Ghosh, Hemantha Kumar Basu and Lila Roy were elected to the Bengal Legislative Assembly.

However, the Bloc was clearly divided along ideological lines. One section was influenced by Marxism, whereas the other upheld 'Subhasism', a syncretic ideology consisting of socialism, nationalism and Indian spiritualism.

Arrah Conference

The Bloc held its 2nd All India Conference in Arrah, Bihar on January 12–14, 1947. S.S. Cavesheer (a leading member of the Subhasist sector) was elected president and Sheel Bhadra Yagee (a leading member of the Marxist sector) was elected general secretary. The party took the name 'All India Forward Bloc'. The conference denounced the understanding between the Congress and the British government for the Independence of India, and called upon the Forward Bloc members present in the Constituent Assembly to withdraw from it. Subsequently, a national council was held in Bauria, West Bengal, which reaffirmed the demand of boycotting the Constituent Assembly as well as issuing a decree that Bloc members of state legislatures would resign.

Split between Yajee and Ruikar

Following Independence and Partition, the party national council met in Varanasi February 1948. The national council meeting was also preceded by a decision of the Indian National Congress in the beginning of the year to expel all dissenting tendencies within the Congress, including the Forward Bloc. Thus the party decided to renounce any links with the Congress once and for all, and reconstruct itself as an independent opposition party. Moreover, it passed a resolution that the party be divided into a Forward Bloc for India and a Forward Bloc for the new nation of Pakistan. This would soon prove to be very controversial. The general secretary Yagee did, in line with the Varanasi resolution, dissolve the Bengal committee of the Forward Bloc and set-up *ad hoc* committees for West Bengal and East Bengal. Now the division between 'Marxists' and 'Subhasists' resurfaced. The 'Subhasists', and S. S. Cavesheer in particular, criticized Yajee's actions. Yagee resigned from the post of general secretary.

The split was now a fact. The 'Subhasist' group, led by Ruiker and Cavesheer, called for a conference in Chandranagar, West Bengal. Their conference was held on December 29–31. On the same dates Yagee organised a conference in Calcutta. Effectively there was now two Forward Blocs, the Forward Bloc led by Ruiker and the Forward Bloc led by Yajee. Yajee was elected general secretary and K. N. Joglekar, chairman of the Yajee-led group. Notably, the Yajee-led group adopted a red flag with a leaping tiger and a hammer and sickle.

Roughly speaking the Yajee's party had its main base in Bihar, Punjab and West Bengal, whereas the Ruiker-led group had its strongholds in Madhya Pradesh and West Bengal. The same year Yajee's party decided to join the United Socialist Organisation of India, a front led by Subhas Chandra Bose's elder brother Sarat Chandra Bose. Joglekar revolted against this decision. His followers, which were found in West Bengal, Bihar, Maharashtra and Uttar Pradesh, rallied to form the Forward Communist Party.

The Yajee-led party did, however survive Joglekar's departure. Yagee was able to push through a merger between the Forward Bloc and the Desh Sevak Party, led by INA officers General Mohan Singh and Colonel Gurbaksh Singh Dhillon, in October 1949. Both had worked closely with Subhas Chandra Bose. They had both been amongst the accused in the Red Fort trials. Now, Mohan Singh was appointed chairman of the Forward Bloc and Dhillon was appointed as its general secretary. This merger gave a considerable moral boost to the party. In June 1951 the majority of the Ruiker-led Forward Bloc reunified with the party. A joint central committee meeting was held on June 23, which confirmed the merger of the two parties. Mohan Singh and Dhillon were re-elected as the party chairman and general secretary.

1952 Elections

In the 1952 general election the party contested as 'Forward Bloc (Marxist)', a denomination that differentiated it from the rump 'Forward Bloc (Ruiker)'.

In Tripura a united front was formed by the Communist Party of India, Tripura Ganatantrik Sangha, Ganamukti Parishad, Ganatantrik Nari Samiti and independents for to contest the election to the Tripura electoral college (whose function was to appoint a Rajya Sabha delegate from Tripura) jointly. The Forward Bloc participated in mass rallies on October 2 and December 2,

1951. However, just before the election the Forward Bloc withdrew from the front and decided to contest three of the 30 seats on their own. None of the Forward Bloc candidates were elected.

The 5th party conference (a 4th party plenum had been held in Ingota, U.P. in 1949) was held in Puri, Orissa on December 28–31, 1952. Mohan Singh was elected chairman and Dhillon as general secretary.

In 1953 a group of party leaders from West Bengal, like Amar Bose, Satyapriya Banerjee and Suhurit Chaudhury, were expelled for breaking party discipline. The expellees formed the Marxist Forward Bloc.

Expulsion of Yagee and Singh

In 1955 the Indian National Congress adopted socialism as its policy. Thus leaders like Yagee and Singh then proposed that as the Congress had become a socialist party, the Forward Bloc ought to merge with it. Singh and Yagee, without consulting the Central Committee nor the party membership, declared the unification of the Forward Bloc into the Congress. Many sections of the party disagreed with this move, and a Central Committee meeting was held in Nagpur May 11–15. The Central Committee decided to expel Singh and Yagee. Hemanta Kumar Bose was elected as the new chairman and R.K. Haldulkar as general secretary. This team would continue in their posts until Bose's murder in 1971. U. Muthuramalingam Thevar from Tamil Nadu was elected as deputy chairman of the party.

Following the 1955 split the party would enjoy a relatively long period without any major splits.

Socialist Unity

In 1964 a unity process was initiated by the Praja Socialist Party, which eventually resulted in the formation of the Samyukta Socialist Party. The Forward Bloc was invited to join the new party, and the Delhi unit of the party did take part in a joint socialist anti-Nehru campaign conference in April 1964. However, the party did not merge into the SSP.

Death of U.M. Thevar

The party stalwart in Tamil Nadu, U. Muthuramalingam Thevar, died on October 30, 1963. Following his death a power-struggle began between two of his disciples, Sasivarna Thevar and P.K. Mookiah Thevar. Mookiah Thevar emerged victorious and Sasivarna Thevar left to form his own party, the Subhasist Forward Bloc. A bye-election for the Aruppukottai Lok Sabha constituency seat vacated by U. Muthuramalingam Thevar's death was held in 1964, in which the Forward Bloc was defeated for the first time.

Progressive Front in Tripura

In 1965 the party joined a 'Progressive Front' in Tripura. The front consisted of the Communist Party of India (Marxist), Communist Party of India, the Forward Bloc and a break-away faction of the Socialist Party.

The front demanded nationwide land reforms, strengthening of the national defence, withdrawal from the Commonwealth, nationalisation of foreign capital, a rational food policy, release of all political prisoners and scrapping of the Indo-American agreement of food supply.

Existence of the new front was declared at a meeting in Agartala on November 17. Mass rallies of the front were held in Belonia on November 28 and then in Birchandra Bazar (near Belonia) on December 1. The front did not last, though, as in the 1967 election the Communist parties aligned with a splinter-group of the Congress Party. The Forward Bloc did not present any candidates in that election.

1968 Split in Tamil Nadu

In 1968 two influential party leaders in Tamil Nadu Velayudham Nayar (then a central committee member of the party) and S. Andi Thevar broke away from AIFB and founded the Revolutionary Forward Bloc. Nayar and Thevar accused the Forward Bloc of having deviated from its socialist principles through its cooperation with the rightwing Swatantra Party.

West Dinajpur Clashes

In July 1969, violent clashes erupted in West Dinajpur district, West Bengal, between peasants aligned with the of Communist Party of India (Marxist) and East Pakistani refugee cultivators, who supported the Forward Bloc. CPI(M) leader Hare Krishna Konar characterized the events as a degeneration of the agrarian struggles in rural West Bengal.

Split in the Indian National Congress

In 1969 a major split in the Indian National Congress. Indira Gandhi had entered into open conflict with the traditional Congress leadership. Effectively two separate Congress parties appeared, the Congress(R) led by Indira and the Congress(O) led by Kamaraj. The split was in many ways a left-right one, with Indira whipping up populism against the established party elites. The Forward Bloc did in some ways welcome the new developments. It appreciated Indira's stands and reformulated its anti-Congress line to focus mainly opposition to the traditional Congress elite (i.e. the Congress(O)). In the 1969 presidential elections, AIFB supported Indira's candidate V.V. Giri. This caused an abrupt break-up of the Swatantra-AIFB alliance in Tamil Nadu, as the Swatantra Party sought to align itself with the Congress(O).

1971–72 Elections

On February 20, just ahead of the 1971 general elections, the All India Forward Bloc chairman Hemantha Kumar Bose was murdered in Calcutta. An emergency central committee meeting was held on February 24, which appointed P.K. Mookiha Thevar as the new chairman of the party.

In the 1971 Lok Sabha election, the Forward Bloc launched 24 candidates around the country. Two were elected, P.K. Mookiah Thevar from Ramanthapuram and Jambuwantrao Dhote from Nagpur.

The party contested 3 seats in the interior of Maharashtra, were it performed well. Dhote, who was then known as *Vidarbha ka Sher* (the Lion of Vidarbha), had joined the Forward Bloc and campaigned for a separate Vidarbha state with the Forward Bloc as his platform. Dhote was hugely popular in the region at the time, and could draw crows of hundreds of thousands to his meetings.

In Tamil Nadu the party contested one seat, Ramanthapuram, with the support of its allies in the Progressive Front (most notably the Congress(R) and Dravida Munnetra Kazhagam). Meanwhile the Forward Bloc played an important role in securing Mukkulathor votes for its Progressive Front allies.

In West Bengal the party contested 10 Lok Sabha seats. The party obtained some significant votage in constituencies like Cooch Behar (22.17%) and Birbhum (19.70%), but in general it was defeated by the CPI(M) candidates.

Moreover the party contested three seats in Bihar, one in Haryana, 1 in Madhya Pradesh, 4 in Uttar Pradesh and 1 in Delhi. In total the candidates of the party obtained 962 971 votes (0.66% of the national vote).

In the 1971 state legislative assembly election in Orissa, the party contested four seats. It got 8393 votes (0.19% of the state-wide vote), but was not close to winning any seat. In Tamil Nadu the party contested 9 seats in the southern part of the state within the framework of the Progressive Front. Out of these nine candidates, seven won. In total its vote stood at 268 721 (1.71% of the state-wide vote). One of its candidate came second and in the Mudukulathor constituency (that had been the centre of the violent 1957 Ramnad riots) the AIFB candidate R. Rathina Thevar came third with 17244 votes (31.02%). The most spectacular victory was that of P.K. Mookiah Thevar (who contested Lok Sabha and assembly elections simultaneously) who got 49292 votes (74.46%) in the Usilampatti constituency, defeating S. Andi Thevar of the Revolutionary Forward Bloc. Lastly in West Bengal the party contested 52 constituencies, but could only win three seats. Its vote stood at 374 141 (2.90% of the state-wide vote).

On March 28, 1972 the party was able to win a seat in the Tamil Nadu Legislative Council (the upper house of the regional parliament) for the first time. S. Sakthi Mohan, the editor of the regional party organ *Kannagi*, was elected with the votes of the AIFB, DMK, PSP, Muslim League and the Tamil Arasu Kazhagam.

In the 1972 state legislative assembly election, the Forward Bloc presented one candidate in Assam, 5 in Bihar and 2 in Madhya Pradesh. In Maharashtra the party contested 26 seats. Like in the 1971 Lok Sabha elections the party did well in the interior areas of the state. It won the Nagpur North and Yeotmal seats, and came second in several others. In total the AIFB candidates in Maharashtra got 363 547 votes (2.4% of the state-wide vote). In West Bengal, were fresh elections to the state assembly were again held in 1972, the Forward Bloc launched 18 candidates. It got 331 244 votes (2.48% of the state-wide vote), but could not win a single seat.

Realignment in Tripura

After having contested the 1972 elections on its own, the Forward Bloc decided to join a 'United Front' led by the Communist parties in Tripura. The front demanded clear-cut policies for procurement and distribution of food grains, stop to spirlalling prices of essential commodities, a land reform legislation for delimitation of Tribal reserve areas and creation of employments opportunities for the unemployed. A 24 hours Tripura Bandh was organised by the front on December 16. On May 3, 1974 the four parties organised a 12-hour Tripura Bandh.

1977 Elections

1977 was a crucial year in Indian political history. For the first time in independent India, the Congress Party was routed in a national election. The Forward Bloc had contested four seats in the Lok Sabha election. In West Bengal it had three candidates which were supported by the Left Front, out of whom all three were elected. Moreover, the party contested one seat in Haryana.

In Tripura a Left Front was formed consisting of the CPI(M), RSP and the Forward Bloc. The Front launched one Forward Bloc candidate, Brajagopal Roy in the Town Bordowali constituency. Roy won the seat with 7800 votes (62.76%). In the beginning of 1978 the Left Front formed a majority government in the state, with Brajagopal Roy appointed minister in the state government.

Recent History

Ahead of the 2000 Bihar legislative election AIFB took part in building a front together with the Bharatiya Jan Congress, the Bihar Vikas Party, the Janata Dal (Secular), the Samajwadi Janata Party and the Nationalist Congress Party. The front vowed to maintain equidistance towards the two major blocs in Bihari politics, the Rashtriya Janata Dal and the National Democratic Alliance, condemning them as 'casteist and communal'.

In 2002 AIFB was one of four leftwing parties that nominated Lakshmi Sehgal as a candidate for the presidency of India. Sehgal, who challenged the main candidate A.P.J. Abdul Kalam, got around 10% of the votes.

Just before the 2006 Tamil Nadu legislative election, the party was joined by the actor Karthik. Karthik was given the post of president of the Tamil Nadu state unit by the national party leadership and was put in charge of the election campaign of the party in the state. The party decided to contest a large number of seats wiuthout joining neither of the two major political blocs in Tamil Nadu. The appointment of Karthik as the new leader of the state unit provoked the sole Forward Bloc legislator and secretary of the state unit, L. Santhanam to leave the party. In the election the party lost its representation in the assembly. A few months later the party leadership expelled Karthik on the grounds of 'anti-party activities'

Ahead of the 2006 West Bengal Legislative Election, a section of the party led by Jayanta Roy, former AIFB Rajya Sabha member, and Chhaya Ghosh, former West Bengal Minister of Agriculture, broke away and formed the Indian People's Forward Bloc. This party aligned itself with the Indian National Congress.

2007 UP Election

In the 2007 assembly election in Uttar Pradesh AIFB launched three candidate, Ram Lakhan in Bisalpur (732 votes, 0.51% of the votes in the constituency), Samar Singh in Fatehpur (870 votes, 0.69%) and Jabar Singh in Hastinapur (503 votes, 0.42%).

FORWARD BLOC TODAY

Ex chairman Late D.D. Shasrti was died in year 2001.AIFB struggles for socialism in India but they consider that their ideology differs from that of Communist Party of India (Marxist) (CPI(M)) and Communist Party of India (CPI), as they build their socialism on foreign ideologues as Karl Marx and Vladimir Lenin, whereas the socialism of AIFB is the Indian socialism of

Subhas Chandra Bose. AIFB has branches throughout the country, but the main strength of the party is concentrated in West Bengal. It is part of the Left Front government in there, and Forward Bloc has various ministers in the state government. Notably though AIFB is cooperating with CPI(M) in West Bengal, Tripura and on the national level, AIFB is not part of the Left Democratic Front in Kerala.

AIFB, together with the Revolutionary Socialist Party, is significantly more hesitant towards supporting the Congress-led governments than the CPI and CPI(M).

In the Lok Sabha elections 2004 the party received 0,4% of votes and three seats (All from West Bengal).

The current general secretary of AIFB is Debabrata Biswas. N. Velappan Nair is the chairman of the party, Dr. Amar Singh Kushwaha the deputy Chairman and Ashok Ghosh the financial secretary. Additional secretaries of the party are Subrata Bose (MP), Dr. Barun Mukherjee, G. Devarajan, Naren Dey, Hafiz Alam Sairani, Bir Singh Mahato, V.P. Saini, Shyamal Roy, G.R. Shivashankar.

Uttar Pradesh

In Uttar Pradesh the party had raising during the 1960-70s by Com.Rameshwar Dayal Sharma (Ex.State president) & Late Rajendra Kumar Tata (Ex.State vice president)of Western UP. Now Com.S.N.Singh Chauhan is the General Secretary of the Uttar Pradesh State Committee.Other members are Dr. Harish Kumar Gupta,Hasraj Akela Jatav, Netra Pal Sharma Advocate,Mohan Singh Rajput, etc. national vice president Com.(Late) Dr.Amar Singh Kushwaha from Kanpur ,& Com.Sanjay Bhattacharya is National president of All India Youth League from Banaras.

Tamil Nadu

In Tamil Nadu, We are by birth of Forward Bloc " Revolution Zindabath"

All India Forward Bloc (State Committee)

V.S.Navamani - Chairman. M.Maheswaran - General Secretary. K.N.K.Sankara Narayanan - Treasurer. "R.S.Mangalam" Ganeshan - State Secretary. "Theni" Senthil Kumar - State Secretary.

All India Forward Bloc (for election 2011)

Balakrishnan - Chairman. P.V.Kathiravan - General Secretary. Maya Thevar - Treasurer. Pasumpon - State Secretary.

All India Forward Bloc groups in Tamil Nadu

Bharathiya Forward Bloc

Pasumpon Forward Bloc

Democracy Forward Bloc

Vallarasu Forward Bloc

National Forward Bloc

All India National Forward Bloc

forward bloc (Santhanam)

and, etc., its not countable.....

Andhra Pradesh

In Andhra Pradesh the party had significant presence during the 1950s, but then declined sharply. In 2005 the party took an initiative to revive its Andhra Pradesh State Committee. A.K. Biswas became the secretary of the Andhra Pradesh State Committee. Other State Committee members includes G. Appa Rao, Malla Reddy, K. Narender, Konda Dayanand and D. Venkatesam. The party is opposed to the Congress-led state government.

Haryana

AIFB has a small state unit in Haryana. The chairman of Haryana state committee is Com. D.K Sharma. In the 2005 election to the Haryana Legislative Assembly AIFB ran a single candidate, Mukhtiar Singh Kaushik in the Nilokheri constituency. Kaushik got 442 votes (0.44%).

Tripura

The Forward Bloc established its presence in Tripura in 1944, founded by Kamala Ranjan Talapatra.Bengali immigrants like Sailesh Sen, Gopi Ballav Saha, Dwijen Deu, Anil Dasgupta, Hiren Nandi and Sati Bhardwaz are the other active members of the party. They took part in various political campaigns. However, around 1955-56 most of the founding core of the party in Tripura joined the RSP. Today, AIFB is a member of the ruling Left Front coalition, but since they've failed to win any seat in the State Legislative Assembly they don't have any minister in that government. In the 2003 Tripura Legislative Election the Tripura State Committee president Brajagopal Roy contested the Town Borowali constituency on behalf of the Left Front. Roy got 9844 votes (43.57%), but was defeated by a Congress candidate. The secretary of the Tripura State Committee of Shyamal Roy (who replaced the former state committee secretary Nisith Das). The AIFB state unit publishes Tripura Bani.

In 2005 the labour fronts of CPI, RSP and AIFB in Tripura formed the Shramik Aikya Manch (Workers United Front), in an attempt to challenge the dominance of the pro-CPI(M) Centre of Indian Trade Unions in the Tripura Trade Union Movement. In the summer of 2005 the AIFB Tripura State Committee vice-president Anil Krishna Sharma was arrested, following clashes between CITU and Shramik Aikya Manch in Northern Tripura.

Kerala

In Kerala, the party is working in all the fourteen districts. The party is seeking an entry into Kerala's Left Democratic Front. The party supported LDF in the last Assembly and Parliament elections. But in the local body election the party contested separately. The mass fronts of the party is also working in the state. V. Ram Mohan is the State General Secretary. AIFB national Secretary G. Devarajan and Chairman N. Velappan Nair are from Kerala.

THE IMPHAL CAMPAIGN

The Imphal Campaign, including the battle of Kohima—the first major town to be captured by the INA inside India—will perhaps go down as one of the most daring and disastrous campaigns in the annals of world military history. General Mutaguchi, commander of the Japanese forces in North Burma since 1943, had been convinced that Imphal should be attacked.

The objects of such an offensive were to forestall any invasion of Burma in 1944 and to establish the Japanese defenses on the frontier mountains. The idea would be first to overwhelm the British in Arakan, involving all their reserves in battle for Chittagong and the gateway to Eastern Bengal.

Then, by April, Kohima and Imphal could be conquered at leisure, without danger of their being reinforced. The monsoon, beginning in May, would postpone operations, and after the rains were over, in the absence of a new British defense posture east of the river Brahmaputra, the entire Assam and East Bengal would lie open to the Indian National Army and the Japanese.

Imphal, the capital of the State of Manipur, lay on a flat, nearly treeless plateau just inside the Indian border. Its elevation was about 3,000 feet, surrounded on all sides by impassable mountains.

The mountain range in the east with 2,000-4,000 foot peaks above the plateau stretches some five hundred miles. To the West and South are the Chin hills of the Arakan range, a formidable stretch of inhospitable terrain. The jungle surrounding this basin is hostile to human habitation. The northern access to the plain from India and Assam lay through Dimapur and the steep

Kohima Road. From Dimapur, a single track railway swept through Assam and Bengal and was an important military objective to both armies.

For the INA the importance of the Imphal campaign was that it was the only major battle in which it would participate with the object of achieving freedom for India. As Salto and Hayashida writes:

> *The Imphal Operation was the final offensive of the East Asia War, mounted by three Burma-based Japanese divisions, and one INA division. The campaign lasted from 15 March to 9 July 1944. The operation has often been compared to the operation Wacht am Rhein or the Battle of the Bulge, which was the final all-out drive launched by Germany towards Ardennes on the Western Front, from December 1944 to January 1945. Both operations al most succeeded and both are termed "gambles" by historians today. If the German push towards Ardennes was Wacht am Rhein, the Japanese-Indian thrust against Imphal might be called "Wacht am Chindwin" although the official Japanese code-name for the action was most prosaic: Operation "U".*

River Chindwin lay across the Indo-Burmese border, and its crossing from the east by an army would signal an invasion of India.

Execution orders for Operation U became operative on 7 January 1944, coinciding with completion of the shifting of the Provisional Government headquarters in Rangoon. In the evening of the same day, Lt. General Masakazy Kawabe, commanding the overall Burma headquarters, held a welcome party in honour of Netaji and his staff officers.

Netaji spoke, and concluded his speech with these words. "My only prayer to the Almighty at this moment is that we may be given the earliest opportunity to pay for our freedom with our own blood.', One INA Division, named after Netaji as Subhash Regiment, was readied for action at the front with the Japanese. Toye writes.

... He spent the whole days... with the Subhash Regiment, reviewing, watching it at exercises and on parade, talking to its officers, exerting his magic on it in a way that he had not attempted before. These were his comrades, the men by whose means he would uphold the rights and honour of India. Everything depended on their achievement in battle; they must absorb all his feelings of confidence, feel the whole of his personal force. On 3 February he bade them farewell: "Blood is calling for blood. Arise! We have no time to lose. Take up your arms. There in front of you is the road. our pioneers have built. We shall march along that road. We shall carve our way through enemy's ranks, or, if God wills, we shall die a martyr's death. And in our last sleep we shall kiss the road which will bring our Army to Delhi. The road to Delhi is the road to Freedom. On to Delhi!"

Mutaguchi set 15 March as the D-day for the beginning of the Imphal campaign. The deployment of well over 120,000 troops along the Chindwin river, a front of some 200 kilometres, went on smoothly and undetected by British spies planted in the area. In the meantime, Netaji received some good news. The Arakan offensive, launched on 4 February, had cut off the 7th Indian Division of the British Army in Mayu valley.

Contributing to this success was the reconnaissance and subversion of an Indian outpost position by Major Misra, the INA Commander in Arakan. At the same time, he received messages from the underground network working inside India under his direction, whose selected trained spies had been sent by submarine.

On Dday, Mutaguchi assembled the war correspondents at his headquarters in central Burma and declared: "I am firmly convinced that my three divisions will reduce Imphal in one month. In order that they can march fast, they carry the lightest possible equipment and food enough for three weeks. All, they will get everything from the British supplies and dumps. Boys! See you again in Imphal at the celebration of the Emperor's birthday on 29 April."

The Japanese-Indian offensive took the British by complete surprise. The Japanese and INA troops literally galloped through mountains and jungles routing the enemy on the way. Prior to the Imphal offensive, an INA detachment under Colonel Saligal had created a breach through the British lines in the Arakan sector. Now the INA's deployment was extended to the Imphal sector.

As the INA under Netaji's command set foot on the Indian soil, the main Japanese force also defeated the obstinate resistance of the enemy on 22 March, broke through the India-Burma border, and advanced from the north and west to encircle Imphal. The initial success of the INA at the Arakan front generated much enthusiasm. In a Special Order of the Day, Netaji referred to the "Glorious and brilliant actions of the brave forces of the Azad Hind Fauj."

On 8 April, Japanese Imperial Headquarters issued a communique which said: "Japanese troops, fighting side by side with the Indian National Army, captured Kohima early on 6 April. A jubilant Netaji at this time started talking with the Japanese about the administration of the liberated and soon-to-be-liberated territories in India.

In response to a call by Netaji, Prime Minister Tojo made an announcement clarifying that all areas of India occupied as a result of Japanese advance would be placed under the jurisdiction of the Provisional Government. This was followed by Netaji's announcement that he was appointing the Finance

Minister of his cabinet, Major-General A.C. Chatterjee, as the governor of the newly liberated areas. Netaji described the march of the INA into India as the event of the century.

He had also just declared the Legion in Europe to be part of the INA and had appointed Nambiar to be a Minister in the Provisional Government; his Chief Commissioner had been installed in the Andamans, his first heroes from the Arakan front had been decorated, and the, INA troops had raised the national standard of free India in Kohima; and now, the fall of Imphal seemed very near.

Did the Imphal Campaign come almost two years too late? What would have happened if Netaji had arrived in East Asia a year earlier by the end of 1942, the Axis had scored successes everywhere.

Rommel was in Egypt, the German invasion of Russia had gone smoothly, Nationalist China was on her knees, and India and Australia were expecting a Japanese invasion. Prospects for the Allies were dark in the Pacific and the Rising Sun was at its zenith from Japan to the Bay of Bengal ... Britain was unable to dispute with the Japanese Navy, and there were not enough British and Indian troops in India to assure its defense. Even air protection was inadequte ... Japanese forces had not pursued retreating British troops beyond the Chindwin river in Burma in May 1942, allegedly because "an invasion was likely to arouse ill-feelings amongst the Indian masses." ... So the Japanese remained east of the Chindwin river, leaving British Indian forces to build up their strength in the Imphal plain.

But above all, in that moment of a golden opportunity, the towering leadership of Netaji, a provisional government, and an Indian National Army worthy of its name—all these were non-existent in East Asia. Japan by itself simply lacked the motivation for extending war into India, let alone think of its independence. The fact remains, however, that the Imphal campaign was indeed first conceived in 1942, right after the conquest of Burma. According to the official history of the British Armed Forces in the Second World War, Soon after the completion of the Japanese conquest of Burma in June 1942, a certain Lt. Col. Hayashi had advocated an attack on Imphal. He considered that the Japanese should strike against India without giving time to the defenders to recuperate from their disastrous retreat, and Imphal's capture would rob them of the best base for launching a counter-offensive against Burma ... 18th division argued that the jungles of Burma were impassable for large bodies of operational troops and that any attack on Indian territory would provoke anti-Japanese feelings in India. About December 1942, therefore, the plan was abandoned.

Lieutenant-General Kuroda Shigetoku, Southern Army Chief of Staff, stated later that if the operation had been carried out in 1942 when first conceived, rather than in 1944, it would have succeeded. According to Lebra, "General Tojo stated in the spring of 1945 that he regretted Japan had missed the opportunity in 1942."

As the INA and the Japanese forces continued to lay siege on Imphal, the Allied air superiority gained strength and the enemy was preparing for counterattack. Shah Nawaz, commanding two battalions of the Subhash Regiment in the Chin Hills, told of the hardships his men were suffering as a result of disease and of supply and transport difficulties. However, owing to communication problems, the news of difficulties his men were undergoing at the front did not reach Netaji in detail.

While there was a stalemate in the front and the offensive came to a halt, there were meetings and jubilations at Rangoon where Netaji collected money and donations in other forms for the conduct of his campaign. He offered to send additional INA regiments to the Front and more troops were despatched. For about a month Operation U went according to plan. Enemy forces were successfully encircled in the Imphal area.

Suddenly, in the middle of April, the military balance began to shift against Japan and the INA. Wingate's airborne unit had already been attacking from air over Burma supply routes. British forces were being supplied by airlift into the besieged Imphal, and reinforcements began to flow in. British forces were being sent to Kohima to the north by both rail and air. Japan had no matching air power to strike back at enemy air operations.

By the end of April the battle strength of Japanese and INA divisions was decreased forty percent. Time for success by surprise attack had already passed and gradually the offensive turned into a defensive battle. The monsoon that followed, brought the ultimate disaster.

As roads became impassable, all supply routes were cut off. Muddy streams flooded roads and valleys, and rivers swelled to sweep away tanks and ammunition. In the wake of the monsoon, disease became rampant. Cholera, malaria, dysentery, beriberi and jungle sores began to take their toll.

The INA and the Japanese started living on rations consisting of rice mixed with jungle grass. The 33rd Division had fought desperately for forty days without being able to penetrate the British lines at Imphal. And now that vast amounts of military supplies were reaching the beleaguered garrison at Imphal, there was virtually no hope for a renewed offensive. On 8 July, on the recommendation of top-ranking Generals including Kawabe and Mutaguchi, Prime Minister Tajo issued the order to halt the operation.

The story of retreat from Imphal is one of the greatest tragedies of World War II. It is a story of misery, hunger and death. Japanese and INA troops, bottled up in the Kawab valley between the Chin Hills in the west and the Chindwin river in the west, began their long trek back through jungles and mountains, headed by division commanders and guards in jeeps and horses.

Officers, supply, communication and medical units followed. Behind them marched thousands of stragglers: rain-soaked, emaciated with fever and malnutrition. Soon, corpses began accumulating along the trek, and they had to be left unburied. Of the 220,000 Japanese troops who began the Imphal Campaign, only 130,000 survived, and of these only 70,000 remained at the front to retreat. INA casualties were over fifty percent. It was a disaster equal in magnitude to Dunkirk and Stalingrad. Lebra writes:

> *When Bose heard the order to retreat he was stunned. He drew himself up and said to Kawabe in ringing tones: "Though the Japanese Army has given up the operation, we will continue it. We will not repent even if the advance of our revolutionary army to attain independence of our homeland is completely defeated. Increase in casualties, cessation of supplies, and famine are not reasons enough to stop marching.*

Even if the whole army becomes only spirit we will not stop advancing toward our homeland. This is the spirit of our revolutionary army." In an article in Azad Hind on 6 November 1944, after the retreat from Imphal, Bose was reported to have "reiterated his firm conviction that final victory in this war would belong to Japan and Germany ... that a new phase of war was approaching in which the initiative would again lie in the hands of the Japanese.-" Each Japanese commander gave his own analysis of the causes of the failure of Operation U, like the problem of the chain of command, lack of air power, on dispersal rather than concentration of forces. However, Netaji thought it was timing, with respect to the monsoon.

He felt that the only chance to take Imphal was before the rains came, and most strategists agreed on this point. From the historic perspective, however, Fujiwara perhaps was the most correct. According to him, the Imphal disaster could have been avoided had the operation been undertaken a year earlier, at a time when the British power in the region was weak.

The delay in launching the Imphal offensive was no doubt due to Netaji's late arrival from Europe to East Asia. The Imphal campaign should have been undertaken at a time when the Axis victories had reached their zenith and the Allied forces were on retreat everywhere.

During the last three months of 1944, Japanese forces had withdrawn to the banks of the Irrawaddy in Burma, where they intended to make a stand.

Netaji enthusiastically offered the reorganized INA First Division, when the Japanese 15th division was ordered to oppose the British. Subsquently, the 2nd Division was also readied for action. In February 1945, the INA held some positions in the region of Mandalay in Burma, giving battle to the advancing enemy.

This was the second campaign of Netaji's army, and it held out tenaciously at Nyaungu for sometime. However, allied troops later crossed the Irrawaddy at several points and the Japanese and INA units were surrounded. There were some desertions.

Despite unique examples of heroism and Netaji's presence in the battlefields, risking his own life in the face of enemy attacks, the second campaign of the INA (which was purely a defensive one) finally had to give way to the gradual reconquest of Burma by the British.

The end of this campaign was followed by a chain of events that included the final Japanese defeat, an alleged plane crash in Formosa in which Netaji reportedly perished, the surrender of the INA to the allied forces and the trial of their leaders at the Red Fort in Delhi, staged by the British. However, all these fateful events, occurring during the final phase of World War II and its aftermath, should be considered parts of an altogether different episode relating to Subhash Chandra Bose and the Indian National Army.

In the present episode we have examined the historical tasks fulfilled by Netaji and his army in Europe and Asia during World War II, and their significance. In recognition of Netaji's historically significant role as a war leader, Guy Wint pays him a rare tribute with these words: "He played ... an extraordinarily decisive part. By accident, and by seizing an exceptional opportunity, he was able to cut a figure which made him outstanding among the comparatively small number of men who influenced the course of the war by their individual qualities."

The Myth of "Freedom through Nonviolence under Gandhi's Leadership"

Modern historians in India are taking a second look at the way the country's freedom was achieved, and in that process are demolishing a number of theories, assumptions and myths preached by the "court historians."

However, in order to grasp the magnitude of the issue, with its many ramifications, it is essential to understand first the concept of freedom as envisaged by Netaji—the ideal which motivated him to wrest it from the hands of the British by the force of arms.

In his entire political career, Subhash Chandra Bose was guided by two cardinal principles in his quest for his country's emancipation: that there could be no compromise with alien colonialists on the issue, and that on no account would the country be partitioned. The Indian geographical unity was to be maintained at all costs.

As we have already seen, the unfortunate turn of events during World War II prevented Netaji's dream of his victorious march to Delhi at the head of his Indian National Army from becoming a reality.

In his and his army's absence in a post-war India, politicians under the leadership of Gandhi and Nehru did exactly what Netaji never wanted: they negotiated and compromised with the British on the issue of freedom, and in their haste to get into power, agreed to a formula of partitioning India presented to them by the British.

The transfer of power was followed by two more developments that were alien to Netaji's philosophy and his blueprint for a free India: introduction of a parliamentary democratic system by Nehru and his decision to keep India in the British Commonwealth of Nations.

It was a truncated freedom, achieved over the bloodbath of millions who had perished in fratricidal religious rioting during the process of partition, as the erstwhile India emerged on the world map as the two nations of India and Pakistan.

Even so, the fragmented freedom that fell as India's share after the British had skilfully played their age-old game of divide and rule came not as a result of Gandhi's civil disobedience and nonviolent movement as the court historians would have us believe; nor was it due to persistent negotiations by Nehru and other Indian National Congress leaders on the conference table, which the British found so easy to keep stalling. The British finally quit when they began to feel the foundations of loyalty being shaken among the British Indian soldiers—the mainstay of the colonial power—as a result of the INA exploits that became known to the world after the cessation of hostilities in East Asia.

Ramesh Chandra Majumdar, the eminent Indian historian who passed away recently, and who by virtue of his challenges to several historical myths can rightly be called the Dean of new historians in India, observed in his book *Three Phases of India's Struggle for Freedom*:

> *There is, however, no basis for the claim that the Civil Disobedience Movement directly led to independence. The campaigns of Gandhi ... came to an ignoble end about fourteen years before India achieved independence ... During the First World War the Indian revolutionaries sought to take advantage of German help in the shape of war materials to free the country by armed revolt. But the attempt did not succeed. During the Second World War Subhash Bose followed the same method and created the INA. In spite of brilliant*

planning and initial success, the violent campaigns of Subhash Bose failed ... The Battles for India's freedom were also being fought against Britain, though indirectly, by Hitler in Europe and Japan in Asia. None of these scored direct success, but few would deny that it was the cumulative effect of all the three that brought freedom to India. In particular, the revelations made by the INA trial, and the reaction it produced in India, made it quite plain to the British, already exhausted by the war, that they could no longer depend upon the loyalty of the seapoys for maintaining their authority in India. This had probably the greatest influence upon their final decision to Quit India.

Despite Japan's defeat and the consequent withering away of the Indian National Army on the India-Burma front, both Subhash Chandra Bose and his INA became household names throughout the country as the returning soldiers were sought to be prosecuted by the British. By then, the Congress leadership under Gandhi and Nehru had pre-empted itself, and the year 1945 seemed relatively calm and uneventful. However, Netaji and his legend worked up a movement all over the country which even a Gandhi could never produce. Echoing this mass upsurge Michael Edwardes wrote in his *Last Years of British India*:

The Government of India had hoped, by prosecuting members of the INA, to reinforce the morale of the Indian army. It succeeded only in creating unease, in making the soldiers feel slightly ashamed that they themselves had supported the British. If Bose and his men had been on the right side—and all India now confirmed that they were—then Indians in the Indian army must have been on the wrong side. It slowly dawned upon the Government of India that the backbone of the British rule, the Indian army, might now no longer be trustworthy. The ghost of Subhash Bose, like Hamlet's father, walked the battlements of the Red Fort (where the INA soldiers were being tried), and his suddenly amplified figure overawed the conference that was to lead to independence.

Apart from revisionist historians, it was none other than Lord Clement Atlee himself, the British Prime Minster responsible for conceding independence to India, who gave a shattering blow to the myth sought to be perpetuated by court historians, that Gandhi and his movement had led the country to freedom. Chief Justice P.B. Chakrabarty of Calcutta High Court, who had also served as the acting Governor of West Bengal in India, disclosed the following in a letter addressed to the publisher of Dr. R.C. Majumdar's book *A History of Bengal*. The Chief Justice wrote:

You have fulfilled a noble task by persuading Dr. Majumdar to write this history of Bengal and publishing it ... In the preface of the book Dr. Majumdar has written that he could not accept the thesis that Indian independence was brought about solely, or predominantly by the nonviolent civil disobedience movement of Gandhi. When I was the acting Governor, Lord Atlee, who had given us independence by withdrawing the British rule from India, spent two days in the Governor's palace at Calcutta during his tour of India. At that time I had a prolonged discussion with him regarding the real factors that had led the British to quit India. My direct question to him was that since Gandhi's "Quit India" movement had tapered off quite sometime ago and in 1947 no such new compelling situation had arisen that would necessitate a hasty British departure, why did they have to leave? In his reply Atlee cited several reasons, the principal among them being the erosion of loyalty to the British Crown among the Indian army and navy personnel as a result of the military activities of Netaji. Toward the end of our discussion I asked Atlee what was the extent of Gandhi's influence upon the British decision to quit India. Hearing this question, Atlee's lips became twisted in a sarcastic smile as he slowly chewed out the word, "m-i-n-i-m-a-l!"

When the new version of the history of the Twentieth Century India, and especially the episode of the country's unique struggle for independence comes to be written, it will no doubt single out but one person who made the most significant and outstanding contribution among all his compatriots toward the emancipation of his motherland from the shackles of an alien bondage. During World War II this man strode across two continents like a colossus, and the footsteps of his army of liberation reverberated through the forests and plains of Europe and the jungles and mountains of Asia. His armed assaults shook the very foundations of the British Empire. His name was Subhash Chandra Bose.

On the Transfer of Power from Britain to India—from 'The Freedom Struggle and the Dravidian Movement' by P.Ramamurti, Orient Longman, 1987

"We have seen that no nonviolent struggle conducted by Mahatma Gandhi in the course of the freedom struggle had achieved its objective. In 1921, the non-cooperation movement was withdrawn before it was started. In 1930 the Civil Disobedience Movement was withdrawn without achieving its limited objective. In 1932, the Civil Disobedience Movement was suspended at Gandhiji's instance and was never revived. In 1941 individual Satyagraha for the right of freedom of speech ended in six months without achieving its aim. The 1942 countrywide struggle for freedom was never started by Gandhiji.

How is it then that the British Government transferred power to the Congress and Muslim League leaders in 1947?

For an answer to this question, one must look into the countrywide upsurge in which military personnel also participated en masse, as anticipated by the communists at the end of the war. First, there was the trial of the Indian National Army. Consequent to the surrender of Japan, the Government arrested the sepoys of the Indian National Army and started a trial on charges of attempting to overthrow the government established by Law in the Red Fort at New Delhi. The Communist Party of India gave a call for countrywide hartals and strikes. The call was responded to in cities, towns and in big villages. In Calcutta the *hartals* and strikes lasted a week and the people took to the streets demanding the unconditional release of the I.N.A. prisoners. The government was forced to release them unconditionally.

When Pandit Jawaharlal Nehru set foot in Jammu and Kashmir, he was arrested by the Princely Raj. Immediately the Communist Party called for countrywide protest demonstrations. The Kashmir Government was forced to release him.

Next came the strikes of police personnel in many provinces, supported by the Communist Party. This was followed by strikes in military cantonments all over the country. The Indian soldiers and air force personnel left the barracks, and held massive rallies in nearby towns shouting slogans like 'Down with British Government" 'Down with Imperialism' and 'Inquilab Zindabad'.

From Kashmir to Travancore, the people of the princely states were fighting to end princely rule. The crowning event of these struggles was the strike by the navymen of the naval ship 'Talwar' stationed near Bombay on 19th February 1946. The British Union Jack was removed and in its place the Congress-League and Communist Party's flags fluttered proudly.

The naval ship 'Hindustan' was ordered to proceed to Bombay to quell the revolt. On reaching Bombay, the navymen of 'Hindustan' refused to fire on their brothers. Then Admiral Godfrey through a radio broadcast ordered the navymen of 'Talwar' and 'Hindustan' to surrender within 24 hours, failing which, he said, 'The entire might of the British Royal Navy would be used to crush the revolt; it does not matter if the entire Indian navy is destroyed in the proces.'

Sardar Patel, on behalf of the Congress, supported Admiral Godfrey and said, 'Discipline in the Navy is of utmost importance and the men should obey the orders of the officers without questioning.'

The fighting navymen had formed a struggle committee which appealed to the Congress, Muslim League and the Communist Party to lend their support. The Communist Party appealed to the people all over the country to demonstrate in support of the struggle; demonstrations and strikes took place all over the country. In Karachi, Cochin, Madras, Calcutta and Chittagong, there was complete strike in all naval establishments. Sardar Patel, on behalf of the Congress, issued an order to the working class of Bombay not to respond to the call of the Communist Party. The people ignored Sardar Patel's call, struck work, observed hartal, demonstrated with the tri-colour flags of the Congress, the green flag of the Muslim League and the red flag of the Communist Party shouting slogans like 'Hindus and Muslims Unite; down, down the British Government', 'Down with imperialism', 'Inquilab Zindabad', etc.

Sardar Patel lamented in a statement that the Congress prestige was sinking. Troops manned by British soldiers were sent to Bombay to quell the demonstrators. They started shooting at unarmed demonstrators indiscriminately. Yet the demonstrations lasted for many days. The official statement of the Central Legislature was that 130 people were killed, which was a conservative estimate. No one knows how many died and how many were wounded since most of the people were not taken to hospitals.

Gandhiji, who was quiet during the struggle, later issued a statement:

> *I can understand if there was unity from top to bottom in this struggle. Only the people at the lower levels were united. This will only lead the country into the hands of the rabble; I would prefer to die in the fire than to live for hundred and twenty-five years.*

Four days after the naval revolt started, on the night of the 23rd February 1946, the British Cabinet held an emergency meeting and decided to transfer political power to the Congress and League leaders.

The British Prime Minister Attlee announced the decision the next day in the House of Commons. The former Prime Minister Churchill and his conservative colleagues bitterly opposed the decision. While replying to the debate, Prime Minister Attlee said:

> *In the conditions prevailing in India today, old remedies are of no use. It is meaningless to talk about them now. The heat in 1946 is not the same as that of 1920 (non-cooperation movement), 1930 (first civil disobedience movement) or 1942 (when the Quit India resolution was passed). (Emphasis mine.)*

Nothing intensifies the national feelings and aspirations of a colonial people like a great war. Those who have had anything to do with the two wars, know what effect the 1914-18 a world war had on the feelings and aspirations of the Indian people. National waves which rise slowly or are accelerated during wartime and rise very high after the war. During the war, they are controlled to some extent; but after the war, they break all shackles and rise very high. Today, in India, no, in the whole Asian continent, they are dashing against the stones and, rocks, breaking them to pieces. I have no doubt about it.

"India alone has to decide what its future will be and what its status will be in the world. I hope that India will decide to stay in the commonwealth. Instead, if it decides to be an independent country, it is our duty to work for peaceful transfer of power in the interim period and make it easy. India has a right to he a sovereign independent country."

Sir Stafford Cripps, intervening in the debate made the position crystal clear. He said:

> *...The Indian Army in India is not obeying the British officers. We have recruited our workers for the war; they have been demobilised after the war. They are required to repair the factories damaged by Hitler's bombers. Moreover, they want to join their kith and kin after five and a half years of separation. Their kith and kin also want to join them. In these conditions if we have to rule India for a long-time, we have to keep a permanent British army for a long time in a vast country of four hundred millions. We have no such army...."*

The countrywide opposition to British rule in which the Indian personnel of the three armies participated, crowned by the naval mutiny, was the direct cause of the decision to transfer power.

The Congress had nothing to do with the entire upsurge. These facts are obscured by Congressmen today. Subsequently, a cabinet mission arrived in India and held talks with both Congress and League leaders. It used the differences between the Congress and the Muslims; Lord Wavel was replaced as Viceroy by Lord Mountbatten, and an interim government dominated by the Congress and the League was formed.

Riots were engineered between Hindus and Sikhs on the one hand, and Hindus and Muslims on the other. On August 15th, United India was divided into India and Pakistan, and power was tranferred to the Congress in India, and the League in Pakistan. India and Pakistan attained independence in the midst of the worst instance in history of mutual killing by two communities.

Death of Subhash Chandra Bose—An enduring political mystery—Anthony Paul, Straits Times, 1 June 2005.

Three days after Japan's surrender ended World War II, a Japanese Mitsubishi Ki.21 medium bomber reportedly took off from Taihoku, a Taipei airfield. The most important of several VIPs on its passenger list was a man who was then one of India's most famous sons-Subhash Chandra Bose, or Netaji (or Revered Leader), of the anti-British Provisional Government of Free India.

To this day, Indians dispute passionately what happened next.

Most accept the official version of events: For reasons unknown, the plane burst into flames on take-off. Badly burnt, Netaji Bose died later that day-Aug 18, 1945.

What are said to be his remains-bone fragments, some teeth and parts of the skull and jaw-were taken to Tokyo and housed at the suburban Renkoji Temple.

Singapore also venerates him indirectly: A modest monument to his greatest accomplishment—the Indian National Army (INA), mobilised in Singapore in the early 1940s for the purpose of driving the British from India-occupies an honoured place on the Esplanade.

But a small, persistent minority of Indians insists that the story of Netaji Bose's death was an elaborate subterfuge. They can point to some fresh support: Earlier this year, an official Indian inquiry, the third since 1956, turned up evidence in Taipei indicating that whatever happened to Netaji Bose, he did not die in a plane crash that day. According to Taipei's current mayor, there are no official records of any such crash.

The conspiracy theorists have several alternative histories, all tortuous. One of the most quoted: Those death reports were a ruse by the leader, his aides and the Japanese to have him escape from victors' justice and flee unscathed to Manchuria. From there, say Netaji Bose's fans, he most probably made his way to the Soviet Union.

Dictator Joseph Stalin, whom he may have met in Moscow in 1941, probably kept him in safe custody, they say, for the day on which he could continue his lifelong struggle against the British imperialists.

Fear of the mischief the anti-British firebrand would cause if he managed to get back to India kept Britain from following up various intelligence leads to Netaji Bose's whereabouts, those sceptical about the official story claim. And Bose's political rivals—those devious accomplices of the British, Mahatma Gandhi and Prime Minister Jawaharlal Nehru—went along with the cover-up.

The Revered Leader is unlikely to be returning to Indian politics—if alive, he would now be 108. Nevertheless, books and newspaper articles, often passionately pro-Bose, continue to be written about India's most enduring political mystery.

Author Anuj Dhar (*Back From The Dead: Inside The Subhash Bose Mystery*; Manas Publications, 2005) tells The Straits Times: 'People may or may not like Netaji, but they have a right to know what happened to him-how he died and where.'

Over the past few months, two developments have brought Netaji Bose back into the headlines. First, there is a much—trumpeted three-hour-long movie with a US$5 million (S$ 8.3 million) budget. Bose: The Forgotten Hero took more than three years to shoot.

Second, the Indian government has extended for six more months the inquiry into the circumstances of Netaji Bose's death or disappearance. In Calcutta, on June 10, the Mukherjee Commission, named after its sole commissioner, retired Supreme Court Justice M. K. Mukherjee, will resume its inquiry, now six years long, into the affair.

Subhash Bose was born in 1896, the son of a well-to-do Bengali lawyer. After securing a Cambridge University honours degree, he returned to India and involved himself in left-wing politics. A powerful orator, he was elected Indian National Congress president in 1938, but was soon forced to resign after a dispute with Mohandas K. Gandhi. Bose advocated the militant overthrow of British rule; Gandhi and acolyte Nehru preferred nonviolent resistance.

Placed under house arrest by the British for his pro-Axis sympathies, he escaped in 1941 and, with clandestine German and Italian help, fled to Germany. From there on, as a biographer puts it, 'his life reads as though written for Hollywood'.

He saw Britain's war with Germany as a chance to wrest India from British rule. Thus in Berlin, this Indian nationalist sought an alliance with Adolph Hitler.

Their one meeting cannot have been very comfortable. In Mein Kampf, the German's racist sermon to his Nazi Party, Hitler had declared: 'Indian agitators...will never achieve (freedom from Britain).'

This view, the Fuhrer had written, was 'quite aside from the fact that I, as a man of Germanic blood, would, in spite of everything, rather see India under English rule than under any other'.

A German information officer's account of the meeting says that Hitler refused attempts by Bose to discuss Mein Kampf's offensive passage. The Fuhrer is reported also to have told the Revered Leader that India 'would not be able to rule itself for another 150 years'.

Nevertheless, Bose received permission to establish a Free India Centre in Berlin and recruit, for an 'Indian Legion', Indians in British uniform whom the Germans had captured, mostly in North Africa.

But the Nazis' racism got in the way of Bose's grander plans-for an Axis-Indian army on the European and Middle Eastern fronts. So he turned to the

Japanese. With his fellow-Asians, then promoting the Greater East Asia Co-Prosperity Sphere, he was somewhat more successful.

In 1943, in an extraordinarily hazardous journey across three oceans, German and Japanese U-boats delivered him to Singapore. Over Japanese-controlled Radio Singapore, he broadcast a stirring appeal to India and the Indian diaspora: 'Give me blood and I will give you freedom!'

At the Capitol Theatre on Oct 21, 1943, he proclaimed the creation of a Japanese-sponsored 'provisional government of Free India' and organised the INA, a force ultimately comprising three divisions totalling about 30,000 troops. Both government and troops hailed him as 'Netaji', an honorific many Indians still use for him today.

Singapore's National Archives' oral history files hold recordings of INA veterans who speak emotionally of those heady days. At the archives last week, I listened to Sikh intelligence officer Mohinder Singh recall with pride and affection his leader's oratory at Singapore's Padang as he addressed troops who would soon be in combat.

'He was a great man, very popular, a great orator,' the old soldier recalled. 'He had a remarkable memory. He would speak first in Hindustani. Then he would repeat the speech word for word in English...But he knew little about military matters.'

In November 1943, the Japanese and the INA captured the Andaman and Nicobar Islands. Suddenly, about two million (of about 400 million then) Indians were no longer under British rule.

Netaji moved his headquarters to Yangon. Four months later, spurred by his war cry Chalo Delhi! (On to Delhi!) the INA crossed the Myanmar border and raised its flag on Indian soil. But the moment did not last long. Unknown to the Japan-Free India alliance, the British had cracked Axis codes. When the INA infiltrated fifth columnists into India, the British picked them up. British forces also acquired air superiority.

Moreover, according to Mr Mohinder Singh, the British, playing for time, were soon joined by a South Asian ally for which the Japanese were unprepared. 'That was 'General Monsoon',' said Mr Singh. 'The Japanese were running out of supplies, and the rains turned their supply routes into mud.'

Even before two atomic bombs in August 1945 ended the war, Japanese and Indian forces in South-East Asia were effectively at a standstill. But the Japan-India axis put a brave face on events. In the war's last months, *a large cenotaph dedicated to an 'Unknown Warrior' of the INA was raised on the Esplanade*(in Singapore)

Several months after the British returned to Singapore, their army dynamited the pillar. Erected on the site by Singapore's National Heritage Board in 1995, the new INA monument is thus, in the words of one tourist brochure, 'a monument to a monument'.

Mr Mohinder Singh told the National Archives that he believed the official story of his leader's death—that he perished in the plane crash. But the recording adds an intriguing detail in support of the notion that Bose might have been trying to reach out to the Russians.

The Soviet Union did not declare war on Japan until Aug 9, 1945. Before this had happened, Mr Singh told his interviewer, a 'Japanese admiral (in Singapore) suggested to Netaji that he might find the Soviet Union would help India'.

Of course, if Bose had been making his way to Manchuria and then Russia on Aug. 18, he could not have been unaware that Moscow now stood with the British-American allies against Japan. But that has not stopped rumours of the Indian being spotted in the Soviet Union over the past half-century.

According to India's Outlook magazine, scholars from Calcutta's Asiatic Society researching India-Soviet ties in Moscow came across recently declassified Soviet files 'that hinted at Bose having been in the USSR after 1945'. One of the scholars, Dr. Purobi Roy, was quoted as saying Soviet military archives mentioned Stalin and Foreign Minister Vyacheslav Molotov discussing in 1946 whether Bose should stay in the Soviet Union or leave. The quest for the truth continues. The Mukherjee Commission has now taken evidence from 127 witnesses and depositions.

The commission's priority will be visiting Russia. Author Dhar told The Straits Times: 'They already have evidence in the form of official papers, affidavits, depositions, etc., all hinting that an inquiry in Russia is most necessary.'

INA War Memorial at the Esplanade, Singapore

Historical Journey of Indian National Army

On 8 July 1945, Bose laid the foundation stone of the INA War Memorial at the Esplanade, Singapore to commemorate the "Unknown Warrior" of the INA. The words inscribed upon the War Memorial were the motto of the INA: Unity (Ittefaq), Faith (Etmad) and Sacrifice (Kurbani). While paying homage to the martyrs of the INA, he said:

> *The future generations of Indians who will be born, not as slaves but as free men, because of your colossal sacrifice, will bless your names and proudly proclaim to the world that you, their forbears, fought and suffered reverses*

in the battle of Manipur, Assam and Burma. But through temporary failure you paved the way to ultimate success and glory.

When the British returned to Singapore in 1945, Lord Mountbatten, Head of South-East Asia Command, ordered the INA Memorial to be destroyed.

In 1995, the site where the INA Memorial once stood was marked by the National Heritage Board of Singapore and new memorial was erected—a monument to a monument'.

The inscription in English reads:

In the final months of the Japanese Occupation of Singapore a memorial dedicated to the Unknown Warrior of the Indian National Army (INA) was constructed at this site.

The local INA was formed in 1942 with Japanese support. It sought to liberate India from the British and consisted mainly of prisoners of war from the British Indian Army. Subhash Chandra Bose who led the INA from 1943 onwards laid a foundation stone at the monument in July 1945. The Urdu words inscribed on the monument read Unity (Ittefaq), Faith (Etmad) and Sacrifice (Kurbani)

When the British returned to Singapore, they demolished the memorial barely two months after its installation.

Aurobindo, Chitranjan Das & Subhash Chandra Bose-Excerpt from *The Relevance of Aurobindo: Early Political Life & Teachings* by Nadesan Satyendra:

Aurobindo also inspired the young lawyer, Chitranjan Das who had defended him in the Alipore trial. Chitranjan Das, later known as Deshabandhu became a fearless fighter for India's freedom and served as President of the Indian National Congress in 1920.

Another young Bengalee, Subhash Chandra Bose followed Aurobindo's footsteps by spurning the Indian Civil Service after having passed the examination in 1920 from Fitzwilliam Hall in Cambridge University. Subhash wrote to his brother Sarat on 22 September 1920, in words reminiscent of Aurobindo:

You will readily understand my mental condition as I stand on the threshold of what the man-in-the-street would call a promising career. There is much to be said in favour of such service. It solves once for all what is the paramount problem for each of us—the problem of bread and butter... But for a man of my temperament who has been feeding on ideas which might be called eccentric—the line of least resistance is not the best line to follow... it is not possible to serve one's country in the best and fullest manner if one is chained to the (Indian) Civil Service. In short, national and spiritual aspirations are not compatible with obedience to Civil Service conditions.

Subhash Chandra Bose wrote again to his brother on 23 February 1921:

> *The principle of serving an alien bureacracy is one to which I cannot reconcile myself. Besides the first step towards equiping oneself for public service is to sacrifice all worldly interests-to burn one's boats as it were-and devote oneself whole heartedly to the national cause... The* illustrious example of Aurobindo Ghosh *looms large before my vision. I feel that I am ready to make the sacrifice which that example demands me.*

Subhash Chandra Bose joined Deshabandu Chitranjan Das in India and in 1921-22 they were both imprisoned by the British in the same Alipore jail which had witnessed Aurobindo's trial some 12 years earlier.

"I had the privilege to be in the same jail with him (Deshabandu Chitranjan Das) for eight months in 1921-22. For a couple of months we were in the Presidency Jail occupying two adjacent celss, and the remaining six months we were in one big hall... in the Alipore Central Jail... That Swaraj in India meant primarily the uplift of the masses... was a matter of conviction with the Deshabandu... Ofcourse, thirty years ago *Swami Vivekananda* spoke in that vein in his book entitled 'Bartaman Bharat', but that message of Swamiji was never echoed from our political platforms...

> *....another reason for the extraordinary influence which he (Deshabandhu) wielded.... was (his) constant experience that through all his actions he had succeeded in establishing Vaishanavism which was very much part of his religious life. Thanks to a fine synthesis between his ideal and his practical life, his entire being was getting progressively saturated with this synthesis... As a result of inner purity, which follows* the pursuit of action without caring for results, *man loses the awareness of the ego. And when the ego is transcended he becomes an instrument for the expression of the Divine Will.."* (Subhash Chandra Bose, letter dated 20 February 1926 to Hemendra Nath Dasgupta. The Essential Writings of Netaji Subhash Chandra Bose, Edited by Sisir K.Bose and Sugata Bose, Oxford University Press, 1997)

Sri Aurobindo, in a significant sense inspired both the spritual and militant aspects of India's struggle for freedom. He was a worthy son of a Bengal which had also given birth to *Ramakrishna Paramahamsa, Swami Vivekananda* and *Rabindranath Tagore*-and that is not to mention *Satyendranath Bose*."

An Estimate

While the Gandhi /Nehru faction of Congress has garnered much of the credit for India's freedom struggle, it is important to remember that India's freedom movement was in fact a movement of the masses and there were a number of great leaders with fierce patriotism and great visionary ideas who sacrificed their entire lives for the nation's cause. Known as *Netaji* (leader), Mr. Bose was a fierce and popular leader in the political scene in pre-independence India. He was the president of the Indian National Congress in 1937 and 1939, and founded a nationalist force called the Indian National Army. He was acclaimed as a semigod, akin to the many mythological heroes like Rama or Krishna, and continues as a legend in Indian mind.

Bose was outspoken in his anti-British stance and was jailed 11 (eleven) times between 1920 and 1941 for periods varying between six months and three years. He was the leader of the youth wing of the Congress Party, in the forefront of the trade union movement in India and organized *Service League*, another wing of Congress. He was admired for his great skills in organization development.

The Influence of Bose

Bose advocated complete freedom for India at the earliest, whereas the Congress Committee wanted it in phases, through a Dominion status. Other younger leaders including Jawaharlal Nehru supported Bose and finally at the historic Lahore Congress convention, the Congress had to adopt *Poorna Swaraj* (complete freedom) as its motto. Bhagat Singh's martyrdom and the inability of the Congress leaders to save his life infuriated Bose and he started a movement opposing the Gandhi-Irvin Peace Pact. He was imprisoned and expelled from India. But defying the ban, he came back to India and was imprisoned again!

Clouds of World War II were gathering fast and Bose warned the Indian people and the British against dragging India into the war and the material losses she could incur. He was elected president of the Indian National Congress twice in 1937 and in 1939, the second time defeating Gandhiji's nominee. He brought a resolution to give the British six months to hand India over to the Indians, failing which there would be a revolt. There was much opposition to his rigid stand, and he resigned from the post of president and formed a progressive group known as the *Forward Block* (1939).

The Second World War broke out in September of 1939, and just as predicted by Bose, India was declared as a warring state (on behalf of the British) by the Governor General, without consulting Indian leaders. The Congress party was in power in seven major states and all state governments resigned in protest.

Subhash Chandra Bose now started a mass movement against utilizing Indian resources and men for the great war. To him, it made no sense to further bleed poor Indians for the sake of colonial and imperial nations. There was a tremendous response to his call and the British promptly imprisoned him. He took to a hunger-strike, and after his health deteriorated on the 11th day of fasting, he was freed and was placed under house arrest. The British were afraid of violent reactions in India, should something happen to Bose in prison.

The Mystery Begins...

Bose suddenly disappeared in the beginning of 1941 and it was not until many days that authorities realized Bose was not inside the house they were guarding! He travelled by foot, car and train and resurfaced in Kabul (now in Afghanistan), only to disappear once again. In November 1941, his broadcast from German radio sent shock waves among the British and electrified the Indian masses who realized that their leader was working on a master plan to free their motherland. It also gave fresh confidence to the revolutionaries in India who were challenging the British in many ways.

The Axis powers (mainly Germany) assured Bose military and other help to fight the British. Japan by this time had grown into another strong world power, occupying key colonies of Dutch, French, and British colonies in Asia. Bose had struck alliance with Germany and Japan. He rightly felt that his presence in the East would help his countrymen in freedom struggle and second phase of his saga began. It is told that he was last seen on land near Keil canal in Germany, in the beginning of 1943. A most hazardous journey was undertaken by him under water, covering thousands of miles, crossing enemy territories. He was in the Atlantic, the Middle East, Madagascar and the Indian ocean. Battles were being fought over land, in the air and there were mines in the sea. At one stage he travelled 400 miles in a rubber dinghy to reach a Japanese submarine, which took him to Tokyo. He was warmly received in Japan and was declared the head of the Indian army, which consisted of about 40,000 soldiers from Singapore and other eastern regions. Bose called it the Indian National Army (INA) and a government by the name "*Azad Hind Government*" was declared on the 21st of October 1943. INA freed the Andaman and Nicobar islands from the British, and were renamed as *Swaraj* and *Shaheed* islands. The government started functioning.

8

Famous Speeches of Bose

BATTLE OF IMPHAL AND ADHERENCE TO FUNDAMENTALS BY NETAJI

History bears indelible imprints of acts of faith and trust, that remain ever bright, fruitful and dynamic ; the climate wherein mistrust and lack of conviction infiltrates and pollutes remains dim and unproductive. The chapters that are created under this unhealthy climate dim insignificant in the history of march of people whereas those that are born of faith in Man and God remain forever phenomental in history. So this act of faith once more helped Netaji Subhash Chandra Bose in raising his moral and political stature in not submitting to Japanese pressure and arrogance *vis-a-vis* the setting up of an Indo-Japanese War Co-Operation Council to function in liberated areas and in deciding fundamentals to India's favour.

The call of Netaji for total mobilization in East and South East Asia found a tremendous echo into the minds of the three million Indians because they found in him a pillar of Indian manhood, courage and conviction and an image of honesty and sacrifice. Now, when the Liberation Forces were to establish and consolidate bases in Liberated Areas, the only compelling thought that naturally Netaji's mind was that such bases must bear an unblemished record of healthy nationalism, robust patriotism, modest yet determined conduct and last but not the least an uncompromising mood for total sacrifice of men and women of India through armed revolution, reflecting the real image of the Provisional Government of Azad Hind. It was a tremendous trial of Netaji's patriotic fervour, statesmanship, intimate sense of history on India's struggles for Freedom, Himalayan patience, keen strategic sense and logical move, and unassailable tact in his pragmatic approach to all problems that were not only delicate in nature but also extremely difficult to solve. Anything derogatory to the dignity, integrity and sovereignty. Of Free India was against the very being of Netaji. But, war is war. To win the war becomes the war aim and everything however noble, is of secondary value. Philosophy and sentiments do not bother those who handle military machine especially at a time when both sides strong and powerful, stand, face to face to onslaught each other. Military expediency then reigns supreme to decide the clear and compelling purpose of military strategist.

The situation becomes more intricate when a dependent country throws herself in military alliance with the powerful enemy of her enemy lodged deeply and strongly in its soil, for the political emancipation of her people. And most intricate the political strategy becomes when the country to be liberated is a great country with a great past having to her credit a glorious history in struggles for freedom in her own way within and that too under the leadership of the greatest man of the age, that is, India.

It is therefore, not the consideration of military triumph alone that was the moot point in discussion with the Japanese Military Command but as every detail involved in total Mobilization of men, money and materials was scrupulously attended to buy Netaji due to his innate faith in Indians by way of exhorting his compatriots to shoulder the sacred task. Netaji was equally emphatic and keen on the question of independence and integrity in role INA's Advance Force and in governance of Liberated Areas.

All discussions therefore with the Japanese civil or military, were held in that context. Temporary military gains were not necessarily all important values to Netaji until and unless Netaji was convinced that such gains would appear commensurate with the ideals of Independence Movement in India itself. How it will act and react psychologically in the minds of the Indian people in general and to what extent such gains would have impact on morals on the political stream of thoughts in minds of men and women in motherland in general was Netaji's concern. What was the image of India, then.

Following the "Quit India', resolution led by Mahatma Gandhi India entered the final phase of her struggle. Its impact on the use of India's manpower and resources by Britain was not so impressive and effective, viewed from practical point of view in so far as Britain's war machine in India was concerned. But it was symbolic of India's stand. All national leaders were incarcerated and hundreds of thousands were within prison walls. Revolutionaries were more active and inflicted great damage on enemy's war efforts. But all in all, cumulative effect of national struggles could not call a halt to Britain's stream-roller in exploiting India's men, money and materials, for her imperialistic end. Britain could also succeed in increasing a sense of hatred and horror against Japanese imperialism and Nazi fascism with all their brutalities and nakedness that appeared only before the mind's eye of intelligentsia and common people. The Congress leaders did, no doubt, stand by Mahatmaji's call but in heart most of them did not like the total collapse of Britain. In fact, they do not think of India, independent of Britain. That the cruelties and hypocrisy of British imperialism far surpassed those inherent in fascism and Japanese imperialism were conveniently forgotten to meet Britain's war needs and to divert people's mind.

The Muslim League helped Britain. The Communist Party of India called the war as the people's war and extended all help and cooperation to Britain not only in her war efforts but also in her organized machination to crush the revolutionary upsurge inherent in the 'Quit India Resolution' and in the call for upsurge by the revolutionaries all over India. The Muslim League, Hindu Mahasabha and the Communist Party of India got all help and assistance in crushing the Inherence Movement. The industrialists, businessmen and traders and job seekers found in war great opportunities to enrich themselves. Educated men and women were reconciled with lucrative jobs. Mahatma Gandhi's call for 'DO or Die' and the revolutionaries march to martyrdom were eloquently manifested by limited people only-a band of patriots-albeit significant but not overwhelming while compared with the total population and the cause involved. A sad contrast, indeed, when one witnessed the total response from the total people to the total mobilization call by Netaji in East and South-East Asia, for the emancipation of motherland.

The Bengal famine-a man-made famine that was created to serve Britain's imperialist's need, took a toll during the period of 1943-44 of four million lives. With all the revolutionary tradition and spiritual and moral values that Bengal was proud of, not a single shot was fired against the criminals-nor a drop of tear was shed outside Bengal in the rest part of India. People died in front of sweetmeat shops, restaurants and hotels but the commonman moved in and out, quite unconcerned and unmoved, as if the 'Quit India Resolution' and the urge of revolutionaries concerned only the followers of the Mahatma and members of revolutionary parties. The people were not to blame-sandwiched as they were between two forces of indecision. The leaders and workers of the Congress took the 'Quit India Resolution', as symbolic and a moral injunction binding on them in India's patriotic stand *vis-a-vis* Britain's war efforts. In absence of a concerted programme for total struggle country wide for independence by striking the enemy—its roots and branches, the people's mind was at bay, bereft of a clear conscince. Again they lacked in that robust conviction that India's strength and power if generated and directed point blank against the only enemy could match in defeating Britain that was strong and powerful and deeply consolidated in our soil, it would equally match in defeating all machinations of Japan or for that matter any other power, if and where faced, once India was free. Indecision seized the mind of the people during the most crucial period when India was in peril. Her resurgent soul should have remained unconquered and asserted to restore her glory.

Netaji Subhash Chandra Bose proved his mettle as patriot, a statesman and diplomat, during the crucial days of India's destiny. The question of military operation in liberating the advance areas of Manipur State. Assam and Bengal, was most important from the viewpoint of the Azad Hind Government and the Japanese military authority. The formation of an Indo-Japanese war cooperation council to conduct war operations on the soil of India was therefore considered a logical step. General Isoda. Chief of the Hikari Kikan. Proposed that a Japanese General be the chairman of the council. Netaji refused to consider the proposal. Japan continued on the insistence for a Japanese chairman of Netaji, equally refused to consider the proposal and insisted on an Indian chairman; in taking this stand he was as uncompromising as he was in his conviction to fight British imperialism. He would not compromise with anything that appeared to him as derogatory to the sovereignty of Free India. He would not concede to anything that would harm India's honour and self-respect of Indian patriots at home.

Any student of history will be amazed at the stand taken by Netaji and at his patriotic fervour. On one side, the powerful Japanese Army that declared war against the two mightiest powers in the world Britain and America and reduced their power to ashes. On other side only three divisions of INA combatant forces. On one side, Japan occupying three fourths of the total area of Asia controlling the destiny of cores of people, on another side the Azad Hind Government functioning—and that too on the territory occupied by Japan on the strength of only three million Indians, and that too scattered all over East and South-East Asia.

On one side, Japan moved fifteen divisions from its Headquarters in Rangoon to Indo-Burma frontiers to march to India, on another side the Supreme command. INA deployed two divisions to face onslaughts of enemy and to liberate the northeastern part of India, at the first outset. Japan's involvement in operation was, therefore, gigantic and stupendous and her military strategy allowed no room for experiments. The main thrust against enemy's position on the soil of India, especially in the north eastern zone was to be given by Japan's mechanized army and air force till INA was prepared to meet the challenge. From the military point of view and in the context of

Japan's strength and involvement she insisted on a Japanese chairman in the council.

But Netaji would not yield. Soon after his arrival from Germany he sounded the Japanese High command on most vital issues and got assurance from Japan of all-out unconditional aid towards India's prosecution of war against Britain and he did not give any promise of military, economic or political concession to Japan in lieu of all her aid. And it was made emphatically clear when General Hideki Tojo, the Prime Minister of Japan declared, "The imperial Japanese Army will fight shoulder to shoulder with the Indian National Army under the leadership of Netaji Subhash Chandra Bose, on Indian soil". It was unequivocally clear.

When he met marshal Terauchi, the supreme commander of Japanese forces inland, air and sea, in East and South-East Asia, Netaji made it clear that the main burden of liberating India through armed forces devolved on Indians and the Indian National Army and that any liberation of India secured through Japanese sacrifices was to him worse than slavery. The joint communique was issued to the effect that the INA soldier must form a spearhead of the advance into India and the Japanese soldier will advance as and when asked by the Commander of the Advance Headquarters of INA. All Japanese commanders were informed accordingly. In his special order of the day issued soon after assuming the office of Supreme Commander of the Indian National Army on August 25, 1943, Netaji said that he deemed it to be against the national honour of India that the soldiers of INA should stay behind in battles of India's independence, while the Japanese advanced into Indian territory. The first drop of blood to be shed on the sacred soil of India would be that of a soldier of the INA.

Now when the declared policy of Japan not to interfere into the vital problems arising out of campaign on Indian soil was there Netaji did not budge an inch and insisted on an Indian chairman in the proposed Indo-Japanese War Cooperation Council. The Azad Hind Government, Netaji said. Declared war against Britain and America and the Indian National Army was fighting the battles of India on Indian soil, under the order of the Government and naturally an Indian general should be the chairman of the council and conduct the battles for India's liberation with Japan as an ally.

But General Isoda, chief of the Hikari Kikan (Liaison Department), Major General Yamamoto, Col. Kogawa and Col. Kitabe were adamant in insisting a Japanese chairman. It was only when Netaji threatened that he would then withdraw from the movement and inform the Tokyo High Command and Marshal Terauchi that these officers of the Hikari Kikan came down and withdrew their suggestion for a Japanese chairman for the council. Netaji however, exercised tremendous self-restraint during those crucial moments and now took Japanese withdrawal of proposal with good grace and humour. The Japanese generals could see the mettle of a man who stood unruffled as a pillar of India's manhood not because of the enormity of men, money and materials at his disposal which was out of proportion while compared with those to be deployed at the mere bidding of the Japanese Military Authority but because of his inner faith in the soul of India and in her people in general and in the mettle of INA forces in particular. Now the problem of the basis of cooperation and action between the Indian National Army and the Japanese Army in the campaign had to be solved. It was a gigantic task involving hundreds, of thousands of armed man belonging to INA and to Japanese army to be deployed to take offensive along the whole Indo-Burma border. This was thoroughly discussed between the Supreme Command, INA and General Kawabe, the Commander-in-Chief of the Japanese army. It was decided that the operation would resume as soon as Netaji ordered them to advance. The following basic guidelines were decided upon :

1. A common strategy in the operation plan will be chalked out by the Commanders of the I. N. A. and Japanese Army Headquarters at Rangoon.
2. The I. N. A. and Japanese army are allies and will enjoy equal status in all respects.
3. The Command of I. N. A. forces and their units will remain in hands of I.N.A. Officers.
4. The smallest unit of I.N.A. forces will be a battalion under an I. N. A. officer. I. N. A. forces should not be split up in small groups. All I.N.A.s units will be composite units and will not be attached to any Japanese formations.
5. To maintain equal status of I. N. A. and Japanese army saluting was to be observed on a reciprocal basis. Junior officers of either army saluting the senior officer of the other army and officer of equal rank of both armies to salute at the same time.
6. I. N. A. forces will be governed by I. N. A. Military Law and Army Act and the Japanese Headquarters will not be within its bounds to interfere in any way with its discipline and regulation. Total Mobilization of men, money and materials on Indian soil will be conducted by the Provisional Government of Azad Hind.
7. Territories liberated in Indian soil must be handed over to the I. N. A. for administration under the over-all command of Major General

Zamani Kiani the Divisional commander who will hand over the charge of administration of liberated areas to Major General A. C. Chatterjee, Governor designate of Liberated Areas and Leader of Azad Hind Dal.

8. Dumps of arms, ammunitions, oil, stores, equipments, machineries and all war materials seized by the Japanese army must be handed over to Provisional Government of Azad Hind.
9. Rule behaviour, looting and rape will not be tolerated. The Commander-in-Chief of Japanese forces accepted and appreciated the order of Netaji Subhash Chandra Bose to INA soldiers to shoot at sight any Indian or Japanese found in looting or raping on Indian soil. The Commander-in-Chief, Burma Army, General Kawabe assured to issue similar orders to the Japanese Army.
10. The only flag that would be permitted to fly over liberated areas is the Indian Tri-colour—the Indian National Flag.

In arriving at the solution of fundamentals Netaji had to work ceaselessly to get over the strong opposition from the Hikari Kikan—the Liaison Department of the Japanese High Command. Without budging an inch from the principle he over ruled the opposition of the General of the Hikari Kikan and his staff and directly negotiated with Marshal Terauchi, Marshal Sugiyama and General Kawabe the commander in chief of the Japanese Forces in Burma. On the question of equal status of I. N. A. with Japanese army the initial Japanese viewpoint that the latter being the senior army should have higher status, was rejected by Netaji. So also the Japanese initial proposal on the question of officers holding the same rank in INA and Japanese army, that the Indian officers should salute first to Japanese officer, was vehemently opposed by Netaji.

On the Japanese proposal that small units or groups of I.N.A. soldiers be attached to larger Japanese formations, was not approved by Netaji for the simple reason that, INA soldiers must remain under the command of INA officers only and also that INA's solidarity should not be allowed to be disintegrated. On the question of military law and Army governing all combatant forces in East & South east Asia, General Kawabe at first proposed that the INA. should be subject to Japanese military law just as all other allied armies, namely the Manchurian army, the China army, the Burmese army and the Thai army were subjected to. Netaji treated the proposal with contempt and eventually succeeded through negotiations with the Japanese High Command in asserting that all combatant forces of the Azad Hind government would be subjected to INA military law and Army Act.

Netaji made it clear to the Japanese High Command that it was India's war of Liberation and that the sacred burdens were to be shouldered by the Indian National Army. He was, therefore, continuously claiming that all war materials seized during the operation on Indian soil were the properties of the Azad Hind Government. The Commander-in-Chief of the Japanese army in Burma vehemently opposed the idea for military reasons. Netaji reminded that the Japanese army would fight shoulder to shoulder with INA, for India's independence which was the declared policy of Japan and not that the INA. would fight shoulder to shoulder with Japan for the cause, Japan had to accede. Regarding the governance of the Liberated Areas the Japanese High Command in Tokyo faced strong resentment from its combined armed forces in Burma on the Azad Hind Government's decision and directive delegate power (a) to Major General Zaman Kiani to control combined armed forces-INA and Japanese on Indian soil and (b) to Major General A. C. Chatterjee, to govern liberated areas as the head of civil administration.

Netaji was determined. Japan had to agree. So the image of a resurgent India appeared before us—an India determined to wage war against British imperialism.

A Free India was thus made conscious to shoulder the sacred burden-all by her sons and daughters with confidence and adherence to fundamentals so that Japanese imperialism could not infiltrate. No wonder, every soldier did his duty with faith in God and country and trust in the leader. And with that implicit faith the Indian National Army advanced through blood bath and liberated Moirang.

The National Flag was hoisted on April 14, 1944 by Col. Malik and the Advance Headquarters of the Liberated Army was established at the residence of Shri H. Nilamani Singh at Moirang while the soil of Moirang and all its surrounding approaches was yet wet with the blood of Martyrs. The names of those national heroes should be entered in golden letters into the Galaxy of Martyrdom and the Historic site where the National Flag was hoisted should be declared as the First National Shrine of India standing ever as the Symbol of India's Unity, Faith and Sacrifice.

NETAJI SUBHASH CHANDRA BOSE THE GREATEST REVOLUTIONARY AND SOCIALIST LEADER

The contributor is the Vice-President of the I. N. A. Martyrs' Memorial Committee Moirang, Manipur. Through his initiative and dedication, the committee could collect contributions from the Centre and State Governments for the memorial. Shri Yajee was also the former President of the All India

Forward Bloc and one of the close associates and confident of Netaji Subhash Chandra Bose.

.. .. .. Editor,

INDIA is going to celebrate the 75th Birth Day of Netaji Subhash Chandra Bose on the 23rd of January, 1971 and on this very day, Shri V. V. Giri, President of Indian Republic and one of the closest associates of Netaji is going to unveil the bronze statue of Netaji in military uniform at Moirang (Manipur) in the premises of the Indian National Army Martyrs' Memorial.

On this solemn occasion, the writer of this article as a colleague and Co-worker of Netaji is to convince the people of India and abroad that Netaji was the greatest revolutionary and socialist leader of India.

Since the very beginning of his political life, Netaji Subhash Chandra Bose as the president of Bharat Navjawan Sabha, All India Trade Union Congress, Indian National Congress, the All India Forward Bloc and the Head of the Provisional Azad Hind Government had always advocated uncompromising struggle against the British Imperialism and had clearly preached that the salvation of India, as of the world depended on full blooded Socialism Scientific Socialism, but he also clearly held that India would evolve her own methods to achieve socialism. Due to his taking help from Germany, Italy and Japan to lead the Indian National Army to liberate India from the clutches of British Imperialism during the Second World War, some interested parties and individuals held wrong notions and created impression that Netaji was not a full-fledged socialist but a national socialist. Though Lenin during the First World War took all help from Germany which was at war with U.K. and Russia, to reach St. Petersburg (now Leningrad) safely to conduct the Great October Revolution, no body doubted his sincerity and called him as agent of Germany.

Now it is a wellknown fact that just after the All India Anti-compromise Conference at Rangrah (Bihar) in March 1940 in which it was decided to start a national struggle against British Imperialism, Netaji consulted some of us on the question of seeking active help from U.S.S.R. and late Lala Shankarlal the then president of Delhi Pradesh Congress Committee and the then General Secretary of the All India Forward Bloc was sent to Japan on a false Passport to finalize this agreement with the Soviet Ambassador in Japan. In the meanwhile, Netaji was arrested in Calcutta in connection with the removal of the Holl-well movement. Lala Shankarlal came back to Calcutta from Japan incognito after finalizing the agreement with the Soviet Ambassador in Japan and through Late Mr. Sarat Chandra Bose the elder brother of Netaji, the message of agreement was communicated to Netaji in Calcutta jail. To come out from the jail and finalize plans to go to U.S.S.R. via Kabul. Netaji started a fast into death. He was released and how he escaped from India to Kabul via Peshawar and again from Kabul to Moscow and Berlin. It is now well known. Due to non-aggression pact with U.K., Stalin and Molotov advised Netaji to take help from Germany and Italy. And Netaji did take help from Germany, Italy and Japan because; these three countries were also fighting U.K. in Second World War.

The writer had to give out this background and reasons as why Netaji had to go to Berlin and Rome because later on the Soviet Press and the Communist Party of India had depicted Netaji as fascist and used vulgar and abusive terms against him. Even after the defeat of the INA in the battlefield, Netaji decided to go U.S.S.R. via Manchuria to continue the struggle against British Imperialism. While going to Manchuria, the fateful an accident took in which he died. It may be remembered here that after the formation of the Azad Hind Government on the 21st of October, 1943, Netaji and his Provisional Azad Hind government declared war against U.S.A. and U.K. but not against U.S.S.R. and China though they were the allies of U.K. in the Second World War. This foreign policy of Azad Hind government proves that Netaji was not against any socialist country.

Presiding over the Third Indian Political Conference held in London on June 10. 1933, Netaji said; "During the nineteenth century, Germany made the most remarkable gift through Marxian philosophy and during twentieth Century Russia had enriched the culture and civilization of the world through her achievement in proletarian revolution and proletarian culture.

The next remarkable contribution to the culture and the civilization of the world. India would be called upon to make." Further he said "we know for example that in Soviet Russia, a new scheme of national (or political) economy has been evolved in keeping with facts and conditions of the land. The same thing will happen to India. In solving our economic problems, Pigeon and Marshall will not be of much help."

As the Editor of "the Forward Bloc" the organ of the All India Forward Bloc, writing on the role of the Forward Bloc said Netaji "that the Forward Bloc would prepare the ground to grow into a Marxist Party". This declaration of Netaji as the president of the All India Forward Bloc in the official organ of the Party proves that he was a genuine scientific Socialist and was neither a national socialist nor a Fabian Socialist. On the 15th of March, 1935, writing a letter to the United Press of India from Vienna, Netaji said "further if I am not mistaken, the Congress Socialist Party seems to be under the influence of Fabian Socialism which was the fashion in England 50 years ago".

The writing in his famous book The Indian Struggle about the post-independence struggle period Netaji said "The party that is going to fight for freedom is the party that is entitled to draw up the constitution of India and rule over the country. If we are to have a socialist economy, socialism cannot be established by the Western Democracy. Socialist reconstruction can be done only by Dictatorship but that Dictatorship should not be of individuals or of the cliques but of general masses "citing the constituent Assembly of Kerensky's government, Netaji said that if Lenin would have joined it, the Bolshevik Government of Lenin would have never come into existence".

Presiding over the fifty first session of the Indian National Congress on Feb. 9, 1938 at Haripura (Gujarat) Netaji said "I am afraid there is lack of clarity in the minds of many congressman as to the Congress in the history of the national struggle. I know that there are friends who think that after freedom is own the Congress Party, having achieved its objectives should wither away. Such a conception is entirely erroneous. The party that wins freedom should be also the party that will put into effect the entire programme of post war reconstructions. Only those who have won can handle it properly.

If it were to forcibly liquidate itself, chaos would follow. I have no doubt in my mind that our chief national problems relating to the eradication of poverty. Illiteracy and disease and to the scientific production and distribution can be effectively tackled along socialistic lines. The very first things which our future national government will have to do would be to set up a Planning Commission for drawing up a comprehensive plan for construction. Last but not the least, the state, on the advice of Planning Commission, will have to adopt a comprehensive scheme for gradually socializing our entire agriculture and industrial system in the sphere of both production and distribution. Extra capital will have to be procured for this whether through internal or external loans or through inflations".

Just after the Haripura Congress Session, Netaji as president of the Au India Congress Committee set up a Planning Commission and appointed Pandit Jawaharlal Nehru as the President, Shri V. V. Giri (the present president of the Indian Republic) as Convenor and Shri H. V. Kamath as the Secretary of the Planning Committee.

Presiding over the All India Forward Bloc Conference at Nagpur in June. 1940 he declared "the All India Forward Bloc as a full-fledged socialist Party within the Indian National Congress and he gave a clarion call to "All power to the Indian people" and observed "We shall also bear in mind that the Forward Bloc will have a role to play in the post Struggle phase of our history. It will have to build up a new India and happy India on the basis of eternal principles of liberty, democracy and socialism" These writings and observations of Netaji Subhash Chandra Bose given here clearly prove that Netaji was not only the greatest revolutionary leader of India but he was also a genuine scientific socialist leader of the country.

Netaji and His I.N.A.

Netaji is a great and illustrious son of India whose memory has an abiding place in the mind of every Indian. It was NETAJI and his Indian National Army who paved the way to India's freedom and struck the last nail in the coffin of British Imperialism The more we look to that great son of BAHRAT for guidance the more pure, patriotic and energetic we shall grow in the service of the motherland. The Goddess of Independence needs blood at its alter, therefore Netaji said "GIVE ME BLOOD I WILL GET YOU FREEDOM" Jallianwala martyrs were the first to give their contribution. Blood donations made by revolutionaries like Bhagat Singh, B.K. Dutt, Udham Singh and many others will also remain immortal in the annals of India's freedom struggle. NETAJI'S Indian National Army gave the puran ahuti.

Those who say that India got Independence without shedding a drop of blood really lessen the importance of those groups the Jallianwala Bagh innocent victims, the Revolutionaries and the heroes of the I. N. A.

It is high time that nation should be kept alive to the memory of all those souls and their sacrifices Let us this day remember NETAJI, his work and his dedicated service to the Country which must serve as a beacon light for generations to come.

The Last Straw that Broke the Back of the British Empire

The contributor of this article Shri Dhillon is one of the heroes of the Redfort Trial. Shri Dhillon joined the Indian Army as a sepoy in 1933. He was commissioned in 1939 and attached to l/14 Punjab Regiment. When the World War II broke out his regiment was in the front fighting with Japanese in Singapore. After the fall of Singapore his regiment joined the surrender to the victorious Japanese Army. With the formation of Indian National Army by Mohan Singh as G.O.C. Shri Dhillon also joined him. When Netaji took over the charge of the Indian National Army as Supreme Commander Shri Dhillon was appointed as the Commander of the 4th Grla. Regt. (Nehru Brigade While fighting against the British in Burma, Commander Dhillbn was captured by the British along with the Divisional Commander Gen. Shahnawaz Khan and Col. P. K. Sahgal and put into trial at Redfort, Delhi in July 1945 for waging war against the ksing.

.. .. .. Editor,

It is difficult to realize in these days of power politics and of the merry game of plucking the golden spoils of office by fair and foul means that hardly a quarter of a century ago we were an enslaved people. The British were our masters completely and entirely. Their might had the sway over land and on sea all the world over. So powerful was the Royal Navy that it was said. "Britannia rules the waves" and she did. One of the pet questions in Geography used to be to show and prove why the Sun never set on the British Empire. In schools children were made to admire the British ways and sing songs of their glory. We used to pray for a happy, glorious and victorious life of the British Sovereign "Long to reign over us." And yet the tallest amongst us were behind bars of the British Jails. The British Government was entrenched behind the Army, the Police and the Administrative Services. Surprisingly there was no dearth of people who really recognized the British Raj as a dispensation of the providence. Others took it with that resignation which is one of our national characteristics. Late in the nineteenth century it required people as great as Swami Vivekananda and the like to awaken our national conscience and restore our spirit.

The story of the Indian Freedom Fight is indeed fascinating. It covers more than a century of continuous struggle unparallel in heroism and self-sacrifice as well as in forms of weapons, strategy, tactics and areas. It was at times spiritual, at times terroristic, at times peaceful, at times violent, at times nonviolent, at times within the country or in a part of it, yet at times without and at times in many forms, at a time and all over the sub-continent as well as in other continents. The last straw, however to break the British back was in the form of the Indian National Army of Netaji Subhash Chandra Bose. Carrying the Tricolor Flag with the emblem of the Leaping Tiger on it and with the slogan, "Chalo Delhi" (on to Delhi) on the lips, from the battlefields of Asia and of Europe, it burst out on the Indian scene like an avalanche overwhelming all and everyone causing a revolutionary and emotional upheaval turning and churning the very depths of the national soul, sparing not even the Indian Armed Forces of the British the very means of keeping India enslaved. They recovered their national conscience. The soul of India became free. The people could no longer tolerate the foreign Rule. The climax came with the Naval uprising in Bombay. The days of Military and Police Raj were over. It could hold no more.

The story of the I.N.A. is a legend in itself. Its historical evidence shows that never, never in the long history of man and war did a people in exile raise an army so big in order to liberate their country from a foreign rule.

In this historic struggle, the part played by the Indians overseas can never be appreciated enough. It was entirely due to these Indians that the Provisional

Government of Free India could attain the status of a duly organized, recognized and a belligerent government enjoying the allegiance of two million people. These Indians were the State with Indian Independence League as the Executive of that State and the I.N.A. as its Army of Liberation.

The Provisional Government of Free India was proclaimed on 21st October 1943 having all the requisites of a government. It had a Cabinet headed by Netaji as the Head of the State, The Prime Minister and the Minister for War and Foreign Affairs. Colonel Doctor Lakshmi (then captain) was the Minister in charge of Women's Organization. She held this portfolio over and above her command of the legendary Rani Jhansi Regiment of a Brigade's strength. Dr. Lakshmi one of the most popular and prosperous Gynecologist in Singapore had to give up her fabulous practice to be in uniform and to undergo all the hardships a combatant has to go through in a war.

Mr. S. A. Ayer held the portfolio of Broadcasting and Publicity

Lt. Col. A. C. Chatterji (later Maj. General) was Finance Minister

The Armed Forces were represented by Lieut. Col.Aziz Ahmed (later Maj. General),

Lieut Col. N. S. Bhagat (later Colonel),

Lt. Col. J. K. Bhonsle (later Maj. General & Chief of the General Staff),

Lt. Colonel Guizara Singh (later Colonel),

Lt. Col. M.Z. Kiani (later Maj. General).

Lt. Col. A. D. Loganathan (later Maj. General),

Lt. Col. Ehsan Qadir (later Colonel),

Lt. Col. Shahnawaz Khan (later Maj. General),

Mr. A.N. Sahay was Secretary with ministerial rank

Messers Karim Ghani Debnath Das, D.M. Khan, A. Yellapa, J. Thivy and Sirdar Isher Singh were Advisorsiand

Shri A. N. Sarkar was the Legal Advisor (all with ministerial rank)

Shri Rash Behari Bose—the very incarnation of service and sacrifice-having vacated the Presidentship of the Indian Independence League and all its offices to make room for the younger Leader Netaji Subhash to come and to take over so as to lead according to his genius stepped aside. Netaji requested him to be the Supreme Advisor. The Senior Leader accepted the post with grace which has been conspicuously absent during the past-independence era.

It is not possible to name the personalities who were fortunate in being ministers on Netaji's Cabinet and took oath on its formation. It cannot be helped in mentioning again the name of General Loganathan. He has tall inspiring personality full of courage, spirit of sacrifice, wit. Humour and the never failing sense of duty. This great man in spite of his ill health accepted to do the most difficult job, the Governership of Andamans and Nicobar Islands which having been annexed to the provisional government had been renamed "Shaheed" and "Sawaraj" respectively.

Though ill health and non-cooperation by the Japanese Forces of Occupation made his job more and more difficult, yet he stood it out. Again he had to act as the G.O.C. Burma Command after Netaji's departure from Rangoon. With the INA Contingent about 6,000 strong he manned the Burmese Capital in the absence of any other Police force or troops during the period between the departure of the Japanese and the arrival of the British. And he was successful in maintaining law and order to the extent that there was not a single case of decoity or of loot during that period-24th April to 4th May 1945. Throughout the difficult stages of the INA, whether it was its formation or the crisis in it, or the move to the battlefields or the withdrawal, this old man held the fort like a Knight from the medieval ages. He was affectionately called "Uncle" by all those who were fortunate enough to approach him. In return the old man would call us all "Uncle" irrespective of the age. While in captivity in the Red Fort he was suffering very badly from an ulcer in the stomach, yet he seldom let us know the agony he was passing through. Shri Ayar says General Shah Nawaz Khan, Colonel Sahgal and I were given Charge Sheets. Overwhelmed with the joy of being one of the first to be tried in the Red Fort on which once we intended to hoist the Tricolor. He furthersays that like a child ran to General Loganathan who was lying in an old sagging cot. I shouted. "Uncle! Uncle! I am going to be senior to you now. We are going to be tried first and shall die first. look! Here is the Charge Sheet of waging war against the king". That day General Loganathan was not well. Forgetting his pains with an effort slowly, very slowly clinching the cherpoy with both hands he set up. Got hold of the Charge Sheet and started reading it to himself as reverently I looked on. As he read through it big tears rolled down from his eyes on to the sunken cheeks and with choked voice he shouted, "No, no, no my son, they can't do that to you when I am living. I being the senior most amongst you, I must be responsible for all what you did. I must be tried and punished first. I must die earlier not to see you suffer". It was this very ulcer developed during the INA days which was responsible for his early death—a martyrdom on the altar of the Indian Freedom.

Logistics of the INA in action are awe-inspiring. It had to operate under ever-increasing difficulties and against fearful odds. Wireless Communication was a rare luxury. We normally had to use runners or at times a dispatch rider on a motorcycle to carry messages to and fro. Often our only means of transport was the good old bullock cart. It was more difficult to find a cover from fire for the oxen than for the men. When they got killed or ran away because of the battle noise, our backs carried the pack and that would be only belongings or rations in the world. Once we hired a cart with a stubborn pair of bullocks. They were too difficult to be controlled. General Shah Nawas Khan personally tried to drive the cart. The pair ran away with the cart and the Divional Commander (Maj. General Shah Nawaz Khan) on it. The owner of the cart had jumped off but the commander would not give in. The situation became worse as an enemy aircraft appeared overhead. In spite of his own predicament Shah Nawaz shouted to us to take cover while he was having the dangerous ride up and down a dry riverbank. It was after a good half an hour that we could retrieve him and that too luckily intact. The athlete in him saved us our commander.

We had a few supporting weapons, but at times lack of ammunition prohibited their use. On 13th February 1945 during my round of the different units of the 4th Guerrilla Regiment (the Nehru Brigade) as I visited No. 1 Battalion posted at Naynngu to oppose the British crossing of Irrawaddy, I learnt that the Battalion had eight machine guns with only two belts of ammunition each. I ordered four of the guns to be thrown into the River to make more ammunition available for the remaining four guns so that the duration of the fire could last a bit longer. It worked. On the following day the assault Crossing of the River by the South Lancashire Regiment failed. They suffered heavy casualties and were compelled to withdraw under the cover of the Artillery and the Aircraft. The object of this article is not to narrate the Battle of Nyanngu and Pagan, that the author may do at some later date. It may suffice here to submit that the odds were of an odd nature and yet we could fight an obviously last battle against the forces of one of the greatest Generals of the War-Field-Marshal Sir William Slim. Now when the din of the battle is twenty-six years away. I cannot help asking myself. "What was our strength? Undoubtedly, Netaji's personality was our greatest strength which could sustain us in spite of our deficiencies in numbers. weapons and resources. I remember an after dinner conversation with him in August 1944 after Imphal had been lost to us. As he was reviewing the war situation, I asked him that as war appeared to have been lost to us and to our allies and we had little hope of taking over the offensive again, what exactly was left for us to fight or what were we fighting for. Netaji's reply was quick, "To pay the price of India's liberty". He further elaborated his point and I was surprised at his frankness and clarity of vision. Little has happened ever since, on the political stages of India, Asia and Europe, which he could not foresee and foretell. He had a very good memory, seven months later in a letter from Rangoon dated 21st March 1945 to me, when I was fighting on the front, he repeated the same concept thus:

> *Whatever, happens to us individually in the course of this heroic struggle, there is no power on earth that can keep India enslaved any longer. Whether we live and work or whether we die fighting, we must, under all circumstances have complete confidence that the cause for which we are striving is bound to triumph. It is the finger of God that is pointing the way towards India's freedom. We have only to do our duty and to pay the price of India's liberty. Our hearts are with you and with all who are with you in the present struggle which is paving the way to our national salvation. Please convey my warmest greetings to all the officers and men under you and accept same yourself.*
>
> JAl HIND. Subhash Chandra Bose."

The letter was worth more than a reinforcement of a hundred guns. It did put a new life into me and into all those who were with me. It is human to be appreciated and human to appreciate.

Netaji was indeed magnanimous, he raised us from the dust to serve the national cause in an unprecedental way. Colonel Shaukat Hayat Malik formerly of the Bahawalpur State Forces earned the decoration of 'Sardar e-Jung' while commanding Bahadur Group (Special Task Brigade) in the Manipur Sector. With the help of Manipurians like Shri Koireng Singh and others who were members of the INA, he hoisted the Tricolour for the first time on the Indian Soil at Moirang after having liberated it from the British. Moirang, situated on the banks of the beautiful Loktak Lake has been a center of the cultural and political activities of the area. The spot chosen for hoisting the Tricolor was considered auspicious and sacred by the people because of its local historical background. Bald, thin tall like a pole standing seven feet high Colonel Malik was great for all the three. While always victorious against the first-two the third one often saw him flat before the end of many a party. "Netaji. Netaji, Netaji my foot, I (pointing to himself) hoisted the Tricolour at Moirang in the State of Manipur," shouted Colonel Malik thumping his foot on the floor. The occasion was a State Banquet given in his honour of other commanders who had fought before the rains in 1944. Netaji heard Col. Malik's outburst with a smile as if nothing had happened, he continued entertaining and talking to the foreign dignitaries including Dr. Ba Maw the Burmese President, present at the function. Colonel Habibur-Rehman the Assistant Chief of the General Staff however quietly got Malik whisked off to a waiting staff car which took the hero to his Bungalow and to the bed. Early next morning as Col. Malik got up, he recalled the previous night's happening. Hurriedly he dressed up and made straight for the Netaji Bhawan.

It was very early in the day but Netaji was already on his desk. On arrival, Col. Malik asked the ADC Captain Shamsher Singh to report to Netaji that Col. Malik requested for an urgent interview.

Immediately he has called in. Salutations over, Col. Malik took out his revolver and presenting it to Netaji said, "I do not deserve to live for a day after what I did last night. But I do not wish to commit a suicide and go to hell. I request you, Sir to shoot me so that I may take the punishment but at the same time may go to heaven because of your sacred hands".

Affectionately Netaji patted him on the back and said, "Shaukat you have been too long under stress and strain. What you need is a rest and a holiday". A few days after, as Shri Aiyar landed at Mingladon Air Port along with Col. S. M. Hussain having flown from Bangkok by Netaji's personal eleven-seater aircraft-AZAD HIND-he found Col. Malik waiting in the lounge. As we wished each other he took me aside and showed his pockets bulging with Currency Notes. He said, "Do you know who gave me this money? Netaji. He has given me fifteen days leave to take a holiday in Bangkok. This plane has specially come to take me". Handing me a couple of hundred rupee notes he said, "You are new to Rangoon, you may need some money. Take it". Inspite of my refusal he put the money into my pocket and hurried away to the waiting plane. What would not Col. Malik do for such a considerate Leader.

Aiyer further says being' a regular soldier, it was natural that I should try to determine the soldier and the commander in Netaji. Once in a battle report, I had mentioned the next likely place where I expected the enemy. I was 500 miles away from Netaji. He sent me a small note scribbled in his own hand suggesting an alternative map reference and advising me to watch the spot for the enemy's next move. When I received his message, I was already fighting the enemy at the spot Netaji had cautioned me to look for.

Given better means of communications, resources and weapons our story might have been a different one. Yet even in defeat, destiny wanted us to play a role the memories of which shall linger as long as India lives.

The I.N.A. apart from serving India as it did, has undoubtedly been also the fore-runner of a freedom movement all over the Asian and African countries. Shri Bhula Bhai Desai had appropriately said during the opening of his Defence Address in the First I.N.A. Trial in the Red Fort of Delhi that, "What is on trial before the court now is the right to wage war with immunity on part of a subject race for their liberation." Is it not so that the age of a liberation of subject races started thence onward, destroying all forms of Empires and Imperialism! It is indeed unfortunate that inspite of our fighting for a free and united India, the powers to be cut up our divine Motherland into pieces.

But having accepted the fact, today it behaves us that in the name of God, in the name of Netaji Subhash, in the name of our Dead Heroes and in the name of bygone and future generations, we try our best to keep our people and country united. Netaji used to recite to himself a quatrain of Kipling, replacing in it India for England. This noble exhortation while an aspiration of Netaji's soul is the vital need of India today. It runs thus :

There is but one task for all

One life for each to give

What stands if freedom fall

Who dies if England live? (Read India for England).

INDIA WILL BE FREE

Message of August 17, 1945, to Indiano in East Asia, retranslated from the Tamil version published by Swatantra India, Singapore. BROTHERS and sisters! A great chapter in the history of India's freedom struggle has come to a close now. India's sons and daughters living in East Asia have secured a permanent place in this chapter. By contributing men, money and supplies to the struggle for Indian independence, you have set up a shining example of patriotism and sacrifice. I can never forget your generous and enthusiastic response to my call of Total Mobilization. Like a perennial spring you sent your sons and daughters to the Azad Hind Fauj and Jhansi Rani Regiment. You gave generous donations in cash and kind to the war fund of the Provisional Government of Azad Hind. In short, you have carried out your duty as the real sons and daughters of India. I am more aggrieved than you by the fact that your sufferings and sacrifices have not yielded immediate results.

Neverthless they have not gone waste, because they have paved the path of deliverance of our motherland and will be a perpetual source of inspiration to Indians living all over the world. The future will bless you and will speak with pride of your sacrifices at the altar of Indian independence and of your solid achievements. At this unprecedented juncture in our history I have a word for you. Do not be disheartened by our temporary defeat ; be cheerful and optimistic. Above all, never lose your faith in the destiny of India. There is no power on earth which can keep India in bondage. India will be free and, that too, soon. JAI-HIND!

Netaji's Dream

Shri Ayer was a close associate of Netaji in his eventful days in his capacity as the Minister of Publicity and Propaganda to the Provisional Government of Azad Hind. Shri Ayer accompanied Netaji up to Saigon in the same plane in his "adventure in to the unknown". When Netaji left Saigon for an unknown destination with Col. Habirbur Rahaman in a Japanese Bomber plane on the 17th August 1945 Shri Ayer was selected on the 19th August to join Netaji out of the five close associates of Netaji and he was the first Indian to lean the sad news of Netaji's death in a plane crash from the Japanese Officers. After returning to India Shri Ayer has been holding high posts of responsibility under Government of India and have been fighting for the cause of NETAJI and INA. Shri Ayer is the author of UNTO HIM A WITNESS and regular contributor to the Netaji and INA literature. Now Shri Ayer lives at Bombay.

.. .. .. Editor,

IMPHAL, Manipur, and Moirang have nostalgic memories for all men and women who played their humble part in the I.N.A. under the leadership of Netaji Subhash Chandra Bose. Moirang the rare sanctity of being the hallowed spot where the immortal heroes of the INA hoisted the National Tricolor on the sacred soil of India for the first time after crossing the Burma border into India. Especially to all those who participated the Indian Independence Movement in East Asia. Moirang is a place of pilgrimage. It will remain a place of pilgrimage to all Indians and for ever. Moirang will go down in history as the spot where the dawn of India' Freedom came into view on the 14th April 1944.

On 21st October 1968. On the occasion of the celebration the Silver Jubilee of the Proclamation of the provisional Government of Azad Hind, Moirang witnessed an impressive ceremony to celebrate the Jubilee and to pay homage to the I.NA Martyrs, a Memorial to whom is fast taking shape in Moirang.

Last year, on 23rd September our Prime Minister Shrimati Indra Gandhi came to Moirang and inaugurated the Museum wing of the INA. Martyrs Memorial Hall. Our President, Siri V. V. Giri, is expected to visit Moirang and install the life size statue of Netaji Subhash Chandra Bose, at the INA. Martyrs Memorial site on 23rd January, 1971, on the occasion of the 75th Birth Anniversary of Netaji Subhash Chandra Bose. When the battle for Imphal was at its height a quarter of a century age, news of its capture by the INA supported by the Japanese forces was eagerly awaited every moment. But it was not to be. The odds against the INA proved formidable. After coming within striking distance of Imphal, the INA had to withdraw.

If Imphal had fallen to the INA, the course of history would have been changed. And independence would have come to India even earlier than 15th August. 1947. Manipur would have been the first liberated territory administered by the Provisional Government of Azad Hind. Netaji had worked out the plan of administration to the minutest detail. A Governor designate had already been nominated for the liberated territories. The Azad Hind Dal had already been recruited and trained for reconstruction work. The Dal was composed of farmers, artisans, administrators, postmen and telegraphists, engineers and doctors. These men were ready to follow the liberation forces to set up civil administration in areas vacated by the withdrawing British authorities. Normal civilian life would have been restored with the least dislocation. Temporary shelters would have been built with the least delay, cultivation of land would have been resumed quickly ; water supply would have been ensured ; medical relief would have been prompt. Money orders and other postal facilities would have been restored. Postage stamps and money order forms were ready ; currency notes of the Azad Hind government were also ready. There would have been no dislocation of normal life for civilians—for want of currency notes or postal stationary.

A full-fledged administration of the Provisional Government of Azad Hind on Indian soil would have been an accomplished fact as a result of meticulous advance planning by Netaji. That was the Dream of Subhash Chandra Bose. The dream did not become a reality. The dream was no less glorious, though it remained only a dream.

Those of us who had the rare good fortune and privilege of being closely associated with Netaji during the twenty-five hectic, fateful months that he spearheaded the Independence Movement in East Asia, were fascinated by the charm and magnetism of the man. Love of the Motherland was a burning passion with him ; his physical and moral courage was the highest order. His thoroughness was striking. From the moment the I.N.A. started advancing towards Imphal, Netaji began drawing up a Proclamation to the people of Manipur. He held a series of consultations with some citizens of Manipur who had crossed the Burma border and reached Rangoon. He wanted to understand the Mind of Manipur before drawing up the Proclamation. Once the proclamation was ready, he had it translated into Manipuri language by citizens of Manipur in the Rangoon camp.

He had an unshakeable faith in his destiny. He carried his life in the palm of his hand. Nobody could persuade him to take shelter when enemy bomber came overhead in swarms and rained bombs on Rangoon and other I.N.A. camping areas. When those near him begged of him to get into underground shelters at the height of the bombing, he would laugh off the suggestion and simply say : "The bomb to kill me has not yet been made."

His moral courage amazed even the Japanese. When news of reverse on the battlefronts began reaching Netaji at his headquarters, he was totally under turbed. He went ahead with his usual routine as if nothing untoward had happened. He never even for a moment lost his faith in the ultimate victory of his efforts. His self-confidence was of an infectious type. And the high-ranking Japanese civilian and military officers often wondered at this supreme self-assurance of Netaji. The secret of Netaji's moral courage was his undying faith in God. He did not give a moment's thought to the immediate success or failure of his campaign for India's liberation from foreign rule. He concentrated all his thoughts and energies on the job in hand. He had knack of turning defeats into victories. When a small group of I.N.A. officers betrayed the cause and went over to the enemy, Netaji refused to be depressed by the betrayal. He used the betrayal as the occasion for a raging, tearing propaganda campaign to rouse the spirit of the entire I.N.A. personal to fever pitch, and made thoroughly sure that there would be no further desertions to the enemy. When news of reverses began trickling from the battlefronts, Netaji took the civilians into confidence, and told them the unpleasant truth that the I.N.A. had failed to capture Imphal. At the same time he appealed to their sense of patriotism and urged them to support the I.N.A. with more men, more money, and more materials to attack Imphal ten times if necessary. Netaji's appeal had an electrifying effect. The civilians rose to the occasion and came forward to pour all they had into Netaji's war chest.

Netaji's finest hour was when news reached him that the Japanese had surrendered to the Anglo-Americans, and that the war was over. This meant an abrupt end to the I.N.A. fighting and a disastrous end to all his dreams. As he was upset only for a few moments. Then he recovered his composure and took supreme command of the entire situation, and issued a series of important orders to the civilian and military wings of the Movement in East Asia and told them in the smallest detail what was to be done by them to look after the entire civilian and military personal. Simultaneously, he held top level consultations with his own colleagues and with the Japanese military authorities as to his own future. He had to make the most momentous decisions about his own immediate plans. He had to take the ultimate decision on the fateful question as to whether he should stay in Singapore and allow himself to be taken prisoner by the Anglo-American forces returning as victors to Singapore and other areas. In those dramatic few days after Japan's surrender, Netaji was extraordinarily cool and calm, and after listening patiently to all that his advisers had to say, finally decided to go on what he himself described as his "adventure into the unknown". The life and achievements of Netaji Subhash Chandra Bose will always serve as a beacon light for the present and future generations of Indians who can draw inexhaustible inspiration from his patriotism, suffering, self sacrifice, and indomitable courage.

Bibliography

Arun, Pseud.: *Testament of Subhas Bose,* Delhi, Rajkamal Pub., 1946.

Bose, Mihir: *The Lost Hero: A Biography of Subhas Chandra Bose*, London, Quartet Books, 1982.

Bose, S. C., *The Indian Struggle, 1920-42,* Bombay, Asia Publishing House, 1964.

Bose, Sisir K., and A. Werth and S.A. Ayer: *A Beacon Across Asia: A Biography of Subhas Chandra Bose,* New Delhi, Orient Longman, 1973.

Chakrabarti, Mohit : *Fire Sans Ire : A Critical Study of Gandhian Non-Violence,* New Delhi, Concept, 2005.

Chakrabarty, B.: *Subhas Chandra Bose and Middle Class Radicalism: A Study in Indian Nationalism, 1928-40,* London / New York, I. B. Taurus, 1990.

Chaudhuri, Kali P.: *Netaji and India,* Shillong, Kali Prasanna Chaudhuri, 1956.

Das, Dipty Moyee : *Gandhi's Doctrine of Truth and Non-Violence : A Critical Study*, New Delhi, Dominant Pub., 2008.

Das, Hari Hara: *Subhas Chandra Bose and the Indian National Movement*, New Delhi, Sterling Publishers, 1983.

Deutsch, Karl: *Political Community and the North Atlantic Area,* Princeton: Princeton University Press, 1957.

Ganpuley, N.G.: *Netaji in Germany: A Little-known Chapter*, Bombay, Bharatiya Vidya Bhavan, 1959.

Gaur, Mahendra : *Indian Political Parties Annual,* Delhi, Kalpaz Pub., 2006.

Ghosh, K. K.: *The Indian National Army: Second Front of the Indian Independence Movement*, Meerut, Meenakshi Prakashan, 1969.

Ghoshal, U. N.: A *History of Indian Political Ideas*. London, 1966.

Haas, Ernst B.: *Beyond the Nation State,* Stanford: Stanford University Press, 1964.

Hari Hara Das: *Subhas Chandra Bose and the Indian National Movement,* New Delhi, 1983.

Harrison, John: *The City in South Asia: Pre-Modern and Modern*, London, Curzon Press, 1980.

Hasan, Mushirul: *India's Partition: Process, Strategy and Mobilization*, New Delhi, Oxford UP, 1993.

Hayashida, T.: *Netaji Subhas Chandra Bose: His Great Struggle and Martyrdom*, Bombay, Allied Publishers, 1970.

Johari, J.C. : *Indian Political System : A Critical Study of the Constitutional Structure and the Emerging Trends of Indian Politics*, 1996.

Joshi, V.C.: *Bhagat Singh and the Process of Modernization in India*, Delhi, 1975.

Kenneth L.: *Ahmedabad: A Study in Indian Urban History*, Berkeley, University of California Press, 1968.

Kitty Kurti: *Subhas Chandra Bose As I Knew Him*, Calcutta, Firma K.L. Mukhopadhyay, 1966.

Krishna, B. : *Indian Freedom Struggle : The Pathfinders From Surendranath Banerjea to Gandhi*, New Delhi, Manohar, 2002.

Maheshwari, S.R.: *Public Administration in India*. The Higher Civil Service, Delhi: Oxford University Press, 2005.

Menon, Ritu and Bhasin, Kamla: *Borders and Boundaries: Women in India's Partition*, New Delhi, Kali for Women, 1998.

Menon, V. P.: *The Transfer of Power in India*, Bombay, Orient Longman, 1957.

Mihir Bose: *The Lost Hero: A Biography of Subhas Chandra Bose*, London/Melbourne/New York, Quartet Books, 1982

Mosher, Frederick C.: *Democracy and the Public Service*, New York: Oxford University Press, 1968.

Nair, A. M.: *An Indian Freedom Fighter in Japan*, Bombay, Orient Longman, 1983.

Noorani, A.G. : *Indian Political Trials : 1775-1947*, New Delhi, Oxford University Press, 2005.

Rai, Ajay Shanker : *Gandhian Satyagraha : An Analytical and Critical Approach*, New Delhi, 2000.

Ray, Sibnarayan : *Gandhi, Gandhism and Our Times : An International Symposium*, Kolkata, Renaissance, 2003.

Roy, Dilip Kumar: *The Subhash I Knew*, Bombay, Nalanda Publications, 1946.

Sharma, K.K. : *Encyclopaedia of Great Personalities of India*, Book Enclave, Jaipur, 2007.

Sharma, S.R. : *Gandhi : Ahimsa and Non Violence in Practice*, Delhi, Cosmo, 2001.

Singhal, Rahul : *The Eternal Saga of Love : Devdas*, Pentagon Paperbacks, Delhi, 2002.

Sopan, Pseud: *Netaji Subhas Chandra Bose. His Life and Work*, Bombay, Azad Bhandar, 1946.

Tagore, Rabindranath : *The Art of Tagore*, New Delhi, Rupa and Co., 2004.

Thomas, Vettickal : *Gandhian Sarvodaya : Realizing a Realistic Utopia*, New Delhi, Gyan Publishing House, 2002.

Thomas, Weber : *Gandhi, Gandhism and the Gandhians*, New Delhi, Roli Books, 2006.

Toye, Hugh: *The Springing Tiger: A Study of a Revolutionary*, London, Cassell, 1959

Index

A

Agreement, 70, 72, 120, 157, 161, 176, 211.

Armed Struggle, 13, 82, 136, 142, 143.

Authoritarian Rule, 12.

Azad Hind, 1, 3, 4, 7, 9, 10, 12, 15, 26, 27, 28, 30, 31, 32, 33, 34, 35, 36, 37, 38, 39, 40, 42, 45, 46, 47, 48, 50, 51, 52, 69, 72, 73, 74, 86, 87, 91, 93, 122, 131, 143, 145, 156, 158, 163, 184, 187, 202, 203, 206, 207, 208, 209, 210, 211, 212, 221, 222, 223.

Azad Hind Government, 1, 4, 30, 39, 40, 69, 74, 86, 202, 206, 207, 210, 211, 212.

B

Bose Mystery, 15, 195.

British Indian Army, 5, 28, 36, 38, 47, 48, 81, 105, 109, 131, 139, 149, 162, 199.

British Military, 106, 146.

British Rule, 1, 2, 7, 13, 37, 55, 57, 62, 63, 65, 93, 95, 97, 114, 120, 124, 191, 192, 195, 197, 198.

C

Cabinet Mission, 149, 194.

Civil Disobedience, 6, 82, 92, 100, 102, 119, 143, 189, 191, 193.

Civil Disobedience Movement, 82, 119, 191, 193.

Civil Service, 2, 96, 97, 115, 121, 129, 199.

Colonial Rule, 81, 172.

Command Structure, 31.

Congress President, 10, 42, 102, 116, 119, 151, 196.

Constituent Assembly, 173, 213.

D

Democracy, 9, 14, 15, 58, 74, 101, 112, 118, 120, 127, 151, 181, 213, 214.

F

Foreign Policy, 212.

Forward Bloc, 1, 3, 6, 10, 19, 37, 103, 171, 172, 173, 174, 175, 176, 177, 178, 179, 180, 181, 211, 212, 213.

Freedom Struggle, 191, 200, 202, 214, 221.

G

Gandhi, 1, 2, 3, 4, 5, 6, 9, 11, 12, 15, 16, 17, 19, 23, 30, 46, 57, 59, 60, 75, 82, 83, 92, 94, 95, 96, 97, 98, 99, 100, 101, 102, 103, 105, 111, 113, 115, 116, 117, 118, 120, 121, 123, 124, 125, 126, 127, 128, 129, 147, 151, 152, 154, 159, 171, 176, 189, 190, 191, 195, 196, 200, 201, 204, 222.

Ghadar Party, 36.
Government Administration, 51.
Governor General, 4, 201.

H

Hindu Mahasabha, 65, 205.

I

Imphal Campaign, 34, 171, 182, 185, 187.
Indian Independence Movement, 85, 118, 140, 152.
Indian National Army, 1, 3, 5, 9, 12, 25, 26, 27, 28, 34, 35, 37, 38, 39, 40, 42, 44, 45, 47, 48, 49, 51, 53, 65, 75, 81, 87, 89, 93, 108, 120, 121, 122, 131, 135, 139, 140, 143, 145, 153, 155, 158, 163, 168, 172, 182, 184, 185, 188, 189, 190, 192, 195, 198, 199, 201, 202, 207, 208, 210, 211, 214, 215.
Indian National Congress, 1, 2, 3, 4, 12, 65, 91, 116, 141, 164, 182, 183, 186, 194, 196, 198, 199, 202, 212, 224.

J

Jallianwala Bagh, 214.
Jawaharlal Nehru, 15, 19, 124, 192, 195, 201, 213.

L

Liberation, 3, 9, 14, 15, 36, 42, 44, 47, 48, 75, 81, 86, 87, 89, 91, 94, 117, 124, 125, 131, 132, 133, 136, 141, 144, 145, 154, 155, 158, 160, 164, 165, 168, 169, 171, 172, 193, 205, 209, 211, 217, 222, 224.

M

Mass Mobilization, 121, 122.
Muslim League, 65, 111, 120, 146, 148, 150, 178, 191, 192, 193, 205.

N

National Integration, 54, 73, 85.
Nationalism, 2, 27, 48, 66, 94, 95, 96, 100, 118, 146, 153, 173, 203.
Non-cooperation Movement, 97, 98, 191, 193.

P

Political Power, 193.
Political Strategy, 204.
Popular Culture, 35.
Projects, 27, 119.
Provisional Government, 4, 10, 12, 13, 15, 17, 47, 49, 50, 51, 52, 53, 69, 82, 91, 93, 122, 131, 143, 145, 146, 183, 184, 185, 194, 203, 208, 209, 215, 216, 221, 222, 223.

Q

Quit India Movement, 105.

S

Sardar Patel, 125, 192, 193.
Second World War, 1, 16, 34, 47, 79, 88, 118, 120, 185, 189, 201, 211, 212.
Socialism, 14, 15, 59, 65, 66, 95, 100, 101, 115, 124, 151, 173, 175, 179, 211, 212, 213, 214.

W

World War II, 1, 8, 16, 27, 28, 36, 37, 45, 118, 141, 153, 164, 169, 187, 188, 189, 191, 194, 201, 214.

❑❑❑